SIBERIA AND THE
EXILE SYSTEM

DRAWN BY HENRY SANDHAM.

ENGRAVED BY T. JOHNSON.

GEORGE KENNAN.

SIBERIA AND THE EXILE SYSTEM

BY GEORGE KENNAN

———

VOLUME ONE

NEW YORK / RUSSELL & RUSSELL

FIRST PUBLISHED IN 1891

REISSUED, 1970, BY RUSSELL & RUSSELL

A DIVISION OF ATHENEUM PUBLISHERS, INC.

L. C. CATALOG CARD NO: 76-77675

PRINTED IN THE UNITED STATES OF AMERICA

PREFACE

THE idea of exploring some of the less known parts of Siberia, and of making, in connection with such exploration, a careful study of the exile system, first took definite form in my mind in the year 1879. From such observations as I had been able to make during a residence of two and a half years in the country, and a subsequent journey of five thousand miles overland to St. Petersburg, it seemed to me that Siberia offered to a competent investigator an extremely interesting and promising field of research. To the Russians, who had possessed it in whole or in part for nearly three centuries, it was, of course, comparatively familiar ground; but to the average American, at that time, it was almost as much a *terra incognita* as central Africa or Thibet. In 1881 the assassination of Alexander II., and the exile of a large number of Russian revolutionists to the mines of the Trans-Baikál, increased my interest in Siberia and intensified my desire not only to study the exile system on the ground, but to investigate the Russian revolutionary movement in the only part of the empire where I thought such an investigation could successfully be made,—namely, in the region to which the revolutionists themselves had been banished. It seemed to me a hopeless task to look for nihilists in the cities of St. Petersburg and Moscow, or to seek there an explanation of the political events and the social phenomena that interested me. Most of the leading actors in the revolutionary drama of 1878-79 were already in Siberia; and if the imperial police could not discover the few who still remained at large in European Russia, it was not at all likely that I could. In Siberia, however, communication with exiled nihilists might perhaps be practicable; and there, if anywhere, was to be obtained the information that I desired.

Circumstances, and the want of time and means for such an extended journey as I wished to make, prevented me from taking any definite steps in the matter until the summer of 1884, when the editor of *The Century Magazine* became interested in my plans, and proposed to me that I should go to Siberia for that periodical and give to it the results of my work. I thereupon made a preliminary excursion to St. Petersburg and Moscow for the purpose of collecting material and ascertaining whether or not obstacles were likely to be thrown in my way by the Russian Government. I returned in October, fully satisfied that my scheme was a practicable one; that there was really nothing in Siberia which needed concealment; and that my literary record—so far as I had made a record—was such as to predispose the Russian Government in my favor, and to secure for me all the facilities that a friendly investigator might reasonably expect.

The opinions which I held at that time with regard to the Siberian exile system and the treatment of political offenders by the Russian Government were set forth fully and frankly in an address that I delivered before the American Geographical Society of New York, in 1882, and in the newspaper controversy to which that address gave rise. I then believed that the Russian Government and the exile system had been greatly misrepresented by such writers as Stépniak and Prince Kropótkin; that Siberia was not so terrible a country as Americans had always supposed it to be; and that the descriptions of Siberian mines and prisons in the just-published book of the Rev. Henry Lansdell were probably truthful and accurate. I also believed, although I did not say, that the nihilists, terrorists, and political malcontents generally, who had so long kept Russia in a state of alarm and apprehension, were unreasonable and wrong-headed fanatics of the anarchistic type with which we in the United States had become so familiar. In short, all my prepossessions were favorable to the Russian Government and unfavorable to the Russian revolutionists. I lay stress upon this fact, not because my opinions at that time had intrinsically any particular weight or importance, but because a just estimate of the results of an investigation cannot be formed without some knowledge of the preconceptions and personal bias of the investigator. I also lay stress upon it for the further reason that it partly explains the friendly attitude towards me which was taken by the Russian Government, the permission which was given me to inspect prisons and mines, and the comparative immunity from arrest, detention, and imprisonment which I enjoyed, even when my movements and associations were such as justly to render me an object of suspicion to the local Siberian authorities. It is very doubtful whether a traveler who had not already committed himself to views that the Government approved would have been allowed to go to Siberia for the avowed purpose of investigating the exile system, or whether, if permitted to go there, he would have escaped serious trouble when it was discovered that he was associating on terms of friendly intimacy with political criminals of the most dangerous class. In my frequent skirmishes with the police, and with suspicious local officials in remote Siberian villages, nothing but the letter which I carried from the Russian Minister of the Interior saved me from summary arrest and imprisonment, or from a search of my person and baggage which probably would have resulted in my expulsion from the empire under guard and in the loss of all my notes and documentary material. That letter, which was my sheet-anchor in times of storm and stress, would never, I think, have been given to me, if I had not publicly defended the Russian Government against some of its numerous assailants, and if it had not been believed that personal pride and a desire to seem consistent probably would restrain me from confessing error, even should I find the prison and exile system worse than I anticipated, and worse than I had represented it to be. How far this belief was well founded, and to what extent my preconceived ideas were in harmony with the facts, I purpose, in the present work, to show.

I wish it to be clearly understood, however, that I do not aim to present a complete and comprehensive picture of Russian society as a whole, nor to survey every part of the vast field occupied by the Russian Government, nor to set forth, in due order and pro-

portion, all of the complex, heterogeneous and inter-related facts
and phenomena that go to make up the composite national life of a
hundred millions of people. A task of such magnitude would ex-
ceed my strength, and would carry me far beyond the limits that I
have set for myself. All that I aim to do is to give the reader a
clear and vivid impression of the scenery, the people, and the cus-
toms of Siberia, to record the results of a careful study of the
exile system, and to consider the attitude of the Russian Government toward its subjects so far — and only so far — as may be necessary to throw light upon the facts, the characters, or the events by
me observed.

Some of the criticisms that have been made upon the articles on
Siberia and the exile system published in *The Century Magazine*
have been based apparently upon the assumption that a survey of
any one particular department of national life must necessarily be
incomplete and misleading, and that the fair-minded investigator
should supplement it by taking into the field of vision a quantity
of unrelated facts and phenomena from a dozen other departments.

" Your articles," certain critics have said, " give a false impression. Your statements with regard to Russian prisons, indiscriminate arrests, and the banishment of hundreds of people to Siberia
without trial may all be true; but there are in Russia, nevertheless,
thousands of peaceful, happy homes, where fathers and brothers
are no more in danger of being arrested and exiled to Siberia than
they would be if they lived in the United States. Russia is not a
vast prison inhabited only by suspects, convicts, and jailors; it is
full of cultivated, refined, kind-hearted people; and its Emperor,
who is the embodiment of all the domestic virtues, has no higher
aim in life than to promote the happiness and prosperity of his beloved subjects."

The obvious reply to such criticism as this is that it wholly mistakes the aim and scope of the work criticised. I did not go to
Russia to observe happy homes, nor to make the acquaintance of
congenial, kind-hearted people, nor to admire the domestic virtues
of the Tsar. I went to Russia to study the working of a penal sys-

tem, to make the acquaintance of exiles, outcasts, and criminals, and to ascertain how the Government treats its enemies in the prisons and mines of Eastern Siberia. Granted, for the sake of argument, that there *are* thousands of happy homes in Russia; that the empire *does* abound in cultivated and kind-hearted people, and that the Tsar *is* devotedly attached to his wife and children; what have these facts to do with the sanitary condition of a tumble-down *étape* in the province of Yakútsk, or with the flogging to death of a young and educated woman at the mines of Kará? The balancing of a happy and kind-hearted family in St. Petersburg against an epidemic of typhus fever in the exile forwarding prison at Tomsk is not an evidence of fairness and impartiality, but rather an evidence of an illogical mind. All that fairness and impartiality require of the investigator in any particular field is that he shall set forth, conscientiously, in due relative proportion and without prejudice, all the significant facts that he has been able to gather in that selected field, and then that he shall draw from the collected facts such conclusions as they may seem to warrant. His work may not have the scope of an encyclopedia, but there is no reason, in the nature of things, why it should not be full, accurate and trustworthy as far as it goes. An investigation of the Indian question in the United States would necessarily deal with a very small part of the varied and complex life of the nation; but it might, nevertheless, be made as fair and complete, within its limits, as Bryce's "American Commonwealth." It would, perhaps, present a dark picture; but to attempt to lighten it by showing that the President of the Republic is a moral man and good to his children, or that there are thousands of happy families in New York that have not been driven from their homes by gold-seekers, or that the dwellers on Commonwealth Avenue in Boston are refined and cultivated people who have never made a practice of selling intoxicating liquor to minors, would be not only illogical, but absurd. If the gloominess of the picture is to be relieved, the proper way to relieve it is to show what has been done to remedy the evils that make it gloomy, and not, by any means, to prove that in some other part of the country, under wholly different conditions, a picture might be drawn that would be cheerful and inspiriting.

In the present work I have tried to deal fairly both with the Government and with the exiles. If the Government's contention is not always set forth as fully as may seem to be desirable, it is simply because most of the Government officials to whom I applied for information, both in Siberia and St. Petersburg, either manifested such a disinclination to talk that I could not pursue the subject, or else made such transparent and preposterous attempts to deceive me that their statements were merely grotesque. It will be seen, however, that a large part—perhaps more than one half—of my information with regard to Siberian prisons and the working of the exile system has been taken directly from official sources, and that a very small part of it—probably less than one-fifth—rests upon the statements of exiles or prisoners. I have appended, in the shape of classified groups of facts, a quantity of information relating to the exile system obtained by going through ten years' files of Siberian newspapers, as well as a mass of statistics from reports of the Russian prison and medical departments to show the sanitary condition of Siberian prisons and the rate of mortality in exile parties. I was assured by honest and intelligent officers of the exile administration in Siberia that these statistics are often "cooked" in such a manner as to show a much more favorable state of affairs than that which in reality exists, but they are the best official evidence obtainable. In other appendices will be found two reports of Governor-general Anúchin to the Tsar with the Tsar's marginal notes; a collection of facts bearing upon the treatment of Russian and Siberian authors by the Minister of the Interior, and of Russian and Siberian periodicals by the bureau of censorship; a small collection of revolutionary documents, and another of laws, rules, and orders of the Government relating to revolutionists, and finally a bibliography of the Russian literature relating to Siberia and the exile system so far as I am acquainted with it.

The system of spelling Russian names that I have adopted is

that sanctioned by the Royal Geographical Society of Great Britain in 1885, and since that time used by it in all of its publications. Its rules are as follows.

1. No change will be made in the spelling of words and names that have become, by long usage, familiar to English readers, such as *Cossack, droshky, Moscow.*

2. The true sound of the word as locally pronounced will be taken as the basis of the spelling, but only an approximation to the sound is aimed at.

3. Vowels are pronounced as in Italian and consonants as in English.

4. One accent only is used, the acute, to denote the syllable on which stress is laid.

5. Every letter is pronounced. When two vowels come together, each one is sounded, though the result, when spoken quickly, is sometimes scarcely to be distinguished from a single sound, as in *ai, au,* and *ei.*

6. The values of the vowels and of the principal consonants are as follows:

a—has the sound of *a* in *father.*   au—has the sound of *ow* in *how.*

e— "   "   " *e* in *benefit.*   ei— "   "   " *ey* in *they.*

i— "   "   " *i* in *ravine.*   zh— "   "   " *s* in *vision.*

o— "   "   " *o* in *mote.*   ch—is soft as in *church.*

u— "   "   " *oo* in *boot.*   g—is hard as in *gun.*

ai— "   "   " *i* in *ice.*   kh—is guttural as in *khan.*

y—is a consonant as in *yard* and is never used as a vowel or a terminal.

An exception will be made to Rule 1 in the case of a few words, such as *Czar, mujik, Nijni,* which are misleading in their common English form, and which have been correctly transliterated by such authorities as Wallace, Ralston, and Morfill.

An exception will also be made to Rule 2 in the case of certain surnames, such as *Kropótkin* and *Tourguénef,* whose possessors have adopted for themselves a definite form of signature in roman letters. A guide, however, to the pronunciation of such surnames will be found in the vocabulary at the end of Volume II.

Before closing this preface I desire to tender my most sincere and hearty thanks to the many friends, acquaintances, and well-wishers throughout European Russia and Siberia who encouraged me in my work, coöperated in my researches, and furnished me with the most valuable part of my material. Some of them are political exiles, who imperiled even the wretched future that still remained to them by writing out for me histories of their lives; some of them are officers of the exile administration who, trusting to my honor and discretion, gave me without reserve the results of their long experience; and some of them are honest, humane prison officials who, after reporting again and again upon the evils and abuses of the prison system, finally pointed them out to me, as the last possible means of forcing them upon the attention of the Government and the world. Most of these people I dare not even mention by name. Although their characters and their services are such as to make their names worthy of remembrance and honor, it is their misfortune to live in a country where the Government regards a frankly expressed opinion as an evidence of "untrustworthiness," and treats an effort to improve the condition of things as an offense to be punished. To mention the names of such people, when they live under such a government, is simply to render them objects of suspicion and surveillance, and thus deprive them of the limited power they still exercise for good. All that I can do, therefore, to show my appreciation of their trust, their kindness, and their aid, is to use the information which they gave me as I believe they would wish it to be used,— in the interest of humanity, freedom, and good government. For Russia and the Russian people I have the warmest affection and sympathy; and if, by a temperate and well-considered statement of the results of my Siberian investigations, I can make the country and the nation better known to the world, and ameliorate, even little, the lot of the "unfortunates" to whom " God is high above and the Tsar is far away," I shall be more than repaid for the hardest journey and the most trying experience of my life.

GEORGE KENNAN.

CONTENTS

ILLUSTRATIONS

ILLUSTRATIONS

ILLUSTRATIONS

MAPS

SIBERIA AND THE
EXILE SYSTEM

SIBERIA AND THE EXILE SYSTEM

CHAPTER I

FROM ST. PETERSBURG TO PERM

THE Siberian expedition of *The Century Magazine* sailed from New York for Liverpool on the second day of May, 1885. It consisted of Mr. George A. Frost, an artist of Boston, and the author of this book. We both spoke Russian, both had been in Siberia before, and I was making to the empire my fourth journey. Previous association in the service of the Russian-American Telegraph Company had acquainted us with each other, and long experience in sub-arctic Asia had familiarized us with the hardships and privations of Siberian travel. Our plan of operations had been approved by *The Century;* we had the amplest discretionary power in the matter of ways and means; and although fully aware of the serious nature of the work in hand, we were hopeful, if not sanguine, of success. We arrived in London on Sunday, May 10, and on Wednesday, the 13th, proceeded to St. Petersburg by rail, via Dover, Ostend, Cologne, Hanover, Berlin, and Eydkuhnen. As the season was already advanced, and as it was important that we should reach Siberia in time to make the most of the summer weather and the good roads, I decided to remain in the Russian capital only five days; but we were unfortunate enough to arrive there just at the beginning of a

1

long series of church holidays, and were able to utilize in the transaction of business only four days out of ten.

As soon as I could obtain an interview with Mr. Vlangálli, the assistant Minister of Foreign Affairs, I presented my letters of introduction and told him frankly and candidly what we desired to do. I said that in my judgment Siberia and the exile system had been greatly misrepresented by prejudiced writers; that a truthful description of the country, the prisons and the mines would, I thought, be advantageous rather than detrimental to the interests of the Russian Government; and that, inasmuch as I had already committed myself publicly to a defense of that Government, I could hardly be suspected of an intention to seek in Siberia for facts with which to undermine my own position. This statement, in which there was not the least diplomacy or insincerity, seemed to impress Mr. Vlangálli favorably; and after twenty minutes' conversation he informed me that we should undoubtedly be permitted to go to Siberia, and that he would aid us as far as possible by giving us an open letter to the governors of the Siberian provinces, and by procuring for us a similar letter from the Minister of the Interior. Upon being asked whether these letters would admit us to Siberian prisons, Mr. Vlangálli replied that they would not; that permission to inspect prisons must in all cases be obtained from provincial governors. As to the further question whether such permission would probably be granted, he declined to express an opinion. This, of course, was equivalent to saying that the Government would not give us *carte-blanche*, but would follow us with friendly observation, and grant or refuse permission to visit prisons as might, from time to time, seem expedient. I foresaw that this would greatly increase our difficulties, but I did not deem it prudent to urge any further concession; and after expressing my thanks for the courtesy and kindness with which we had been received I withdrew.

At another interview, a few days later, Mr. Vlangálli gave me the promised letters and, at the same time, said that he would like to have me stop in Moscow on my way to Siberia and make the acquaintance of Mr. Katkóff, the well-known editor of the *Moscow Gazette*. He handed me a sealed note of introduction to Baron Búhler, keeper of the imperial archives in Moscow, and said that he had requested the latter to present me to Mr. Katkóff, and that he hoped I would not leave Moscow without seeing him. I was not unfamiliar with the character and the career of the great Russian champion of autocracy, and was glad, of course, to have an opportunity of meeting him; but I more than suspected that the underlying motive of Mr. Vlangálli's request was a desire to bring me into contact with a man of strong personality and great ability, who would impress me with his own views of Russian policy, confirm my favorable opinion of the Russian Government, and guard me from the danger of being led astray by the specious misrepresentations of exiled nihilists, whom I might possibly meet in the course of my Siberian journey. This precaution — if precaution it was — seemed to me wholly unnecessary, since my opinion of the nihilists was already as unfavorable as the Government itself could desire. I assured Mr. Vlangálli, however, that I would see Mr. Katkóff if possible; and after thanking him again for his assistance I bade him good-by.

In reviewing now the representations that I made to high Russian officials before leaving St. Petersburg I have not to reproach myself with a single act of duplicity or insincerity. I did not obtain permission to go to Siberia by means of false pretenses, nor did I at any time assume a deceptive attitude for the sake of furthering my plans. If the opinions that I now hold differ from those that I expressed to Mr. Vlangálli in 1885, it is not because I was then insincere, but because my views have since been changed by an overwhelming mass of evidence.

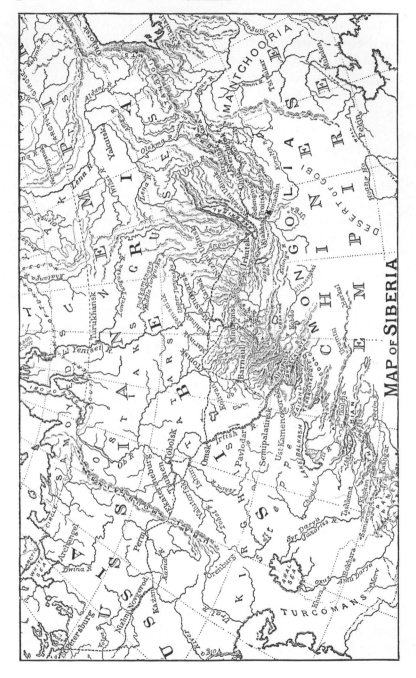

MAP OF SIBERIA

On the afternoon of May 31, having selected and purchased photographic apparatus, obtained all necessary books and maps, and provided ourselves with about fifty letters of introduction to teachers, mining engineers, and Government officials in all parts of Siberia, we left St. Petersburg by rail for Moscow. The distance from the Russian capital to the Siberian frontier is about 1600 miles; and the route usually taken by travelers, and always by exiles, is that which passes through the cities of Moscow, Nízhni Nóvgorod, Kazán, Perm, and Ekaterínburg. The eastern terminus of the Russian railway system is at Nízhni Nóvgorod, but, in summer, steamers ply constantly between that city and Perm on the rivers Vólga and Káma; and Perm is connected with Ekaterínburg by an isolated piece of railroad about 180 miles in length, which crosses the mountain chain of the Urál, and is intended to unite the navigable waters of the Vólga with those of the Ob.[1]

Upon our arrival in Moscow I presented my sealed note of introduction to Baron Búhler, and called with him at the office of the *Moscow Gazette* for the purpose of making the acquaintance of its editor. We were disappointed, however, to find that Mr. Katkóff had just left the city and probably would be absent for two or three weeks. As we could not await his return, and as there was no other business to detain us in Moscow, we proceeded by rail to Nízhni Nóvgorod, reaching that city early on the morning of Thursday, June 4.

To a traveler visiting Nízhni Nóvgorod for the first time there is something surprising, and almost startling, in the appearance of what he supposes to be the city, and in the scene presented to him as he emerges from the railway station and walks away from the low bank of the Óka River in the direction of the Vólga. The clean, well-paved

[1] During our stay in Siberia this railroad was extended to Tiumén, on one of the tributaries of the Ob, so that St. Petersburg is now in communication, by rail or steamer, with points in Siberia as remote as Semipalátinsk and Tomsk, the former 2600 and the latter 2700 miles away.

streets; the long rows of substantial buildings; the spacious boulevard, shaded by leafy birches and poplars; the canal, spanned at intervals by graceful bridges; the picturesque tower of the water-works; the enormous cathedral of Alexánder Névski; the Bourse; the theaters; the hotels; the market places — all seem to indicate a great populous center of life and commercial activity; but of living inhabitants there is not a sign. Grass and weeds are growing in the middle of the empty streets and in the chinks of the travel-worn sidewalks; birds are singing fearlessly in the trees that shade the lonely and deserted boulevard; the countless shops and warehouses are all closed, barred, and padlocked; the bells are silent in the gilded belfries of the churches; and the astonished stranger may perhaps wander for a mile between solid blocks of buildings without seeing an open door, a vehicle, or a single human being. The city appears to have been stricken by a pestilence and deserted. If the new-comer remembers for what Nízhni Nóvgorod is celebrated, he is not long, of course, in coming to the conclusion that he is on the site of the famous fair; but the first realization of the fact that the fair is in itself a separate and independent city, and a city that during nine months of every year stands empty and deserted, comes to him with the shock of a great surprise.

The fair-city of Nízhni Nóvgorod is situated on a low peninsula between the rivers Óka and Vólga, just above their junction, very much as New York City is situated on Manhattan Island between East River and the Hudson. In geographical position it bears the same relation to the old town of Nízhni Nóvgorod that New York would bear to Jersey City if the latter were elevated on a steep, terraced bluff four hundred feet above the level of the Hudson. The Russian fair-city, however, differs from New York City in that it is a mere temporary market — a huge commercial *caravansarái* where 500,000 traders assemble every year to buy and to sell commodities. In September it has fre-

THE FAIR-CITY OF NÍZHNI NÓVGOROD.

quently a population of more than 100,000 souls, and contains merchandise valued at $75,000,000; while in January, February, or March all of its inhabitants might be fed and sheltered in the smallest of its hotels, and all of its goods might be put into a single one of its innumerable shops. Its life, therefore, is a sort of intermittent commercial fever, in which an annual paroxysm of intense and unnatural activity is followed by a long interval of torpor and stagnation.

It seems almost incredible at first that a city of such magnitude — a city that contains churches, mosques, theaters, markets, banks, hotels, a merchants' exchange, and nearly seven thousand shops and inhabitable buildings, should have so ephemeral a life, and should be so completely abandoned every year after it has served the purpose for which it was created. When I saw this unique city for the first time, on a clear frosty night in January, 1868, it presented an extraordinary picture of loneliness and desolation. The moonlight streamed down into its long empty streets where the unbroken snow lay two feet deep upon the sidewalks; it touched with silver the white walls and swelling domes of the old fair-cathedral, from whose towers there came no clangor of bells; it sparkled on great snowdrifts heaped up against the doors of the empty houses, and poured a flood of pale light over thousands of snow-covered roofs; but it did not reveal anywhere a sign of a human being. The city seemed to be not only uninhabited, but wholly abandoned to the arctic spirits of solitude and frost. When I saw it next, at the height of the annual fair in the autumn of 1870, it was so changed as to be almost unrecognizable. It was then surrounded by a great forest of shipping; its hot, dusty atmosphere thrilled with the incessant whistling of steamers; merchandise to the value of 125,000,000 rubles lay on its shores or was packed into its 6000 shops; every building within its limit was crowded; 60,000 people were crossing every day the pontoon bridge that connected it with the old town; a military band was playing airs from Offenbach's operas on the great boulevard in front of the governor's house; and through all the streets of the reanimated and reawakened city poured a great tumultuous flood of human life.

I did not see the fair-city again until June, 1885, when I found it almost as completely deserted as on the occasion of my first visit, but in other ways greatly changed and improved. Substantial brick buildings had taken the place of the long rows of inflammable wooden shops and sheds; the streets in many parts of the city had been neatly paved; the number of stores and warehouses had largely increased; and the lower end of the peninsula had been improved and dignified by the erection of the great Alexánder Névski cathedral, which is shown in the center of the illustration on page 7, and which now forms the most prominent and striking architectural feature of the fair.

It was supposed that, with the gradual extension of the Russian railway system, and the facilities afforded by it for the distribution of merchandise throughout the empire in small quantities, the fair of Nízhni Nóvgorod would lose most of its importance ; but no such result has yet become apparent. During the most active period of railway construction in Russia, from 1868 to 1881, the value of the merchandise brought annually to the fair rose steadily from 126,000,000 to 246,000,000 *rúbles*,[2] and the number of shops and stores in the fair-city increased from 5738 to 6298. At the present time the volume of business transacted during the two fair-months amounts to something like 225,000,000 *rúbles*, and the number of shops and stores in the fair exceeds 7000.

The station of the Moscow and Nízhni Nóvgorod railway is situated within the limits of the fair-city, on the left bank of the river Óka, and communication between it and the old town on the other side is maintained in summer by means of a steam ferry, or a long floating bridge consisting of a roadway supported by pontoons. As the bridge, at the time of our arrival, had not been put in position for the season, we crossed the river on a low, flat barge in tow of a small steamer.

The view that one gets of the old fortified city of Nízhni Nóvgorod while crossing the Óka from the fair is both striking and picturesque. The long steep bluff upon which it is situated rises abruptly almost from the water's edge to the height of four hundred feet, notched at intervals by deep V-shaped cuts through which run the ascending roads to the upper plateau, and broken here and there by narrow terraces upon which stand white-walled and golden-domed cathedrals and monasteries half buried in groves of trees. In the warm, bright sunshine of a June day the snowy walls of the Byzantine churches scattered along the crest of the bluff ; the countless domes of blue, green, silver, and gold

[2] The value of the Russian *rúble* is about half a dollar.

rising out of dark masses of foliage on the terraces; the smooth, grassy slopes which descend here and there almost to the water's edge; and the river front, lined with steamers and bright with flags—all make up a picture that is hardly surpassed in northern Russia. Fronting the Vólga, near what seems to be the eastern end of the ridge, stands the ancient *krémlin*,[3] or stronghold of the city, whose high, crenelated walls descend the steep face of the bluff toward the river in a series of titanic steps, and whose arched gateways and massive round towers carry the imagination back to the Middle Ages. Three hundred and fifty years ago this great walled enclosure was regarded as an absolutely impregnable fortress, and for more than a century it served as a secure place of refuge for the people of the city when the fierce Tatárs of Kazán invaded the territories of the Grand Dukes. With the complete subjugation of the Tatár khanate, however, in the sixteenth century, it lost its importance as a defensive fortification, and soon began to fall into decay. Its thirteen towers, which were originally almost a hundred feet in height, are now half in ruins; and its walls, which have a circuit of about a mile and a quarter, would probably have fallen long ago had they not been extraordinarily thick, massive, and deeply founded. They make upon one an impression of even greater solidity and strength than do the walls of the famous *krémlin* in Moscow.

Upon landing from the ferry-boat in the old town of Nízhni Nóvgorod, we drove to a hotel in the upper part of the city, and after securing rooms and sending our passports to the chief of police, we walked down past the *krémlin* to

3 A *krémlin*, or, to use the Russian form of the word, a *kreml*, is merely a walled enclosure with towers at the corners, situated in a commanding position near the center of a city, and intended to serve as a stronghold, or place of refuge, for the inhabitants in time of war. It differs from a castle or fortress in that it generally incloses a larger area, and contains a number of buildings, such as churches, palaces, treasuries, etc., which are merely protected by it. It is popularly supposed that the only *krémlin* in Russia is that of Moscow; but this is a mistake. Nízhni Nóvgorod, Kazán, and several other towns in the part of Russia that was subject to Tatár invasion, had strongholds of this kind.

A PART OF THE OLD TOWN OF NÍZHNI NÓVGOROD.

the river front.   Under the long bluff upon which the city
and the *krémlin* stand, and between the steep escarpment and
the river, there is a narrow strip of level ground which is
now given up almost wholly to commerce and is known as
the "lower bazar." Upon this strip of land are huddled together in picturesque confusion a multitude of buildings of
the most heterogeneous character and appearance.   Pretentious modern stores, with gilded signs and plate-glass windows, stand in neighborly proximity to wretched hucksters'
stalls of rough, unpainted boards; banks, hotels, and steam-
ship offices are sandwiched in among ship-chandlers' shops,
old-clothes stalls, and *traktírs;*[1] fantastic, highly colored
churches of the last century appear in the most unexpected
places, and give an air of sanctity to the most disreputable
neighborhoods; and the entire region, from the river to the
bluff, is crowded with wholesale, retail, and second-hand
shops, where one can buy anything and everything—from
a paper of pins, a wooden comb, or a string of dried mushrooms, to a ship's anchor, a church bell, or a steam-engine.
In a single shop of the lower bazar I saw exposed for sale
a set of parlor chairs, two wicker-work baby-carriages, a
rustic garden seat, two cross-cut log saws, half a dozen battered *samovárs*, a child's cradle, a steam-engine, one half of
a pair of elk horns, three old boilers, a collection of telescopes,
an iron church-cross four feet in height, six or eight watches,
a dilapidated carriage-top, feather dusters, opera-glasses,
log chains, watch charms, two blacksmith's anvils, measuring
tapes, old boots, stove covers, a Caucasian dagger, turning
lathes, sleigh bells, pulleys and blocks from a ship's rigging,
fire-engine nozzles, horse collars, an officer's sword, axe
helves, carriage cushions, gilt bracelets, iron barrel-hoops,
trunks, accordions, three or four soup plates filled with old
nails and screws, carving-knives, vises, hinges, revolvers,
old harnesses, half a dozen odd lengths of rusty stove-pipe,
a tin can of "mixed biscuits" from London, and a six-foot

[1] A *traktír* is a public tea-house.

bath tub. This list of articles, which I made on the spot, did not comprise more than a third part of the dealer's heterogeneous stock in trade; but I had not time for a careful and exhaustive enumeration. In a certain way this shop was illustrative and typical of the whole lower bazar, since nothing, perhaps, in that quarter of the city is more striking than the heterogeneity of buildings, people, and trades. The whole river front is lined with landing-stages and steamers; it is generally crowded with people from all parts of the empire, and it always presents a scene of great commercial activity. Steamers are departing almost hourly for the lower Vólga, the frontier of Siberia, and the far-away Caspian; huge black barges, which lie here and there at the landing-stages, are being loaded or unloaded by gangs of swarthy Tatár stevedores; small, unpainted one-horse *telégas*, which look like longitudinal halves of barrels mounted on four wheels, are carrying away bags, boxes, and crates from the piles of merchandise on the shore; and the broad, dusty street is thronged all day with traders, peddlers, peasants, longshoremen, pilgrims, beggars, and tramps.

Even the children seem to feel the spirit of trade that controls the city; and as I stood watching the scene on the river front, a ragged boy, not more than eight or nine years of age, whose whole stock in trade consisted of a few strings of dried mushrooms, elbowed his way through the crowd with all the assurance of an experienced peddler, shouting in a thin, childish treble, "Mushrooms! Fine mushrooms! Sustain commerce, gentlemen! Buy my mushrooms and sustain commerce!"

The diversity of popular types in the lower bazar is not perhaps so great in June as it is in September, during the fair, but the peculiarities of dress are such as to make almost every figure in the throng interesting and noteworthy to a foreign observer. There are swarthy Tatárs in round skull caps and long, loose *khaláts;*[1] Russian peas-

---

[1] A loose, waistless coat resembling a dressing-gown.

ants in greasy sheepskin coats and huge wicker-work shoes, with their legs swathed in dirty bandages of coarse linen cloth and cross-gartered with hempen cords; disreputable-looking long-haired, long-bearded monks, who solicit alms for hospitals or churches, receiving contributions on small boards covered with black velvet and transferring the money deposited thereon to big tin boxes hung from their necks and secured with enormous iron padlocks; strolling dealers in *kvas*,[1] mead, sherbet, and other seductive bright-colored drinks; brazen-throated peddlers proclaiming aloud the virtues of brass jewelry, salted cucumbers, strings of dried mushrooms, and cotton handkerchiefs stamped with railroad maps of Russia; and, finally, a surging crowd of wholesale and retail traders from all parts of the Vólga River basin.

The first thing that strikes the traveler on the threshold of southeastern Russia is the *greatness* of the country — that is, the enormous extent of its material resources, and the intense commercial activity manifested along its principal lines of communication. The average American thinks of southeastern Russia as a rather quiet, semi-pastoral, semi-agricultural country, which produces enough for the maintenance of its own half-civilized and not very numerous population, but which, in point of commercial activity, cannot bear comparison for a moment with even the most backward of our States. He is not a little astonished, therefore, at Nízhni Nóvgorod, to find the shipping of the Vólga occupying six or eight miles of river front; to learn that for its regulation there is in the city a shipping court with special jurisdiction; that the *prístan*, or, as a Western steamboatman would say, the levee, is under control of an officer appointed by the Minister of Ways and Communications and aided by a large staff of subordinates; that the number of steamers plying on the Vólga and its tributaries is greater than the number on the Missis-

[1] A drink made by fermenting rye flour in water.

sippi;[1] that $15,000,000 worth of products come annually down a single tributary of the Vólga—namely, the Káma, a stream of which few Americans have ever heard; and, finally, that the waters of the Vólga River system float annually nearly 5,000,000 tons of merchandise, and furnish employment to 7000 vessels and nearly 200,000 boatmen. It may be that an ordinarily well-educated American ought to know all these things; but I certainly did not know them, and they came to me with the shock of a complete surprise.

On the morning of Saturday, June 6, after having visited the fair-city and the *krémlin* and made as thorough a study of Nízhni Nóvgorod as the time at our disposal would permit, we embarked on one of the Kámenski Brothers' steamers for a voyage of nearly a thousand miles down the Vólga and up the Káma to Perm.

It has been said that Egypt is the creation of the Nile. In a different sense, but with equal truth, it may be said that eastern Russia is the creation of the Vólga. The ethnological composition of its population was mainly determined by that river; the whole history of the country has been intimately connected with it for more than a thousand years; the character and pursuits of all the east-Russian tribes have been greatly modified by it; and upon it now depend, directly or indirectly, the welfare and prosperity of more than 10,000,000 people. From any point of view, the Vólga must be regarded as one of the great rivers of the world. Its length, from the Váldai hills to the Caspian Sea, is nearly 2300 miles; its width below Tsarítsin, in time of high water, exceeds 30 miles, so that a boatman, in crossing it, loses sight entirely of its low banks and is virtually at sea; it washes the borders of nine provinces, or administrative divisions of the empire, and on its banks stand 39 cities and more than 1000 villages and settlements. The most important part of the river, commercially, is that lying

---

[1] In 1880 there were on the upper and the lower Mississippi 681 steamers. The number on the Vólga and its tributaries is about 700.

between Nízhni Nóvgorod and the mouth of the Káma,
where there ply, during the season of navigation, about 450
steamers. As far down as the so-called "Samára bend,"
the river presents almost everywhere a picture of busy life
and activity, and is full of steamers, barges, and great hulks,
like magnified canal-boats, loaded with goods from eastern
Russia, Siberia, and Central Asia. The amount of merchan-

WATER CARRIER IN A VÓLGA RIVER VILLAGE.

dise produced, even in the strip of country directly tributary
to the Vólga itself, is enormous. Many of the agricultural
villages, such as Lískovo, which the steamer swiftly passes
between Nízhni Nóvgorod and Kazán, and which seem,
from a distance, to be insignificant clusters of unpainted
wooden houses, load with grain 700 vessels a year.

The scenery of the upper Vólga is much more varied and
picturesque than one would expect to find along a river

running through a flat and monotonous country. The left bank, it is true, is generally low and uninteresting; but on the other side the land rises abruptly from the water's edge to a height of 400 or 500 feet, and its boldly projecting promontories, at intervals of two or three miles, break up the majestic river into long, still reaches, like a series of placid lakes opening into one another and reflecting in their tranquil depths the dense foliage of the virgin forest on one side and the bold outlines of the half-mountainous shore on the other. White-walled churches with silver domes appear here and there on the hills, surrounded by little villages of unpainted wooden houses, with elaborately carved and decorated gables; deep valleys, shaggy with hazel bushes, break through the wall of bluffs on the right at intervals, and afford glimpses of a rich farming country in the interior; and now and then, in sheltered nooks half up the mountain-side overlooking the river, appear the cream-white walls and gilded domes of secluded monasteries, rising out of masses of dark-green foliage. Sometimes, for half an hour together, the steamer plows her way steadily down the middle of the stream, and the picturesque right bank glides past like a magnificent panorama with a field of vision ten miles wide; and then suddenly, to avoid a bar, the vessel sweeps in towards the land, until the wide panorama narrows. to a single vivid picture of a quaint Russian hamlet which looks like an artistically contrived scene in a theater. It is so near that you can distinguish the features of the laughing peasant girls who run down into the foreground to wave their handkerchiefs at the passing steamer; or you can talk in an ordinary tone of voice with the *muzhíks* in red shirts and black velvet trousers who are lying on the grassy bluff in front of the green-domed village church. But it lasts only a moment. Before you have fairly grasped the details of the strange Russian picture it has vanished, and the steamer glides swiftly into a new reach of the river, where there is not a sign of human

habitation, and where the cliffs on one side and the forest
on the other seem to be parts of a vast primeval wilderness.

Fascinated by the picturesque beauty of the majestic Vólga and the ever-changing novelty of the scenes successively
presented to us as we crossed from side to side, or swept
around great bends into new landscapes and new reaches of
tranquil water, we could not bear to leave the hurricane
deck until long after dark. The fresh, cool air was then

A VÓLGA RIVER HAMLET.

filled with the blended fragrance of flowery meadows and
damp forest glens; the river lay like an expanse of shining
steel between banks whose impenetrable blackness was intensified rather than relieved by a few scattered spangles of
light; and from some point far away in the distance came
the faint voice of a timber rafter, or a floating fisherman,
singing that song dear to the heart of every Russian boatman — *V'nis po mátushke po Vólge* [Down the Mother Vólga].

After drinking a few tumblers of fragrant tea at the little
center-table in the steamer's small but cozy cabin, we un-

rolled the blankets and pillows with which we had provided ourselves in anticipation of the absence of beds, and bivouacked, as Russian travelers are accustomed to do, on the long leather-covered couches that occupy most of the floor space in a Russian steamer, and that make the cabin look a little like an English railway carriage with all the partitions removed.

About five o'clock in the morning I was awakened by the persistent blowing of the steamer's whistle, followed by the stoppage of the machinery, the jar of falling gang-planks, and the confused trampling of a multitude of feet over my head. Presuming that we had arrived at Kazán, I went on deck. The sun was about an hour high and the river lay like a quivering mass of liquid silver between our steamer and the smooth, vividly green slopes of the high western bank. On the eastern side, and close at hand, was a line of the black hulls with yellow roofs and deck-houses that serve along the Vólga as landing-stages, and beside them lay half a dozen passenger steamers, blowing their whistles at intervals and flying all their holiday flags. Beyond them and just above high-water mark on the barren, sandy shore was a row of heterogeneous wooden shops and lodging-houses, which, but for a lavish display of color in walls and roofs, would have suggested a street of a mining settlement in Idaho or Montana. There were in the immediate foreground no other buildings; but on a low bluff far away in the distance, across a flat stretch of marshy land, there could be seen a mass of walls, towers, minarets, and shining domes, which recalled to my mind in some obscure way the impression made upon me as a child by a quaint picture of "Vanity Fair" in an illustrated copy of the "Pilgrim's Progress." It was the famous old Tatár city of Kazán. At one time, centuries ago, the bluff upon which the *krémlin* of Kazán stands was washed by the waters of the Vólga; but it has been left four or five miles inland by the slow shifting of the river's bed to the westward; and the distant view of the

city which one now gets from the shore is only just enough
to stimulate the imagination and to excite, without gratify-
ing, the curiosity.

The *prístan* or steamer-landing of Kazán, however, is
quite as remarkable in its way as the city itself. The build-
ers of the shops, hotels, and "rooms for arrivers" on the
river bank, finding themselves unable, with the scanty materials at their command, to render their architecture striking and admirable in form, resolved to make it at least
dazzling and attractive in color; and the result is a sort of
materialized architectural aurora borealis, which astounds
if it does not gratify the beholder. While our steamer was
lying at the landing I noted a chocolate-brown house with
yellow window shutters and a green roof ; a lavender house
with a shining tin roof; a crimson house with an emerald
roof; a sky-blue house with a red roof; an orange house
with an olive roof; a house painted a bright metallic green
all over; a house diversified with dark-blue, light-blue, red,
green, and chocolate-brown; and, finally, a most extraordinary building which displayed the whole chromatic scale
within the compass of three stories and an attic. What permanent effect, if any, is produced upon the optic nerves
of the inhabitants by the habitual contemplation of their
brilliantly colored and sharply contrasted dwellings I am
unable to say; but I no longer wonder that *prekrásni*, the
Russian word for "beautiful," means literally "very red";
nor that a Russian singer imagines himself to be using a
highly complimentary phrase when he describes a pretty
girl as *krásnaya dévitsa* [a red maiden]. When I think of
that steamboat-landing at Kazán I am only surprised that
the Russian language has not produced such forms of met-
aphorical expression as "a red-and-green maiden," "a purple
scarlet-and-blue melody," or "a crimson-yellow-chocolate-
brown poem." It would be, so to speak, a red-white-and-
blue convenience if one could express admiration in terms
of color, and use the whole chromatic scale to give force to
a superlative.

About seven o'clock passengers began to arrive in carriages and *droshkies* from the city of Kazán, and before eight o'clock all were on board, the last warning whistle had sounded, the lines had been cast off, and we were again under way. It was Sunday morning, and as the weather was clear and warm we spent nearly the whole day on the hurricane deck, enjoying the sunshine and the exhilarating sense of swift movement, drinking in the odorous air that came to us from the forest-clad hills on the western bank, and making notes or sketches of strange forms of boats, barges, and rafts which presented themselves from time to time, and which would have been enough to identify the Vólga as a Russian river even had we been unable to see its shores. First came a long, stately "caravan" of eight or ten huge black barges, like dismantled ocean steamers, ascending the river slowly in single file behind a powerful tug; then followed a curious kedging barge, with high bow and stern and a horse-power windlass amidships, pulling itself slowly up-stream by winding in cables attached to kedge anchors which were carried ahead and dropped in turn by two or three boats' crews; and finally we passed a little Russian hamlet of ready-made houses, with elaborately carved gables, standing on an enormous timber raft 100 feet in width by 500 in length, and intended for sale in the tree-less region along the lower Vólga and around the Caspian Sea. The bareheaded, red-shirted, and blue-gowned population of this floating settlement were gathered in a picturesque group around a blazing camp-fire near one end of the raft, drinking tea; and I could not help fancying that I was looking at a fragment of a peasant village which had in some way gotten adrift in a freshet and was miraculously floating down the river with all its surviving inhabitants. Now and then there came to us faintly across the water the musical chiming of bells from the golden-domed churches here and there on the right bank, and every few moments we passed a large six-oared *lódka* full of men and women in bright-colored costumes, on their way to church service.

About eleven o'clock Sunday morning we left the broad, tranquil Vólga and turned into the swifter and muddier Káma, a river which rises in the mountains of the Urál on

A PEASANT WOMAN OF SIMBIRSK.

the Siberian frontier, and pursues a southwesterly course to its junction with the Vólga, fifty or sixty miles below Kazán. In going from one river to the other we noticed a marked change, not only in the appearance of the people, villages, boats, and landing-stages, but in the aspect of the whole country. Everything seemed stranger, more primitive, and, in a certain sense, wilder. The banks of the Káma were less thickly inhabited and more generally covered with forests than those of the Vólga; the white-walled monasteries which had given picturesqueness and human interest to so many landscapes between Nízhni Nóvgorod and Kazán were no longer to be seen; the barges were of a ruder, more primitive type, with carved railings and spirally striped red-and-blue masts surmounted by gilded suns; and the crowds of peasants on the landing-stages were dressed in costumes whose originality of design and crude brightness of color showed that they had been little affected by the sobering and conventionalizing influence of Western civilization. The bright colors of the peasant costumes were attributable perhaps, in part, to the fact that, as it was Sunday, the youths and maidens came down to the steamer in holiday attire; but we certainly had not before seen in any part of Russia young men arrayed in blue, crimson, purple, pink, and violet shirts, nor young women dressed in lemon-yellow gowns, scarlet aprons, short pink over-jackets, and lilac head-kerchiefs.

Our four days' journey up the river Káma was not marked by any particularly noteworthy incident, but it was, nevertheless, a novel and a delightful experience. The weather was as perfect as June weather can anywhere be; the scenery was always varied and attractive, and sometimes beautifully wild and picturesque; the foliage of the poplars, aspens, and silver-birches that clothed the steep river-banks, and in places overhung the water so as almost to sweep the hurricane deck, had the first exquisite greenness and freshness of early summer; and the open glades and meadows, which the steamer frequently skirted at a distance of not more than fifteen or twenty feet, were blue with forget-me-nots or yellow with the large double flowers of the European trollius. At every landing-place peasant children offered for sale great bunches of lilies-of-the-valley, and vases of these fragrant flowers, provided by the steward, kept our little dining-saloon constantly filled with delicate perfume. Neither in the weather, nor in the scenery, nor in the vegetation was there anything to suggest an approach to the frontier of Siberia. The climate seemed almost Californian in its clearness and warmth; flowers blossomed everywhere in the greatest profusion and luxuriance; every evening we heard nightingales singing in the forests beside the river; and after sunset, when the wind was fair, many of the passengers caused *samovárs* to be brought up and tables to be spread on the hurricane deck, and sat drinking tea and smoking cigarettes in the odorous night air until the glow of the strange northern twilight faded away over the hills. So comfortable, pleasant, and care-free had been our voyage up the Káma that when, on Wednesday, June 10, it ended at the city of Perm, we bade the little steamer *Alexander* good-by with a feeling of sincere regret.

CHAPTER II

IN the city of Perm, where we spent one night, we had
our first skirmish with the Russian police; and although
the incident has intrinsically little importance, it is perhaps
worth recital as an illustration of the suspicion with which
strangers are regarded on the great exile route to Siberia,
and of the unlimited power of the Russian police to arrest
and examine with or without adequate cause. Late in the
afternoon on the day of our arrival, Mr. Frost and I set out
afoot for the summit of a high hill just east of the town,
which we thought would afford a good point of view for a
sketch. In making our way toward it we happened to pass
the city prison; and as this was one of the first Russian
prisons we had seen, and was, moreover, on the exile route to
Siberia, we naturally looked at it with interest and attention.
Shortly after passing it we discovered that the hill was
more distant than we had supposed it to be; and as the
afternoon was far advanced, we decided to postpone our
sketching excursion until the following day. We thereupon
retraced our steps, passed the prison the second time, and
returned to our hotel. Early the next morning we again
set out for the hill; and as we did not know any better or
more direct route to it we took again the street that led
past the prison. On this occasion we reached our destination. Mr. Frost made a sketch of the city and its suburbs,
and at the expiration of an hour, or an hour and a half, we
strolled homeward. On a large, open common near the pri-

son we were met by two *dróshkies,* in which were four officers armed with swords and revolvers, and in full uniform. I noticed that the first couple regarded us with attentive

THE CITY OF PERM.

scrutiny as they passed; but I was not as familiar at that time as I am now with the uniforms of the Russian police and gendarmes, and I did not recognize them. The two officers in the second *dróshky* left their vehicle just before reaching us, walked away from each other until they were forty or fifty feet apart, and then advanced on converging lines to meet us. Upon looking around I found that the first pair had left their carriages and separated in a similar way behind us, and were converging upon us from that direction. Then for the first time it flashed upon my mind that they were police officers, and that we, for some inconceivable reason, were objects of suspicion, and were about to be arrested. As they closed in upon us, one of them, a good-looking gendarme officer about thirty years of age, bowed to us stiffly, and said, "Will you permit me to inquire who you are?"

"Certainly," I replied; "we are American travelers."

"Where are you from?"

"Of course from America."

"I mean where did you come from last?"

"From St. Petersburg, Moscow, and Nízhni Nóvgorod."

"Where are you going?"

"To Siberia."

"Ah! To Siberia! To what part of Siberia?"

"To all parts."

"Allow me to inquire what you are going to Siberia for?"

"We are going there to travel."

"What is the object of your travels?"

"To see the country and the people."

"But tourists [with a contemptuous intonation] are not in the habit of going to Siberia. You must have some particular object in view. Tell me, if you please, exactly what that object is."

I explained to him that American travelers—if not tourists—are in the habit of going everywhere, and that the objects they usually have in view are the study of people and places, and the acquirement of knowledge. He did not seem, however, to be satisfied with this vague general statement, and plied me with all sorts of questions intended to elicit a confession of our real aims and purposes in going to such a country as Siberia. Finally he said with increasing seriousness and severity, "Yesterday you deigned to walk past the prison."

"Yes," I replied.

"What did you do that for?"

"We were going up on the hill to get a view of the town."

"But you did not go up on the hill — you merely walked past the prison, looked at it attentively as you passed, and then came back."

I explained that the hour was late and that after passing the prison we decided to postpone our excursion to the top of the hill until morning.

"Both in going and returning," he continued, "you devoted all your attention to the prison. This morning it was the same thing over again. Now, what were you looking at the prison in that way for?"

When I understood from these questions how we happened to fall under suspicion, I could not help smiling in the officer's face; but as there was no responsive levity, and as all four officers seemed to regard this looking at a prison as an exceedingly grave offense, I again went into explanations.

"Where are you staying in the city?" inquired one of the police officers.

"At the Bourse hotel."

"How long do you intend to remain here?"

"We intended to leave here to-night."

"For Ekaterínburg?"

"For Ekaterínburg."

"Where did you learn to speak Russian?" inquired the chief of gendarmes, taking up the examination in turn.

"In Siberia," I replied.

"You have been there before then?"

"I have."

"Do you speak German?"

"Very imperfectly—I have studied it."

"What were you doing in Siberia before ?"

"Trying to build a telegraph line—but may I be permitted to inquire what is the object of all these questions ?"

The gendarme officer, to whom my statements were evidently unsatisfactory, made no reply except to ask, rather peremptorily, for my passport. When informed that our passports were at the hotel he said that we must regard ourselves as under arrest until we could satisfactorily establish our identity and explain our business in Perm. We were then separated, Mr. Frost being put into one *dróshky* under guard of the gendarme officer, while I took my seat in another beside a gray-bearded official whom I took to be the chief of police. The driver of my *dróshky* happened to be a highway robber of a hackman who had tried that very morning to make me pay three times the usual rate for five minutes' ride, and when he saw me taken into custody he was unable to conceal his delight.

"They're a bad lot, your high nobility," he said to the chief of police as we drove away in the direction of the town ; "only a little while ago they hired my *dróshky* and then tried to cheat me out of half my fare."

"How much did they give you ?" asked the police officer with assumed sympathy.

The driver hesitated.

"Fifty *kopéks*," I said indignantly, "and it was twice what he ought to have had."

The driver began to asseverate, by all he held sacred, that he had not received half as much as the service was worth; but before he had spoken a dozen words, the chief of police, who evidently knew exactly how far we had ridden in a *dróshky* that morning, interrupted him with a stern command "Malchí razbóinik ! [Shut your mouth, you brigand.] They gave you three times as much as you were entitled to, and still you complain ! A stick on the bare back is what you need—twenty blows laid on hot !"

The astonished driver, not daring to make any reply to the all-powerful chief of police, relieved his feelings by flogging his horse, and we were borne in a tornado of dust to the door of the Bourse hotel.

I invited the officers to my room, gave them cigarettes, offered to get them tea, and treated them in every way as if they were guests; but this unexpected courtesy seemed to puzzle rather than placate them. They evidently regarded us as political conspirators about to make an attempt to release somebody from the Perm prison, and when I handed my passport to the young gendarme officer with a polite "Izvóltia" [It is at your service], he looked at me as if I were some new species of dangerous wild animal not classified in the books, and consequently of unknown power for evil. Our passports did not seem, for some reason, to be satisfactory; but the production of the letter of recommendation from the Russian Minister of Foreign Affairs brought the comedy of errors to an abrupt termination. The gendarme officer's face flushed a little as he read it, and after a whispered consultation with the chief of police he came to me with some embarrassment and said that he hoped we would pardon what was evidently an "unfortunate misunderstanding"; that they had taken us for two important German criminals (!) of whom they were in search, and that in detaining us they were only doing what they believed to be their duty. He hoped that they had not treated us discourteously, and said that it would gratify them very much if we would shake hands with them as an evidence that we did not harbor any resentment on account of this "lamentable mistake." We shook hands solemnly with them all, and they bowed themselves out. This little adventure, while it interested me as a practical illustration of Russian police methods, made me feel some anxiety with regard to the future. If we were arrested in this way before we had even reached the Siberian frontier, and for merely looking at the outside of a prison, what probably would happen to us when we should seriously begin our work of investigation ? [1]

Perm, which is the capital of the province of the same name, is a city of 32,000 inhabitants, situated on the left bank of the river Káma about 125 miles from the boundary line of European Russia. It is the western terminus of the Urál Mountain railway, and through it passes nearly the whole of the enormous volume of Siberian commerce. In outward appearance it does not differ materially from other Russian provincial towns of its class. It is cleaner and apparently more prosperous than Nízhni Nóvgorod, but it is much less picturesque than the latter both in architecture and in situation.

[1] Almost every foreign traveler who has made a serious attempt to study Russian life and has gone for that purpose into the country has been arrested at least once. Lansdell, the English clergyman, was arrested near this same city of Perm in 1882, as a distributor of revolutionary pamphlets [*Athenæum*, September 16, 1882]; Mackenzie Wallace was arrested "by mistake" on the bank of the Pruth as he returned from Austria in 1872 [Wallace's *Russia*, page 209]; and even the great German scientist, Baron von Humboldt, did not wholly escape suspicion. The Russian historical review *Rússkaya Stariná* has recently published a letter from a police prefect in the little Siberian town of Ishím, written in 1829, when Humboldt was in that part of the empire making scientific reseaches. The letter, which is addressed to the governor-general, is as follows :

" A few days ago there arrived here a German of shortish stature, insignificant appearance, fussy, and bearing a letter of introduction from your Excellency to me. I accordingly received him politely ; but I must say that I find him suspicious, and even dangerous. I disliked him from the first. He talks too much and despises my hospitality. He pays no attention to the leading officials of the town and associates with Poles and other political criminals. I take the liberty of informing your Excellency that his intercourse with political criminals does not escape my vigilance. On one occasion he proceeded with them to a hill overlooking the town. They took a box with them and got out of it a long tube which we all took for a gun. After fastening it to three feet they pointed it down on the town and one after another examined whether it was properly sighted. This was evidently a great danger for the town which is built entirely of wood ; so I sent a detachment of troops with loaded rifles to watch the German on the hill. If the treacherous machinations of this man justify my suspicions, we shall be ready to give our lives for the Tsar and Holy Russia. I send this despatch to your Excellency by special messenger."

A letter more characteristic of the petty Russian police officer was never penned. The civilized world is to be congratulated that the brilliant career of the great von Humboldt was not cut short by a Cossack bullet or a police saber, while he was taking sights with a theodolite in that little Siberian town of Ishím.

On Thursday, June 11, at half-past nine o'clock in the evening, we left Perm by the Urál Mountain railroad for Ekaterínburg. As we were very tired from two days spent almost wholly in walking about the streets of the former city, we converted two of the extension seats of the railway carriage into a bed, and with the help of our blankets and pillows succeeded in getting a very comfortable night's rest.

When I awoke, about eight o'clock on the following morning, the train was standing at the station of Bíser near the summit of the Uráls. The sun was shining brightly in an unclouded sky; the morning air was cool, fresh, and laden with the odor of flowers and the resinous fragrance of mountain pines; a cuckoo was singing in a neighboring grove of birches; and the glory of early summer was over all the earth. Frost made hasty botanical researches beside the railroad track and as far away from the train as he dared to venture, and came back with alpine roses, daisies, wild pansies, trollius, and quantities of other flowers to me unknown.

The scenery of the Urál where the railroad crosses the range resembles in general outline that of West Virginia where the Baltimore and Ohio railroad crosses the Alleghanies; but it differs somewhat from the latter in coloring, owing to the greater preponderance in the Urál of evergreen trees. All the forenoon, after leaving Bíser, the train swept around great curves in a serpentine course among the forest-clad hills, sometimes running for an hour at a time through a dense larch wood, where there was not a sign of human life; sometimes dashing past placer mining camps, where hundreds of men and women were at work washing auriferous gravel; and sometimes coming out into beautiful park-like openings diversified with graceful clumps of silver birch, and carpeted with turf almost as smooth and green as that of an English lawn. Flowers were everywhere abundant. Roses, dandelions, violets, wild strawberries, and lilies of the valley were in blossom all along the track, and occasionally we crossed an open glade in the heart of the forest where the grass was almost entirely hidden by a vivid sheet of yellow trollius.

We were greatly surprised to find in this wild mining region of the Urál, and on the very remotest frontier of European Russia, a railroad so well built, perfectly equipped, and luxuriously appointed as the road over which we were traveling from Perm to Ekaterínburg. The stations were the very best we had seen in Russia; the road-bed was solid and well ballasted; the rolling stock would not have suffered in comparison with that of the best lines in the empire; and the whole railroad property seemed to be in the most perfect possible order. Unusual attention had been paid evidently to the ornamentation of the grounds lying adjacent to the stations and the track. Even the *verst-posts* were set in neatly fitted mosaics three or four feet in diameter of colored Urál stones. The station of Nízhni Tagíl, on the Asiatic slope of the mountains, where we stopped half an hour for dinner, would have been in the highest degree creditable to the best railroad in the United States. The substantial station building, which was a hundred feet or more in length, with a covered platform twenty

A RAILROAD VERST POST.

feet wide extending along the whole front, was tastefully painted in shades of brown and had a red sheet-iron roof. It stood in the middle of a large, artistically planned park or garden, whose smooth, velvety greensward was broken by beds of blossoming flowers and shaded by the feathery foliage of graceful white-stemmed birches; whose winding walks were bordered by neatly trimmed hedges; and whose air was filled with the perfume of wild roses and the murmuring plash of falling water from the slender jet of a sparkling fountain. The dining-room of the station had a floor of polished oak inlaid in geometrical patterns, a high dado of dark carved wood, walls covered with oak-grain paper, and a stucco cornice in relief. Down the center of the room ran a long dining-table, beautifully set with tasteful china, snowy napkins, high glass epergnes and crystal candelabra, and ornamented with potted plants, little cedar trees in green tubs, bouquets of cut flowers, artistic pyramids of polished wine-bottles, druggists' jars of colored water, and an aquarium full of fish, plants, and artificial rock-work. The chairs around the table were of dark hard wood, elaborately turned and carved; at one end of the room was a costly clock, as large as an American jeweler's "regulator," and at the other end stood a huge bronzed oven, by which the apartment was warmed in winter. The waiters were all in evening dress, with low-cut waistcoats, spotless shirt-fronts, and white ties; and the cooks, who filled the waiters' orders as in an English grill-room, were dressed from head to foot in white linen and wore square white caps. It is not an exaggeration to say that this was one of the neatest, most tastefully furnished, and most attractive public dining-rooms that I ever entered in any part of the world; and as I sat there eating a well-cooked and well-served dinner of four courses, I found it utterly impossible to realize that I was in the unheard-of mining settlement of Nízhni Tagíl, on the Asiatic side of the mountains of the Urál.

Early in the evening of Friday, June 12, we arrived at Ekaterínburg. The traveler who has not studied attentively the geography of this part of the Russian empire is surprised to learn, upon reaching Ekaterínburg, that although he has passed out of Europe into Asia he has not yet entered Siberia. Most readers have the impression that the boundary of European Russia on the east is everywhere coterminous with that of Siberia; but such is by no means the case. The little stone pillar that marks the Asiatic line stands beside the railway track on the crest of the Urál mountain divide; while the pillar that marks the Siberian line is situated on the Ekaterínburg-Tiumén post road, more than a hundred miles east of the mountains. The effect of this arrangement of boundaries is to throw a part of the European province of Perm into Asia, and thus to separate Siberia from Russia proper.

Ekaterínburg, which although not the largest is the most cultivated and enterprising town in this part of the empire, is situated on the eastern slope of the Uráls in the Asiatic portion of the province of Perm, about one hundred and fifty miles from the Siberian frontier. It impresses the traveler at once as a city that makes some pretensions to wealth, taste, and cultivation. The well-built and architecturally effective railway station, with its circumjacent lawn and glowing flower-beds, the polished private carriages and *droshkies* with coachmen in livery that stand behind it, the well-dressed, prosperous looking gentlemen that alight from the train and enter the waiting vehicles, and the white globes of electric lights hanging here and there over the broad streets, are all significant evidences of enterprise, success, and prosperity. And it is not without reason that Ekaterínburg shows signs of wealth. The famous mineral region of which it is the center yields annually about $3,335,000 worth of gold, 5000 pounds of platinum, 6,700,000 pounds of copper, 280,000 tons of pig iron, 140,000 tons of hard coal, 16,000 tons of manganese, and 277,000 tons of salt; to say nothing of quantities of malachite, jasper, beryl, topaz, agate, emeralds, and other precious or semi-precious stones.[1] Of this wealth, which is

---

[1] The precise quantities of the principal minerals taken from the mines of the Urál, in the province of Perm, in 1884, are as follows:

PRODUCTION OF		PRODUCTION OF	
Russia as a whole:	*Province of Perm:*	*Russia as a whole:*	*Province of Perm:*
Lbs.	Lbs.	Short Tons.	Short Tons.
Gold ....78,408........ ..	10,944	Iron...... 559,901	280,082
Platinum.....4,932..........	4,932	Coal .....4,318,583..........	139,014
Copper ..13,668,732.. 6,652,988		Manganese 24,323...	15,845
		Salt 1,179,023	277,048

produced almost at their doors, the inhabitants of Ekaterínburg have naturally taken their share; and they have used
it to secure for themselves all the luxuries and opportunities for self-culture that are within their reach. They have
organized, for example, the " Urál Society of Friends of
Natural Science," which holds regular meetings and pub-
lishes its proceedings and the papers read by its members;
they have established a museum of anatomy in connection
with the Nevyánsk hospital, and a small but promising
museum of natural history under the patronage of the scientific society; they sustain two newspapers;[2] they boast of
having occasionally a season of opera; and they recently
carried to a successful conclusion a scientific, agricultural,
and industrial exhibition that attracted public attention
throughout Russia and brought visitors to Ekaterínburg
from almost all parts of the empire. These evidences of
culture and enterprise, judged by an American standard,
may seem trifling and insignificant; but they are not so

The number of *zavods* or " works " in
the province, including blast-furnaces,
rolling-mills, and manufactories, exceeds one hundred; and in the production of wrought iron, chrome iron,
platinum, and copper Perm takes first
rank among the provinces of the empire.

[2] About the time that we passed
through Ekaterínburg, the censorship
of one of these papers—the "Week"—
was transferred to Moscow. This compelled the editor to send to Moscow,
in advance, a proof of every item or
article that he desired to use; and as
the distance from the place of publication to the place of censorial supervision and back was about 1500 miles, the
"Week's" news was sometimes three
weeks old before it ceased to be dangerous. By this time, of course, it had
ceased to be interesting. Whether the
paper survived this blow or not, I am
unable to say. The two numbers of it
that appeared while we were in that

part of the empire contained nothing
but advertisements. The editor, I presume, was waiting for the expurgated
proofs of his local and telegraphic news
to get back from Moscow; and it probably did not occur to him to fill up his
reading columns with a few of the titles
of the Autocrat of all the Russias, or a
chapter or two of genealogies from the
Old Testament.

The other newspaper in Ekaterínburg
is called " The Active Correspondent,"
but how any "correspondent" ventures
to be " active " in a country where
mental activity is officially regarded as
more dangerous to the state than moral
depravity, I do not know. I invite the
attention of the reader to the list of
periodicals that have been punished or
suppressed on account of their " pernicious activity" since the accession
to the throne of Alexander III. It includes every newspaper published in
Siberia. See Appendix B.

common in Russia as to justify a traveler in passing them
without notice.

In external appearance Ekaterínburg does not differ
essentially from the typical Russian town of its class.

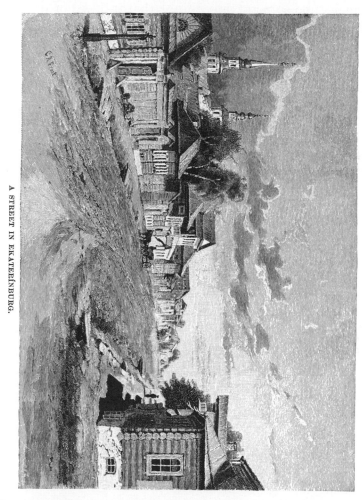

A STREET IN EKATERÍNBURG.

There are the same wide, unpaved streets that one sees
everywhere in Russia, the same square log houses with
ornamented window casings and flatly pyramidal tin roofs,
the same high board fences between the scattered dwel-

lings, the same white-walled churches with colored or gilded domes, and the same *gastínnoi dvor* or city bazar. In the bazars of these Russian provincial towns you may find, if you search diligently, almost everything that the empire produces, and a great many things that it does not produce. In roaming through *gastínnoi dvor* of Ekaterínburg a day or two after our arrival, we happened to get into what seemed to be a small grocery. The chief clerk or proprietor, a bright-faced, intelligent young peasant, answered good-humoredly all our questions with regard to his business and stock in trade, allowed us to taste certain Asiatic commodities that were new to us, and gave us as much information as he could concerning a lot of Russian and Chinese nuts that lay in open bags on the counter, and that attracted our attention because many of them were new to us. After we had examined them all, and tested experimentally a few of them, the young groceryman said, "I have in the back part of the shop some very curious nuts that were sold to me a year or two ago as 'African nuts.' Whether they ever came from Africa or not I don't know,— the Lord only *does* know,— but the people here don't like the taste of them and won't buy them. If you will condescend to wait a moment I will get a few."

"What do you suppose they are?" inquired Mr. Frost as the young man went after the "African" nuts.

"Brazil nuts, very likely," I replied, "or possibly cocoanuts. I don't believe anybody here would know either of them by sight, and they are the only tropical nuts that I can think of."

In a moment the young groceryman returned, holding out toward us a handful of the fruit of the plant known to science as *Arachis hypogaea*.

"Why, those are *peanuts!*" shouted Mr. Frost in a burst of joyful recognition. "Americanski peanuts," he explained enthusiastically to the groceryman, "kushat khorosho" [American peanuts eat. well], and he proceeded to illustrate this luminous statement by crushing the shell of one of them and masticating the contents with an ostentatious, pantomimic show of relish. Suddenly, however, the expression of his face changed, as if the result had not fully justified his anticipations, and spitting out the crushed fragments of the "African" nut he said, "They have n't been roasted."

"Nada zharit!" [It is necessary to fry] he remarked impressively to the groceryman, "Amerikanski toujours zharit" [American always to fry].

"Zharit!" exclaimed the young groceryman, to whom fried nuts were a startling novelty,—"How is it possible to fry them?"

I explained to him that Mr. Frost meant to say roast them, and that in America raw peanuts are not regarded as fit to eat. To roast a nut, however, seemed to the groceryman quite as extraordinary as to fry one, and when he was informed that the peanut is not the fruit of a tree, but of an herbaceous plant, and that it grows underground, his astonishment was boundless. His practical, commercial instincts, however, soon resumed their sway; and when we left his shop he was already preparing to roast a quantity of the "wonderful American underground nuts," with a view to sending them out again for trial as samples of a new importation. I trust that his enterprise has been crowned with success, and that the idlers of Ekaterínburg, who obstinately declined to consume African nuts raw, have learned, long ere this, to eat American peanuts roasted, and to like them at least as well as the Russian fruits of idleness—the sunflower seed and the melon seed.[1]

The pleasantest experience that we had during our brief stay in Ekaterínburg was a visit that we made to Mr. N. J. Nesterófski, the cultivated and hospitable superintendent

[1] Loungers and idlers in Russian villages, and in municipal parks, sometimes sit for hours on wooden benches in the shade, watching the passers-by, or talking with one another, while they shell and eat the seeds of the watermelon and the great Russian sunflower.

of the Berózef gold mines. I had brought a letter of introduction to him from one of his friends in St. Petersburg;
but upon reaching Ekaterínburg I discovered that he lived
ten or fifteen miles away in what was known as the Berózef
mining district. I sent the letter to him, however, at the
first opportunity, and on Monday, June 15th, he drove into
the city with a carriage and took us out to his house. The
route thither lay through a rather wild, lonely region, not
noticeably mountainous but densely wooded, with a still,
black pond here and there in the midst of the evergreens,
and a thin fringe of buttercups or golden trollius on either
side of the road to relieve a little the somber gloom of the
forest. Mr. Nesterófski's house, which was situated in rather
a large mining village of unpainted log cabins, was a complete surprise to travelers who had expected to find in that
wild part of the Urál little more than the bare necessaries
of life. Although built of squared logs, it was high and
spacious, with a metallic roof, ornamented window-casings,
and a substantial storm house at the head of the front steps.
Our host pressed an electric bell button at the door, and in
a moment we were admitted by a neatly dressed maid-servant to a spacious hall, where we removed our overcoats
and goloshes. We were then shown into the drawing room,
a beautiful apartment hung with paper of a delicate gray
tint, lighted by three long windows, filled with the perfume of fuchsias, geraniums, and splendid cinnamon pinks,
and luxuriously furnished with rugs, easy chairs, long mir-
rors, and a grand piano. Before I recovered from the state
of breathless surprise into which I was thrown by this
unexpected display of luxury, I found myself shaking hands
with Mrs. Nesterófski, a pleasant-faced lady thirty or thirty-
five years of age, who welcomed us with warm-hearted hospitality, insisted that we must be hungry after our long
ride, and invited us to come out at once to luncheon. We
took seats in the dining-room at a cozy little table, just big
enough for four, upon which were vodka, excellent sherry

and claret, bread and butter, Edam and cream cheese, sardines, fresh lettuce and radishes; and as soon as we had made a beginning by drinking the customary "fifteen drops," and nibbling at the bread, cheese, and radishes, the neat little maid-servant brought to us delicious, hot *Pozhárski* cutlets with new potatoes. And all this in an unheard-of mining camp in the Asiatic wilderness of the eastern Urál! If I may judge of the expression of my own face from the expression that irradiated the face of my comrade, Mr. Frost, I must have been fairly beaming with surprise, delight, and half-suppressed enthusiasm.

After luncheon Mr. Nesterófski escorted us through what he called the *fabrik*, a six-stamp quartz mill, where we were shown the whole process of quartz crushing and washing, the amalgamation of the gold, and the roasting of the amalgam to get rid of the mercury. It was substantially the same process that I had already seen in California and Nevada. Gold is obtained, in the Berózef district, both from quartz mines and from open placers; and after we had inspected the quartz-crushing machinery of the *fabrik*, we were taken, in a sort of Irish jaunting car known as a *dalgúshka*, to one of the nearest of the placer mines—the Andréyefski *priisk*. It was merely an extensive excavation in the midst of the forest, where 150 men and women were hard at work shoveling earth into small one-horse carts for transportation to the "machine." As fast as the carts were loaded they were driven up an inclined plane to the top of a huge iron cauldron, or churn, into which their contents were dumped. In this churn revolved horizontally in different planes half a dozen sharp iron blades, and over the blades fell continually a small stream of water. The auriferous earth, agitated incessantly by the revolving blades and drenched by the falling water, was thoroughly broken up and disintegrated, and it finally made its escape, with the water in which it was partially dissolved, through an opening at the base of the churn. From its place of exit the muddy stream ran down a series of wooden flumes or sluices, in the bottoms of which were pockets and transverse ledges to catch the heavier particles of gold and the black sand with which the gold was mixed. After it had passed through these flumes, the stream was again raised, by means of an Archimedean screw, to a height of twenty or thirty feet, and turned into another series of sluices, where it finally parted with its last and lightest flakes of precious metal. From 460 to 560 tons of earth were churned and washed in this manner every day, with a product ranging in value from $235 to $285, the average yield of the auriferous earth being about 51 cents a ton. Mr. Nesterófski said that he expected to get three puds, or about 131 pounds (troy) of gold out of the Andréyefski *priisk* before the end of the working season. This would represent a value of about $30,000. The average number of men and women employed in the placer was 150. They worked from 5 A.M. to 5 P.M., with from one to two hours' rest at noon, and their wages ranged from 17 cents a day for girls and women to 50 cents a day for men that furnished their own horses and carts. Out of these wages they had to pay $2 a hundredweight for coarse wheaten flour, 5 cents a pound for second quality meat, and about 75 cents a hundredweight for oats. Nothing, of course, but the direst necessity will force a woman to toil strenuously in a gold placer eleven hours a day for a dollar and two cents a week; and yet I saw many women, and a number of young girls, engaged in such work and receiving such wages, in the Andréyefski *priisk*. The life of men in the Siberian gold placers is a life of terrible hardship, privation, and suffering; but for the women it must be worse than penal servitude.

We did not leave the *priisk* until late in the afternoon, when the last sluice had been "cleaned up" for the night, the last flake of gold separated with a magnet from the heavy "iron sand," and a little more than a pound of gold dust locked up in an iron flask as the proceeds of 500 tons of

earth churned and washed that day. We then drove back
to Mr. Nesterófski's house, where we found dinner waiting
for us. It consisted of "fifteen drops" to wash down a preliminary *zakúska* or appetizer of rye bread and pickled
fish; then vegetable soup with little crescent-shaped meat
pies; spinach and mashed potatoes served together as a
course; cutlets of brains; small birds on toast; delicious
charlotte russe; chocolate cake, and macaroons with sherry,
claret, and white Crimean wine *ad libitum*.

I thought, after the delicious and tastefully served lunch
at noon, that Mr. Nesterófski could hardly have any more
surprises in store for us, but he was not yet at the end of
his resources. After dinner he suggested, in a nonchalant,
matter-of-fact sort of way, that we light cigarettes and take
our coffee out in the garden. It did not seem to me possible
that he could have much of a garden, on the 15th of June,
in latitude 57° north, and in the mountains of the Urál; but
I was quite willing, nevertheless, to go into the yard and see
how, in that latitude and at that season of the year, he managed to have lettuce, radishes, and new potatoes. We went
out upon a broad piazza in the rear of the house, and then
descended a flight of steps into the prettiest and most tastefully arranged garden that I had seen in Russia. The winding walks were neatly graveled and bordered with beds
of blossoming, verbena-like flowers; graceful birches, with
snowy stems and drooping, feathery foliage, stood here and
there in the grass plots, like fountains of foaming water
breaking aloft into light-green, down-drifting spray; wild
cherry trees, in full blossom, relieved the darker foliage with
their nebulous masses of misty white; while currant bushes,
raspberry bushes, and strawberry vines, in the outlying region away from the house, gave promise of an abundant
summer fruitage. At the extreme end of the yard, beyond
the vegetable garden, stood a large conservatory filled with
plants, flowers, and fruits of various kinds, among which were
dwarf palms and cactuses, good-sized oranges and lemons,

and half-ripe pineapples. Lemons, oranges, and pineapples in the mountains of the Urál on the threshold of Siberia! Could anything be more out of harmony with the impressions received from the elementary geographies of childhood? Mr. Nesterófski apologized for the half-ripe state of the pineapples, as if it was really a very humiliating and discreditable thing, and as if travelers from America had every right to expect, in the mountains of Asiatic Russia, navel oranges as big as foot-balls, and dead-ripe pineapples with sweet, spicy juice oozing out of every pore. We assured him, however, that apologies were wholly unnecessary, and that if he had shown us pine cones, instead of pineapples, our brightest anticipations would have been fully realized.

After inspecting the conservatory, the vegetable garden, and the flower garden, we seated ourselves at a little rustic table under the trees near the croquet lawn, and were there served with fragrant coffee and delicious cream. Although it was half-past eight o'clock in the evening, the sun had not yet set, and it was warm enough to sit out of doors without hat or wrap. We talked, smoked, and sipped coffee for half an hour or more, and then Mrs. Nesterófski proposed a game of croquet. The suggestion was received with acclamation, the wickets were set, and at nine o'clock at night we began knocking the balls around in bright sunshine and with birds singing in all parts of the garden. Mrs. Nesterófski and I played against her husband and Mr. Frost; and after a hard struggle beat them, hands down, by five wickets. It was a highly entertaining, if not a strictly scientific, game. Mr. Frost at that time spoke Russian very imperfectly, using French or English words when he could not remember their Russian equivalents; I myself was wholly out of practice; neither of us knew the Russian croquet rules, and our trilingual attempts to advise or consult our partners, at critical stages of the game, excited so much merriment that we were hardly able to make a strike, to say nothing of a carom. More than once I became so weak from laughter at the kaleidoscopic combinations of broken language in Mr. Frost's speech that I had to go away and sit down under a tree to recover my breath. I have no doubt Mr. Frost will say that if the mosaic of my conversation did not have as many pieces in it as his, it was only because I did not know so many tongues; and that, in the touching and plaintive words of the Portuguese grammar, "It is difficult to enjoy well so much several languages."

By the time we had finished our game and refreshed ourselves with delicately flavored caravan tea it was after ten o'clock, and time to think of getting back to Ekaterínburg. Our warm-hearted and hospitable host urged us to stay with him for the rest of the night, and return to the city some time the next day; but as we intended to set out the next day for the Siberian frontier it did not seem best to yield to the temptation. The horses were therefore ordered, and at half-past ten the carriage appeared at the door. We expressed to Mr. and Mrs. Nesterófski, as well as we could in Russian, our grateful appreciation of their cordiality and kindness, thanked them for the great pleasure they had given us, bade them good-night and good-by, and drove back to Ekaterínburg. The streets of the city, when we entered it, were still filled with the soft glow of the long northern twilight; but there was not a sign nor a sound of life in them save the slow, measured "ting!— ting!— ting!" of the triangles carried by the night watchmen, and struck, now and then, as a warning to "vagrom" men. I had heard of "belling the cat," but I never saw a practical illustration of it until I came into Ekaterínburg that night, and found a policeman with a Chimes-of-Normandy attachment prowling up and down our street in search of evil-doers. Of course the wary evil-doer fled from the sound of that watchman's triangle as a schooner in thick weather would flee from the warning boom of a fog bell, while the innocent and the righteous drew near in conscious rectitude and were promptly taken to the lock-up.

TÁRANTÁS AT A POST STATION.

We should probably have shared the fate, as well as the characteristics, of the latter if we had not found shelter in our room before the nearest policeman could get to us. He evidently regarded us as suspicious characters, and walked back and forth under our window striking his triangle impressively, until we put out our light.

At the time when we made our journey to Siberia, the railroad from Ekaterinburg, the last Russian town, to Tiumen, the first Siberian town, had not been completed. There was in operation, however, between the two cities an excellent horse express service, by means of which travelers were conveyed over the intervening two hundred miles of country in the comparatively short time of forty-eight hours. The route was let by the Government to a horse express company, which sold through tickets, provided the traveler with a vehicle, and carried him to his destination with relays of horses stationed along the road at intervals of about eighteen miles. The vehicle furnished for the traveler's use in summer is a large, heavy, four-wheeled carriage called a *tárantás*, which consists of a boat-shaped body without seats, a heavy leathern top or hood, and a curtain by which the vehicle can be closed in stormy weather. The body of the *tárantás* is mounted upon two or more long stout poles, which unite the forward with the rear axletree, and serve as rude springs to break the jolting caused by a rough road. The traveler usually stows away his baggage in the bottom of this boat-shaped carriage, covers it with straw, rugs, and blankets, and reclines on it with his back supported by one or more large, soft pillows. The driver sits sidewise on the edge of the vehicle in front of the passenger and drives with four reins a team of three horses harnessed abreast. The rate of speed attained on a good road is about eight miles an hour.

On the evening of June 16, having bought through tickets, selected a *tárantás*, and stowed away our baggage in it as skilfully as possible, we climbed to our uncomfortable seat

on Mr. Frost's big trunk, and gave the signal for a start.
Our gray-bearded driver gathered up his four reins of

A CARAVAN OF FREIGHT WAGONS.

weather-beaten rope, shouted "Nu rodníya!" [Now, then,
my relatives!] and with a measured jangle, jangle, jangle,
of two large bells lashed to the arch over the shaft-horse's
back we rode away through the wide unpaved streets of

Ekaterínburg, across a spacious parade-ground in front of the soldiers' barracks, out between two square white pillars surmounted by double-headed eagles, and then into a dark, gloomy forest of pines and firs.

When we had passed through the gate of Ekaterínburg, we were on the "great Siberian road"—an imperial highway which extends from the mountains of the Urál to the head-waters of the Amúr River, a distance of more than three thousand miles. If we had ever supposed Siberia to be an unproductive arctic waste, we soon should have been made aware of our error by the long lines of loaded wagons which we met coming into Ekaterínburg from the Siberian frontier. These transport wagons, or *obózes*, form a characteristic feature of almost every landscape on the great Siberian road from the Urál mountains to Tiumén. They are small four-wheeled, one-horse vehicles, rude and heavy in construction, piled high with Siberian products, and covered with coarse matting securely held in place by large wooden pins. Every horse is fastened by a long halter to the preceding wagon, so that a train of fifty or a hundred *obózes* forms one unbroken caravan from a quarter of a mile to half a mile in length. We passed five hundred and thirty-eight of these loaded wagons in less than two hours, and I counted one thousand four hundred and forty-five in the course of our first day's journey. No further evidence was needed of the fact that Siberia is not a land of desolation. Commercial products at the rate of one thousand five hundred tons a day do not come from a barren, arctic waste.

As it gradually grew dark towards midnight, these caravans began to stop for rest and refreshment by the roadside, and every mile or two we came upon a picturesque bivouac on the edge of the forest, where a dozen or more *obóz* drivers were gathered around a cheerful camp-fire in the midst of their wagons, while their liberated but hoppled horses grazed and jumped awkwardly here and there along the road or among the trees. The gloomy evergreen forest, lighted up from beneath by the flickering blaze and faintly tinged above by the glow of the northern twilight, the red and black Rembrandt outlines of the wagons, and the group of men in long *kaftáns* and scarlet or blue shirts gathered about the camp-fire drinking tea, formed a strange, striking, and peculiarly Russian picture.

We traveled without stop throughout the night, changing horses at every post station, and making about eight miles an hour over a fairly good road. The sun did not set until half-past nine and rose again at half-past two, so that it was not at any time very dark. The villages through which we passed were sometimes of great extent, but consisted almost invariably of only two lines of log-houses standing with their gables to the road, and separated one from another by inclosed yards without a sign anywhere of vegetation or trees. One of these villages formed a double row five miles in length of separate houses, all fronting on the Tsar's highway. Around every village there was an inclosed area of pasture-land, varying in extent from two hundred to five hundred acres, within which were kept the inhabitants' cattle; and at the point where the inclosing fence crossed the road, on each side of the village, there were a gate and a gate-keeper's hut. These village gate-keepers are almost always old and broken-down men, and in Siberia they are generally criminal exiles. It is their duty to see that none of the village cattle stray out of the inclosure, and to open the gates for passing vehicles at all hours of the day and night. From the village commune they receive for their services a mere pittance of three or four roubles a month, and live in a wretched hovel made of boughs and earth, which throughout the year is warmed, lighted, and filled with smoke by an open fire on the ground.

On the second day after our departure from Ekaterínburg, as we were passing through a rather open forest between the villages of Márkova and Tugulímskaya, our driver suddenly pulled up his horses, and turning to us

said, " Vot granítsa " [Here is the boundary]. We sprang
out of the *tárantás* and saw, standing by the roadside, a

BIVOUAC OF FREIGHT WAGON DRIVERS.

square pillar ten or twelve feet in height, of stuccoed or
plastered brick, bearing on one side the coat-of-arms of the
European province of Perm, and on the other that of the

Asiatic province of Tobólsk. It was the boundary post of Siberia. No other spot between St. Petersburg and the Pacific is more full of painful suggestions, and none has for the traveler a more melancholy interest than the little opening in the forest where stands this grief-consecrated pillar. Here hundreds of thousands of exiled human beings — men, women, and children; princes, nobles, and peasants — have bidden good-by forever to friends, country, and home. Here, standing beside the square white boundary post, they have, for the last time, looked backward with love and grief at their native land, and then, with tear-blurred eyes and heavy hearts, they have marched away into Siberia to meet the unknown hardships and privations of a new life.

No other boundary post in the world has witnessed so much human suffering, or been passed by such a multitude of heart-broken people. More than 170,000 exiles have traveled this road since 1878, and more than half a million since the beginning of the present century. In former years, when exiles were compelled to walk from the places of their arrest to the places of their banishment, they reached the Siberian boundary post only after months of toilsome marching along muddy or dusty roads, over forest-clad mountains, through rain-storms or snow-storms, or in bitter cold. As the boundary post is situated about half-way between the last European and the first Siberian *étape*, it has always been customary to allow exile parties to stop here for rest and for a last good-by to home and country. The Russian peasant, even when a criminal, is deeply attached to his native land; and heart-rending scenes have been witnessed around the boundary pillar when such a party, overtaken, perhaps, by frost and snow in the early autumn, stopped here for a last farewell. Some gave way to unrestrained grief; some comforted the weeping; some knelt and pressed their faces to the loved soil of their native country, and collected a little earth to take with them into

THE SIBERIAN BOUNDARY POST.

exile; and a few pressed their lips to the European side of the cold brick pillar, as if kissing good-by forever to all that it symbolized.

At last the stern order " Stróisa! " [Form ranks!] from the under officer of the convoy put an end to the rest and leave-taking, and at the word "March!" the gray-coated troop of exiles and convicts crossed themselves hastily all together, and, with a confused jingling of chains and leg-fetters, moved slowly away past the boundary post into Siberia.

Until recently the Siberian boundary post was covered with brief inscriptions, good-bys, and the names of exiles scratched or penciled on the hard cement with which the pillar was originally overlaid. At the time of our visit, however, most of this hard plaster had apparently been pounded off, and only a few words, names, and initials remained. Many of the inscriptions, although brief, were significant and touching. In one place, in a man's hand, had been written the words " Prashchái Márya! " [Good-by, Mary!] Who the writer was, who Mary was, there is nothing now left to show; but it may be that to the exile who scratched this last farewell on the boundary pillar " Mary" was all the world, and that in crossing the Siberian line the writer was leaving behind him forever, not only home and country, but love.

After picking a few flowers from the grass at the base of the boundary pillar, we climbed into our carriage, said "Good-by" to Europe, as hundreds of thousands had said good-by before us, and rode away into Siberia.

CHAPTER III

THE FLOWERY PLAINS OF TOBÓLSK

IN crossing the boundary line between the provinces of Perm and Tobólsk, we entered a part of the Russian empire whose magnitude and importance are almost everywhere underestimated. People generally seem to have the impression that Siberia is a sub-arctic colonial province about as large as Alaska; that it is everywhere cold, barren, and covered during the greater part of the year with snow; and that its sparse population is composed chiefly of exiles and half-wild aborigines, with a few soldiers and Government officials here and there to guard and superintend the *ostrógs*, the prisons, and the mines. Very few Americans, if I may judge from the questions asked me, fully grasp and appreciate the fact that Siberia is virtually a continent in itself, and presents continental diversities of climate, scenery, and vegetation. We are apt, unconsciously, to assume that because a country is generally mapped upon a small scale it must necessarily occupy only a small part of the surface of the globe; but the conclusion does not follow from the premises. If a geographer were preparing a general atlas of the world, and should use, in drawing Siberia, the same scale that is used in Stieler's "Hand Atlas" for England, he would have to make the Siberian page of his book nearly twenty feet in width to accommodate his map. If he should use for Siberia the scale adopted by Colton, in his "Atlas of the

United States," for New Jersey, he would have to increase the width of his page to fifty-six feet. If he should delineate Siberia upon the scale of the British ordnance survey maps of England (the "six-inch maps") he would be compelled to provide himself with a sheet of paper 2100 feet wide, and his atlas, if laid out open, would cover the whole lower part of New York City from the Battery to Wall street. These illustrations are sufficient to show that if Siberia were charted upon a scale corresponding with that employed in mapping other countries, its enormous geographical extent would be much more readily apprehended, and would appeal much more strongly to the imagination.

Siberia extends in its extreme dimensions from latitude 40.17 (the southern boundary of Semiréchinsk) to latitude 77.46 (Cape Cheliúskin), and from longitude 60 east (the Uráls) to longitude 190 west (Bering strait). It therefore has an extreme range of about 37 degrees, or 2500 miles, in latitude, and 130 degrees, or 5000 miles, in longitude. Even these bare statistics give one an impression of vast geographical extent; but their significance may be emphasized by means of a simple illustration. If it were possible to move entire countries from one part of the globe to another, you could take the whole United States of America from Maine to California and from Lake Superior to the Gulf of Mexico, and set it down in the middle of Siberia, without touching anywhere the boundaries of the latter territory. You could then take Alaska and all the States of Europe, with the single exception of Russia, and fit them into the remaining margin like the pieces of a dissected map; and after having thus accommodated all of the United States, including Alaska, and all of Europe, except Russia, you would still have more than 300,000 square miles of Siberian territory to spare — or, in other words, you would still leave unoccupied in Siberia an area half as large again as the empire of Germany.[1] The single province of Tobólsk, which in comparison with the other Siberian provinces ranks only fourth in point of size, exceeds in area all of our northern States from Maine to Iowa taken together. The province of Yeniséisk is larger than all of the United States east of the Mississippi River and the territory of Yakútsk is thirteen times as large as Great Britain, thirty-four times as large as the State of Pennsylvania, and might be divided into a hundred and eighty-eight such States as Massachusetts; and yet Yakútsk is only one of eleven Siberian colonies.

A country of such vast extent must necessarily include all varieties of topography and scenery, and all sorts of climate. Disregarding for the present local and partial exceptions, taking climate and topography together and beginning at the arctic ocean, Siberia may be roughly divided into three broad east-and-west zones, or belts of country.

[1] COMPARATIVE AREAS.

Siberia.	Square Miles.	Europe.	Square Miles.
Tobólsk	570,290	France	204,177
Tomsk	333,542	Germany	211,196
Steppe territories	560,324	Great Britain	120,832
Yeniséisk	992,874	Greece	25,014
Irkútsk	309,191	Italy	110,620
Yakútsk	1,517,132	Montenegro	3,630
Trans-Baikál	240,781	Netherlands	12,648
Amúr region	239,471	Portugal	32,528
Maritime territories	730,024	Roumania	48,307
		Servia	18,750
Total	5,493,629	Spain	193,199
		Sweden	170,979
Am. and Europe.	Square Miles.	Norway	123,205
		Switzerland	15,892
U. S. and Alaska	3,501,404	European Turkey	125,289
Austria-Hungary	240,942		
Belgium	11,373	Total	5,184,109
Denmark	14,124		

Siberian provinces	5,493,629
The United States, Alaska, and Europe	5,184,109
Difference in favor of Siberia	309,520

They are as follows : 1. The great northern *túndra* or
the treeless region of moss steppes, extending along the
whole arctic sea-coast from Nóvaya Zémlaya to Bering
strait. 2. The forest region, which, with occasional breaks,
occupies a wide belt through the middle of the country
from the Urál mountains to the Okhótsk sea. 3. The fertile and arable region which lies along the Central Asiatic
and Mongolian frontier, and extends from Ekaterínburg
and Órenburg to the coast of the Pacific. The northern
and southern boundaries of these great transcontinental
belts of country cannot be exactly defined, because they
are more or less irregular. In some places, as for example
in the valleys of the great rivers, the central forests make
deep indentations into the barren region that lies north of
them; while in others the northern steppes break through
the central forests and even encroach upon the beautiful
and fertile region along the southern frontier. Generally
speaking, however, the imaginary zones or belts into which
I have for convenience divided Siberia correspond with
actual physical features of the country.

I will now take up these zones of climate and topography
separately and sketch hastily the character of each. 1. The
great northern *túndra*. The northern coast of Siberia, between the southern extremity of Nóvaya Zémlaya and
Bering strait, is probably the most barren and inhospitable
part of the whole Russian empire. For hundreds of miles
back from the arctic ocean the country consists almost entirely of great desolate steppes, known to the Russians as
túndras, which in summer are almost impassable wastes of
brownish-gray, arctic moss, saturated with water, and in
winter trackless deserts of snow, drifted and packed by
polar gales into long, hard, fluted waves. The Siberian
túndra differs in many essential particulars from all other
treeless plains. In the first place, it has a foundation of
permanently frozen ground. Underlying the great moss
túndras that border the Léna river north of Yakútsk there

is everywhere a thick stratum of eternal frost, beginning in winter at the surface of the ground, and in summer at a point twenty or thirty inches below the surface, and extending in places to a depth of many hundred feet. What scanty vegetation, therefore, the *túndra* affords roots itself and finds its nourishment in a thin layer of unfrozen ground —a mere veneering of arable soil—resting upon a substratum of permanent ice. This foundation of ice is impervious, of course, to water, and as the snow melts in summer the water completely saturates the soil to as great a depth as it can penetrate, and, with the continuous daylight of June and July, stimulates a dense growth of gray, arctic moss. This moss, in course of time, covers the entire plain with a soft, yielding cushion, in which a pedestrian will sink to the knee without finding any solid footing. Moss has grown out of decaying moss, year after year, and decade after decade, until the whole *túndra*, for thousands of square miles, is one vast, spongy bog. Of other vegetation there is little or none. A clump of dwarf berry-bushes, an occasional tuft of coarse, swamp grass, or a patch of storm-and-cold-defying *kedróvnik* [*Pinus cembra*] diversifies perhaps, here and there, the vast, brownish-gray expanse; but, generally speaking, the eye may sweep the whole circle of the horizon and see nothing but the sky and moss.

An observer who could look out upon this region in winter from the car of a balloon would suppose himself to be looking out upon a great frozen ocean. Far or near, he would see nothing to suggest the idea of land except, perhaps, the white silhouette of a barren mountain range in the distance, or a dark, sinuous line of dwarf berry-bushes and trailing pine, stretching across the snowy waste from horizon to horizon, and marking the course of a frozen arctic river. At all seasons, and under all circumstances, this immense border land of moss *túndras* is a land of desolation. In summer, its covering of water-soaked moss struggles into life, only to be lashed at intervals by pitiless whips of icy rain until it is again buried in snow; and in winter, fierce gales, known to the Russians as *púrgas*, sweep across it from the arctic ocean and score its snowy surface into long, hard, polished grooves called *zastrúgi*. Throughout the entire winter, it presents a picture of inexpressible dreariness and desolation. Even at noon, when the sealike expanse of storm-drifted snow is flushed faintly by the red, gloomy light of the low-hanging sun, it depresses the spirits and chills the imagination with its suggestions of infinite dreariness and solitude; but at night, when it ceases to be bounded even by the horizon because the horizon can no longer be distinguished, when the pale, green streamers of the aurora begin to sweep back and forth over a dark segment of a circle in the north, lighting up the whole white world with transitory flashes of ghostly radiance, and adding mystery to darkness and solitude, then the Siberian *túndra* not only becomes inexpressibly lonely and desolate, but takes on a strange, half terrible unearthliness, which awes and yet fascinates the imagination.

The climate of this great northern *túndra* is the severest in the Russian empire, if not the severest in the known world. As you go eastward from the Urál mountains through this barren zone, the mean annual temperature gradually decreases; until, shortly after crossing the river Léna, you reach, in latitude 67.34, on the border of the great *túndra*, a lonely Yakút settlement called Verkhoyánsk, or the upper settlement of the Yána, a village that is known throughout Siberia, and is beginning to be known throughout the world, as the Asiatic pole of cold. The fact is familiar to most readers that the magnetic pole, and probably the pole of greatest cold, do not coincide with the geographical pole. There are two points in the northern hemisphere, one in the American arctic archipelago and one in northeastern Siberia, where the cold is more severe than in any region lying farther north that has yet been explored. The Siberian pole of cold is at or near Verkhoyánsk. A long series of Russian observations made at this settlement shows the following mean temperatures: For the whole year, four degrees above zero Fahr.; mean temperature for December, 46 degrees below; for January, 55 degrees below; for February, 54 degrees below; or an average temperature of 51 degrees below zero for the three winter months. In 1869, the thermometer at Verkhoyánsk went repeatedly below —70 degrees, and fell once to —81 degrees Fahr.[1]

Immediately south of the great northern *túndra,* and extending, with occasional breaks, from the Urál mountains to the Okhótsk sea, lies the second of the three zones into which I have provisionally divided Siberia—the zone of forests. As you go southward from the arctic ocean and get gradually into a less rigorous climate, trees begin to make their appearance. At first there are only a few stunted and storm-twisted larches struggling for existence on the edge of the *túndra;* but they gradually grow larger and more abundant, pines and firs make their appearance, then birch, willow, and poplar, until at last you enter a vast primeval forest, through which you may travel in a straight line for weeks together. This zone of forests has an area of hundreds of thousands of square miles, and stretches almost entirely across Siberia. Along its northern boundary the climate, although less rigorous than the climate of the *túndra,* is still severe; but long before you get through to its southern edge, the temperature grows milder, poplars, aspens, elms, and the Tatár maple take the places of firs,

[1] The record is given by the eminent Russian meteorologist Dr. Woeikof, who vouches for the trustworthiness of the observations, and an account of them may be found in the English scientific journal, *Nature,* for March 10, 1881. Dr. Búnge, who has recently returned from an expedition to the coast of the arctic ocean and the New Siberian islands, reports a minimum temperature at Verkhoyánsk of —87°; and a previous record of —82° may be found in the Irkútsk newspaper *Sibír* for September 18, 1883. The best of thermometers, however, at temperature lower than —60° are very inaccurate; and these observations are to be taken with proper allowance for instrumental error. But, even with such allowance, they show that Verkhoyánsk is probably the coldest place on the globe.

larches, and pines, and you come out at last into the more
open, fertile, and arable zone of southern Siberia. This
beautiful and picturesque country presents, at least in summer, nothing that would even remotely suggest an arctic
region. The soil is a rich, black loam, as fertile as the soil of
an English garden; flowers grow everywhere in the greatest
profusion; the woods are full of rhododendron, wild cherry,
and flowering acacia; the country is neither all plain nor
all forest, but a blending of both; it is broken just enough
by hills and mountains to give picturesqueness to the landscape; and during half the year it is fairly saturated with
golden sunshine. I do not wish, of course, to convey the
idea that in this country it is always summer. Southern
Siberia has a winter and a severe one, but not, as a rule,
much severer than that of Minnesota, while its summer is
warmer and more genial than that of many parts of central
Europe. A glance at the map is sufficient to show that a
considerable part of Western Siberia lies farther south than
Nice, Venice, or Milan; and that the southern part of the
Siberian territory of Semiréchinsk is nearer the equator
than Naples. In a country that stretches from the latitude
of Italy to the latitude of central Greenland, one would naturally expect to find, and as a matter of fact one does find,
many varieties of climate and scenery. On the Taimir
peninsula, east of the gulf of Ob, the permanently frozen
ground thaws out in summer to a depth of only a few
inches, and supports only a scanty vegetation of berry-
bushes and moss; while in the southern part of Western
Siberia water-melons and cantaloupes are a profitable crop;
tobacco is grown upon thousands of plantations; and the
peasants harvest annually more than 50,000,000 bushels of
grain. In the fertile and arable zone of southern Siberia
there are a dozen towns that have a higher mean temperature for the months of June, July, and August than the city
of London. In fact, the summer temperature of this whole
belt of country, from the Uráls to the Pacific, averages six

degrees higher than the mean summer temperature of England. Irkútsk is five degrees warmer in summer than Dublin; Tobólsk is four degrees warmer than London; Semipalátinsk exactly corresponds in temperature with Boston; and Viérni has as hot a summer as Chicago.[1]

To the traveler who crosses the Uráls for the first time in June nothing is more surprising than the fervent heat of Siberian sunshine and the extraordinary beauty and profusion of Siberian flowers. Although we had been partly prepared, by our voyage up the Káma, for the experience that awaited us on the other side of the mountains, we were fairly astonished, upon the threshold of Western Siberia, by the scenery, the weather, and the flora. In the fertile, blossoming country presented to us as we rode swiftly eastward into the province of Tobólsk there was absolutely nothing even remotely to suggest an arctic region. If we had been blindfolded and transported to it suddenly in the middle of a sunny afternoon, we could never have guessed to what part of the world we had been taken. The sky was as clear and blue and the air as soft as the sky and air of California; the trees were all in full leaf; birds were singing over the flowery meadows and in the clumps of birches by the roadside; there were a drowsy hum of bees and a faint fragrance of flowers and verdure in the air; and the

[1] COMPARATIVE SUMMER TEMPERATURES.

Siberia.	Fahr.	America and Europe.	Fahr.
Viérni	70.7	Chicago, Ill.	71.3
Blagovéshchensk	68.6	Buffalo, N. Y.	69.0
Semipalátinsk	68.2	Milwaukee, Wis	68.6
Khabarófka	67.3	Boston, Mass.	68.2
Vladivostók	65.6	Portland, Me.	66.6
Akmolínsk	65.1	Moscow, European Russia	65.0
Omsk	65.1	St. Petersburg	61.0
Barnaúl	63.7	London, England	60.0
Krasnoyársk	63.0	Dublin, Ireland	57.0
Tobólsk	62.4		
Tomsk	62.2	Mean summer temperature of 12	
Irkútsk	61.5	Siberian cities and towns	65.3
		Mean summer temperature in 9	
		American and European cities.	65.2

sunshine was as warm and bright as that of a June afternoon in the most favored part of the temperate zone.

The country through which we passed between the post stations of Cheremíshkaya and Sugátskaya was a rich, open, farming region, resembling somewhat that part of western New York which lies between Rochester and Buffalo. There were no extensive forests, but the gently rolling plain was diversified here and there by small patches of woodland, or groves of birch and poplar, and was sometimes cultivated as far as the eye could reach. Extensive stretches of growing wheat and rye alternated with wide fields of black plowed land not yet sown, and occasionally we crossed great expanses of prairie, whose velvety greensward was sprinkled with dandelions, buttercups, and primroses, and dotted in the distance with grazing cattle and sheep. Sometimes, for miles together, the road ran through unfenced but cultivated land where men and women in bright-colored dresses were plowing, harrowing, or weeding young grain; sometimes we plunged into a dense cool forest, from the depths of which we could hear the soft notes of shy cuckoos, and then we came out into a great sea of meadow blue with forget-me-nots, where field sparrows and warblers were filling all the air with joyous melody. Flowers met the eye everywhere in great variety and in almost incredible profusion. Never had we seen the earth so carpeted with them, even in California. The roadside was bright with wild roses, violets, buttercups, primroses, marsh-marigolds, yellow peas, iris, and Tatár honeysuckles; the woods were whitened here and there by soft clouds of wild-cherry blossoms, and the meadows were literally great floral seas of color. In some places the beautiful rose-like flowers of the golden trollius covered hundreds of acres with an almost unbroken sheet of vivid yellow; while a few miles farther on, the steppe, to the very horizon, was a blue ocean of forget-me-nots. I do not mean simply that the ground was sprinkled with them, nor merely that they grew in great abundance;

I mean that the grass everywhere was completely hidden by them, so that the plain looked as if a sheet of blue gauze had been thrown over it, or as if it were a great expanse of tranquil water reflecting a pale-blue sky. More than once these forget-me-not plains, when seen afar, resembled water so closely as to deceive us both.

Throughout the whole distance from Ekaterínburg to Tiumén, wherever the country was open, the road was bordered on each side by a double or triple row of magnificent silver-birches, seventy or eighty feet in height, set so closely together that their branches interlocked both along the road and over it, and completely shut out, with an arched canopy of leaves, the vertical rays of the sun. For miles at a time we rode, between solid banks of flowers, through this beautiful white-and-green arcade, whose columns were the snowy stems of birches, and whose roof was a mass of delicate tracery and drooping foliage. The road resembled an avenue through an extensive and well-kept park, rather than a great Siberian thoroughfare, and I could not help feeling as if I might look up at any moment and see an English castle, or a splendid country villa. According to tradition these birches were planted by order of the Empress Catherine II., and the part of the great Siberian road which they shade is known as " Catherine's Alley." Whether the object of the great *Tsarítsa* was to render less toilsome and oppressive the summer march of the exiles, or whether she hoped, by this means, to encourage emigration to the country in which she took so deep an interest, I do not know ; but the long lines of beautiful birches have for more than a century kept her memory green, and her name has doubtless been blessed by thousands of hot and tired wayfarers whom her trees have protected from the fierce Siberian sunshine.

Almost the first peculiarity of a West Siberian landscape that strikes a traveler from America is the complete absence of fences and farm-houses. The cultivated land of the peasants is regularly laid out into fields, but the fields are not inclosed, and one may ride for two or three hours at a time through a fertile and highly cultivated region without seeing a single fence, farm-house, or detached building. The absence of fences is due to the Siberian practice of inclosing the cattle in the common pasture which surrounds the village, instead of fencing the fields that lie outside. The absence of farm-houses is to be explained by the fact that the Siberian peasant does not own the land that he cultivates, and therefore has no inducement to build upon it. With a very few exceptions, all of the land in Siberia belongs to the Crown. The village communes enjoy the usufruct of it, but they have no legal title, and cannot dispose of it nor reduce any part of it to individual ownership. All that they have power to do is to divide it up among their members by periodical allotments, and to give to each head of a family a sort of tenancy-at-will. Every time there is a new allotment, the several tracts of arable land held under the Crown by the commune may change tenants; so that if an individual should build a house or a barn upon the tract of which he was the temporary occupant, he might, and probably would, be forced sooner or later to abandon it. The result of this system of land tenure and this organization of society is to segregate the whole population in villages, and to leave all of the intervening land unsettled. In the United States, such a farming region as that between the Uráls and Tiumén would be dotted with houses, granaries, and barns; and it seemed very strange to ride, as we rode, for more than eighty miles, through a country that was everywhere more or less cultivated, without seeing a single building of any kind outside of the villages.

Another peculiarity of Western Siberia which strongly impresses an American is the shabbiness and cheerlessness of most of its settlements. In a country so fertile, highly cultivated, and apparently prosperous as this, one naturally expects to see in the villages some signs of enterprise, comfort, and taste; but one is almost everywhere disappointed.

A West Siberian village consists of two rows of unpainted one-story log-houses with A-shaped or pyramidal roofs, standing directly on the street, without front yards or front doors. Between every two houses there is an inclosed side yard, around which stand sheds, granaries, and barns; and from this side yard or court there is an entrance to the house. The court-yard gate is sometimes ornamented with

A SIBERIAN PEASANT'S HOUSE, BARN, AND COURT-YARD GATE.

carved or incised wood-work, as shown in the above illustration; the window-shutters of the houses are almost always elaborately painted, and the projecting edges of the gable roofs are masked with long strips of carved or decorated board; but with these exceptions the dwellings of the peasants are simple log structures of the plainest type, and a large proportion of them are old, weather-beaten, and in bad repair. The wide street has no sidewalks; it is sometimes a sea of liquid mud from the walls of the houses on one side to the walls of the houses on the other; and there is not a tree, nor a bush, nor a square yard of grass in the settlement. Bristly, slab-sided, razor-backed pigs lie here and there in the mud, or wander up and down the street in search of food, and the whole village makes upon an American an impression of shiftlessness, poverty, and squalor. This impression, I am glad to say, is in most cases deceptive. There is in all of these villages more or less individual comfort and prosperity; but the Siberian peasant does not seem to take any pride in the external appearance of his premises, and pays little attention to beautifying them or keeping them in order. The condition of the whole village, moreover, indicates a lack of public spirit and enterprise on the part of its inhabitants. As long as an evil or a nuisance is endurable, there seems to be no disposition to abate it, and the result is the general neglect of all public improvements. Much of this seeming indifference is doubtless attributable to the paralyzing influence of a paternal and all-regulating Government. One can hardly expect the villagers to take the initiative, or to manifest public spirit and enterprise, when nothing whatever can be done without permission from the official representatives of the Crown, and when the very first effort to promote the general well-being is likely to be thwarted by some bureaucratic "regulation," or the caprice of some local police officer. All that the peasants can do is to obey orders, await the pleasure of the higher authorities, and thank God that things are no worse.

Almost the only indication of taste that one sees in a West Siberian settlement, and the only evidence of a love of the beautiful for its own sake, is furnished by the plants and flowers in the windows of the houses. Although there may not be a tree nor a blade of grass in the whole village, the windows of nine houses out of ten will be filled with splendid blossoming fuchsias, oleanders, cactuses, geraniums, tea-roses, and variegated cinnamon pinks. One rarely finds, even in a florist's greenhouse, more beautiful flowers than

may be seen in the windows of many a poor Siberian peasant's dwelling.   Owing to some peculiarity in the composition of the glass, these windows are almost always vividly
iridescent, some of them rivaling in color the Cesnola glass
from Cyprus.   The contrast between the black, weather-
beaten logs of the houses and the brilliant squares of irides-
cence that they inclose—between the sea of liquid mud in
the verdureless streets and the splendid clusters of conservatory flowers in the windows—is sometimes very striking.

On the walls of many of the log houses in the villages
through which we passed were unmistakable evidences of
the existence, in Western Siberia, of an organized volun-
teer fire department.   These evidences took the form, generally, of rough pictorial representations, in red paint, of
the fire-extinguishing apparatus that the houses contained.
On the gable end of one cabin, for example, there would be
a rudely drawn outline of a fire-bucket; on another a picture of a ladder; while on a third would appear a graphic
sketch of a huge broad-ax that looked red and bloodthirsty enough to have belonged to Ivan the Terrible.   In
the event of a fire, every householder was expected to
make his appearance promptly, armed and equipped with
the implement pictorially represented on the wall of his
house.   I made a careful inventory of the fire-extinguishing apparatus promised by the mural sketches along one
village street through which we passed, and found it to
consist of seven axes, eleven buckets, three ladders, one
sledge-hammer, one barrel mounted on wheels, two pulling-
down hooks, and a pair of scissors.   Exactly in what way
they use scissors in Siberia to put out fires I am unable to
explain.   I gave the subject a great deal of thought, but
arrived only at conjectural conclusions.   Mr. Frost was of
opinion that the house decorated with the picture of the
scissors was the home of the "exchange editor"; but I insisted, as a newspaper man, that the "exchange editor" could
not be expected to run to fires, even in as benighted a coun-

try as Siberia, and that, moreover, no Russian editor would
dare to *look* at a fire — much less *run* to one—without
written permission from the press-censor, countersigned
by the chief of police, and indorsed by the procureur of the
Holy Synod and the *glávni nachálnik* of the Department
of Public Safety.   In my judgment, therefore, it was probable that the house was the residence of the tailor who
cut out and fitted uniforms for the firemen whenever it
became necessary for them to act in their official capacity.
It would have a very demoralizing tendency, of course,
and would unsettle the public mind, if a fire should be ex-
tinguished by men who passed buckets in their shirt-sleeves.
It was of the utmost importance, therefore, that the firemen
should be able to find the house of the duly authorized
tailor and get their uniforms made at the earliest possible
moment after the sounding of the alarm.   I tried to make
Mr. Frost see what a terrible state of things would exist if
there were no picture of scissors to designate the tailor's
house, and the firemen should be unable to find it when a
fire had broken out in the next street and they wanted
their uniforms cut and fitted instantly.   But the graphic
picture that I drew of the horrors of such a situation did
not seem to touch his callous sensibilities.   He had not
lived long enough in Russia to really feel and appreciate
the importance of getting into a uniform before under-
taking to do anything.

As we approached Tiumén we left behind us the open
plains and the beautiful farming country that had so much
surprised and delighted us, and entered a low, swampy,
and almost impenetrable forest, abounding in flowers, but
swarming with mosquitoes.   The road, which before had
been comparatively smooth and dry, became a quagmire
of black, tenacious mud, in which the wheels of our heavy
tárantás sank to the hubs, and through which our progress
was so slow that we were four hours in traversing a single
stretch of about eighteen miles.   Attempts had apparently

been made here and there to improve this part of the route by laying down in the soft, marshy soil a corduroy of logs; but the logs had sunk unequally under the pounding wheels of ten thousand loaded freight wagons, leaving enormous transverse ruts and hollows filled with mud, so that the only result of the "improvement" was to render the road more nearly impassable than before, and to add unendurable jolting to our other discomforts. At last, weary of lurches, jolts, and concussions, we alighted, and tried walking by the roadside; but the sunshine was so intensely hot, and the mosquitoes so fierce and bloodthirsty, that in twenty minutes we were glad to climb back into the *tárantás* with our hands full of flowers, and our faces scarlet from heat and mosquito bites. Upon comparing our impressions we found that we were unanimously of the opinion that if we had been the original discoverers of this country, we should have named it either Florida or Culexia, since flowers and mosquitoes are its distinctive characteristics and its most abundant products.

At the gate-keeper's lodge of one of the last villages that we passed before reaching Tiumén, we were greeted with the ringing of a large hand-bell. The sound was strangely suggestive of an auction, but as we stopped in front of the village gate the bell-ringer, a bareheaded man in a long black gown, with a mass of flaxen hair hanging over his shoulders and a savings-bank box suspended from his neck, approached the *tárantás* and called our attention to a large, brownish picture in a tarnished gilt frame resting on a sort of improvised easel by the roadside. It was evidently an *ikón* or portrait of some holy saint from a Russian church; but what was the object of setting it up there, and what relation it bore to us, we could not imagine. Finally the bell-ringer, bowing, crossing himself, and invoking blessings on our heads, implored us, *Khristá rádi* [for Christ's sake], to contribute to the support of the holy saint's church, which, it appeared, was situated somewhere in the vicinity. This combination of an auctioneer's bell, a saint's image, a toll-gate, and a church beggar, greatly amused Mr. Frost, who inquired whether the holy saint owned the road and collected toll. The gate-keeper explained that the saint had nothing to do with the road, but the church was poor, and the "noble gentlemen" who passed that way were accustomed to contribute to its support; and (removing his hat) "most of the noble gentlemen remembered also the poor gate-keeper." Of course the two noble gentlemen, with mosquito-bitten faces, rumpled hair, soiled shirt-collars, and mud-bespattered clothing, sitting with noble dignity on a luxurious steamer-trunk in a miry *tárantás*, could not resist such an appeal as this to their noble sympathies. We gave the gate-keeper a few copper coins with directions to put half of them into the savings bank of the black-robed deacon, and having thus contributed to the support of two great Russian institutions, the church and the grog-shop, we rode on.

Late in the afternoon of Thursday, June 18, we came out of the forest into an extensive marshy plain, tinted a peculiar greenish-yellow by swamp grass and buttercups, and our driver, pointing ahead with his whip, said, "There is Tiumén." All that we could see of the distant city was a long line of pyramidal board roofs on the horizon, broken here and there by the white stuccoed walls of a Government building, or the green-domed belfries and towers of a Russo-Greek church. As we approached it we passed in succession a square marble column marking the spot where the citizens of Tiumén bade good-by to the Grand Duke Vladímir in 1868; a squad of soldiers engaged in target practice, stepping forward and firing volleys by ranks to the accompaniment of a flourish of bugles; a series of long, low sheds surrounded by white-tilted emigrant wagons, and finally, in the suburbs, the famous exile forwarding prison.

There were two or three hotels in the town, but upon the recommendation of our driver we went to the "Rooms for

Arrivers," or furnished apartments, of one KVálski, who
occupied a two-story brick house near the bank of the river
in the eastern part of the city. About six o'clock in the
evening we finally alighted from our muddy *tárantás* in
KVálski's court-yard, having made a journey of two hundred
and four miles in two days, with eleven changes of horses,
and having spent more than forty hours without sleep, sitting in a cramped and uncomfortable position on Mr. Frost's
trunk. My neck and spine were so stiff and lame from incessant jolting that I could not have made a bow to the Tsar
of all the Russias, and I was so tired that I could hardly
climb the stairs leading to the second story of KVálski's
house. As soon as possible after dinner we went to bed, and
for twelve hours slept the sleep of exhaustion.

CHAPTER IV

THE TIUMÉN FORWARDING PRISON

TIUMÉN, where we virtually began our Siberian journey as well as our investigation of the exile system, is a town of 19,000 inhabitants, situated 1700 miles east of St. Petersburg, on the right bank of the river Túra just above the junction of the latter with the Toból. The chief interest that the place had for us lay in the fact that it contains the most important exile forwarding prison in Siberia, and the *Prikáz o Sílnikh*, or Chief Bureau of Exile Administration. Through the Tiumén prison pass all persons condemned to banishment, colonization, or penal servitude in Siberia, and in the Tiumén *prikáz* are kept all the records and statistics of the exile system.

Russian exiles began to go to Siberia very soon after its discovery and conquest—as early probably as the first half of the seventeenth century. The earliest mention of exile in Russian legislation is in a law of the Tsar Alexéi Mikháilovich in 1648.[1] Exile, however, at that time, was regarded not as a punishment in itself, but as a means of getting criminals who had already been punished out of the way. The Russian criminal code of that age was almost incredibly cruel and barbarous. Men were impaled on sharp stakes, hanged, and beheaded by the hundred for crimes that would not now be regarded as capital in any civilized country in the world; while lesser offenders were flogged with the *knut* and bastinado, branded with hot irons, muti-

[1] *Poln. Sobr. Zakonof, tom.* I. *Ulozhenie, gl.* XIX, p. 13. [Full Collection of Russian Laws, Vol. I. Penal Code, Ch. XIX, p. 13.]

lated by amputation of one or more of their limbs, deprived of their tongues, and suspended in the air by hooks passed under two of their ribs until they died a lingering and miserable death.[1] When criminals had been thus *knuted*, bastinadoed, branded, or crippled by amputation, Siberian exile was resorted to as a quick and easy method of getting them out of the way; and in this attempt to rid society of criminals who were both morally and physically useless Siberian exile had its origin. The amelioration, however, of the Russian criminal code, which began in the latter part of the seventeenth century, and the progressive development of Siberia itself gradually brought about a change in the view taken of Siberian exile. Instead of regarding it, as before, as a means of getting rid of disabled criminals, the Government began to look upon it as a means of populating and developing a new and promising part of its Asiatic territory. Toward the close of the seventeenth century, therefore, we find a number of *ukázes* abolishing personal mutilation as a method of punishment, and substituting for it, and in a large number of cases even for the death penalty, the banishment of the criminal to Siberia with all his family.[2] About the same time exile, as a punishment, began to be extended to a large number of crimes that had previously been punished in other ways; as, for example, desertion from the army, assault with intent to kill, and vagrancy when the vagrant was unfit for military service and no land-owner or village commune would take charge of him. Men were exiled, too, for almost every conceivable sort of minor offense, such, for instance, as fortune-telling, prize-fighting, snuff-taking,[3] driving with reins,[4]

[1] *Izsledoványia o Protsénte Sóslannikh v Sibír; E. N. Anúchina; Vedénie.* [An Investigation of the Percentages of Siberian Exiles; by E. N. Anuchin; Introduction.] Memoirs of the Imperial Russian Geographical Society, Statistical Section, St. Petersburg, 1873.

[2] Full Collection of Russian Laws, Vol. I, Nos. 105, 343, and 441, and Vol. II, Nos. 772, 970, 1002, and 1004.

[3] The snuff-taker was not only banished to Siberia, but had the septum between his nostrils torn out.

[4] This was punished as a Western or European innovation. The old Russian driver had been accustomed to ride his horse or run beside it.

begging with a pretense of being in distress, and setting fire to property accidentally.[1]

In the eighteenth century the great mineral and agricultural resources of Siberia began to attract to it the serious and earnest attention of the Russian government. The discovery of the Daúrski silver mines, and the rich mines of Nérchinsk in the Siberian territory of the Trans-Baikál, created a sudden demand for labor, which led the government to promulgate a new series of *ukázes* providing for the transportation thither of convicts from the Russian prisons. In 1762 permission was given to all individuals and corporations owning serfs, to hand the latter over to the local authorities for banishment to Siberia whenever they thought they had good reason for so doing.[2] With the abolition of capital punishment in 1753, all criminals that, under the old law, would have been put to death, were condemned to perpetual exile in Siberia with hard labor.

In the reign of Catherine II. the demand for laborers in Siberia became more and more imperative, by reason of the discovery of the rich and important mines of Ekaterínburg, and the establishment of large manufactories in Irkútsk; and the list of crimes and offenses punishable by exile grew larger and larger. Jews were exiled for refusing or neglecting to pay their taxes for three successive years; serfs were exiled for cutting down trees without leave; noncommissioned officers of the army were exiled for second offenses of various kinds, and bad conduct of almost any sort became a sufficient warrant for deportation to Siberia.

Up to the close of the eighteenth century, very little attention was paid to the treatment of the exiles *en route*, and still less to the proper organization and control of the exile system. *Kolódniks*, as the exiles were then called, were

[1] Full Collection of Russian Laws, Vol. VIII, Nos. 5611, 5632, 5441, and Vol. IX, No. 6406. See also a paper entitled "Exile in Russia in the Seventeenth Century," by Professor Sergéyefski, read at the annual meeting of the St. Petersburg Juridical Society, March 8, 1887.

[2] Full Collection of Russian Laws, Vol. XIII, Nos. 10,086 and 9643, and Vol. XV, No. 11,116.

simply driven in troops, like cattle, from one provincial town to another, sometimes begging their way because no provision had been made for their subsistence, and sometimes starving to death on the road. No one knew who they were, whence they had come, what crimes they had committed, or whither they were going. Hardened murderers, who should have been sent to the mines for life, were set at liberty in Siberia as colonists; while unfortunate peasants who had merely lost their passports, or incurred the resentment of some hot-tempered land-owner, were kept at hard labor in the mines until they perished from privation and cruel treatment. The exile system, in short, was nothing but a chaos of disorder, in which accident and caprice played almost equally important parts.[1]

Early in the nineteenth century, steps were taken by the Government to remedy some of the evils that had become apparent under this lax system of administration, and to subject the methods of exile to stricter control. In 1811 a suitable force of regular guards was organized to convoy exile parties, and all exiles were furnished with identifying documents, called *statéini spíski*, to show who they were and whither they were bound. In 1817 *étapes*, or exile station-houses, were erected along the most important routes; and in 1823, upon the initiative of the great Russian reformer Count Speránski, the present *Prikáz o Sílnikh*, or Bureau of Exile Administration, was established in Tobólsk. It has

---

[1] Count Speránski, for example, refers to a case in which a peasant from the Russian province of Kostromá was condemned to forced colonization for having innocently bought a stolen horse. Through confusion and error he was not set at liberty in Siberia, as he ought to have been, but was transported as a murderer to the Berózef mines, where he worked twenty-three years underground. See Speránski's explanation of his projected "Exile Statutes," *Vostóchnoe Obozrénie*, No. 7, 1887, p. 2.

As an illustration of the extent to which caprice was carried, it is only necessary to refer to one of the many arbitrary acts of the notorious Siberian governor Tréskin. Taking a spite, for some reason, against one of the councilors of the *Kazónaya Paláta*, or State Chamber, Tréskin banished the latter from the province of Irkútsk, with instructions that he should not be allowed to live more than ten days in any one place. The unfortunate exile spent the remainder of his life in wandering aimlessly about Siberia. *Sibir i Kátorga* [Siberia and Penal Servitude], S. Maximof, St. Petersburg, 1871, Vol. III, p. 8.

since been removed to Tiumén. The duties of this bureau are of a two-fold nature. In the first place it sorts and classifies all exiles, upon their arrival in Tiumén, and keeps a full and accurate record of them, and in the second it watches and controls, through six subordinate bureaus, their transportation and distribution throughout Siberia. These subordinate bureaus, which are known as *expedítsii o sílnikh*, are situated in Kazán, Perm, Tobólsk, Tomsk, Krasnoyársk, and Irkútsk. They are aided in their work of supervision and control by three inspectors of exile transportation, each of whom looks after one division of the great exile route. At the time of our journey, Colonel Vinokúrof was inspector of exile transportation for Western Siberia with headquarters at Tiumén, while Colonel Zagárin occupied a similar position in Eastern Siberia with headquarters at Krasnoyársk.

Since the organization of the *Prikáz o Sílnikh* in 1823, a careful and accurate record has been kept of all the exiles that have crossed the Siberian frontier; and from the books of this great central bureau may now be obtained the fullest statistical information with regard to the working of the exile system. The first questions that naturally rise in one's mind in connection with this subject are, "How many persons are banished to Siberia annually, and how many have been sent there in all?" From the records of the *Prikáz o Sílnikh* it appears that between the years 1823 and 1887 inclusive there were sent to Siberia 772,979 exiles, as follows:

From 1823 to 1832	98,725	*Brought forward*	593,914
From 1833 to 1842	86,550	In 1878	17,790
From 1843 to 1852	69,764	In 1879	18,255
From 1853 to 1862	101,238	In 1880	17,660
From 1863 to 1872	146,380	In 1881	17,183
From 1873 to 1877	91,257	In 1882	16,945
		In 1883	19,314
Total	593,914	In 1884	17,824
		In 1885	18,843
		In 1886	17,477
		In 1887	17,774
Total[1]			772,979

[1] The statistics of exile in this chapter are all from official sources, as are also the facts, unless otherwise stated.

Exiles to Siberia may be grouped, according to the nature of their sentences, into four great classes, namely:

1. *Kátorzhniki* or hard-labor convicts.

2. *Poseléntsi* or penal colonists.

3. *Sílni* or persons simply banished.

4. *Dobrovólni* or women and children that go to Siberia voluntarily with their exiled husbands or parents. Persons belonging to the first two classes, who are always supposed to be criminals, are deprived of all civil rights and must remain in Siberia for life. Persons belonging to the third class, who are not necessarily criminals, retain some of their civil rights and may return to European Russia at the expiration of their terms of banishment. Convicts and penal colonists go to their places of destination in five-pound leg-fetters and with half-shaven heads, while simple exiles wear no fetters and are not personally disfigured. Exiles of the third class comprise:

a. Vagrants (persons without passports who refuse to disclose their identity).

b. Persons banished by sentence of a court.

c. Persons banished by the village communes to which they belong.

d. Persons banished by order of the Minister of the Interior.

The relative proportions of these several classes for 1885, the year that I spent in Siberia, may be shown in tabular form as follows:

Penal Class.	Males.	Females.	Total.
I. Hard-labor convicts [kátorzhniki], punished by sentence of a court	1,440	111	1,551
II. Penal colonists [poseléntsi], punished by sentence of a court	2,526	133	2,659
III. Exiles — *a.* Vagrants	1,646	73	1,719
b. Exiled by judicial sentence	172	10	182
c. Exiled by village communes	3,535	216	3,758
d. Exiled by executive order	300	68	361
IV. Voluntaries [dobrovólni], accompanying relatives	2,068	3,468	5,536
Totals	11,687	4,079	15,766

An analysis of this classified statement reveals some curious and suggestive facts. It shows in the first place that the largest single class of exiles (5536 out of 15,766) is composed of women and children who go to Siberia voluntarily with their husbands and fathers.[1] It shows, in the second place, that out of the 10,230 persons sent to Siberia as criminals, only 4392, or less than a half, have had a trial by a court, while 5838 are exiled by "administrative process"— that is, by a mere order from the Minister of the Interior.[2] Finally, it shows that more than one-third of the involuntary exiles (3751 out of 10,230) were sent to Siberia by village communes, and not by the Government.

Every *mir*, or village commune, in Russia has the right to banish any of its members who, through bad conduct or general worthlessness, have rendered themselves obnoxious to their fellow-citizens and burdensome to society. It has also the right to refuse to receive any of its members who, after serving out terms of imprisonment for crime, return to the *mir* and ask to be re-admitted. Released prisoners

[1] The records of the Bureau of Exile Administration for the four years ending with the year of my visit to Siberia show that the numbers and percentages of women and children who voluntarily accompanied their husbands and fathers to Siberia are as follows:

Year.	Whole number of exiles.	Women and children.	Percentage.
1882	16,945	5,276	31
1883	19,314	6,311	33
1884	17,824	6,067	34
1885	18,843	5,536	28
Totals	72,926	23,190	31

[2] The proportion of the judicially sentenced to the administratively banished varies little from year to year. In the ten-year period from 1867 to 1876 inclusive, there were sent to Siberia 151,585 exiles; 48.80 per cent. went under sentences of courts, and 51.20 per cent. were banished by administrative process. In the seven-year period from 1880 to 1886 inclusive, there passed through the Tiumén forwarding prison 120,065 exiles, of whom 64,513, or 53.7 per cent., had been tried and condemned by courts, and 55,552, or 46.3 per cent., had been banished by orders from the Minister of the Interior. A prison reform commission appointed by Alexander II. in the latter part of the last decade reported that on an average 45.6 per cent. of all the exiles sent to Siberia went under sentences of courts, and 54.4 per cent. were banished by administrative process.

whom the *mir* will not thus readmit are exiled to Siberia by administrative process.

The political offenders that are exiled to Siberia do not constitute a separate penal class or grade, but are distributed among all of the classes above enumerated. I was not able to obtain full and trustworthy statistics with regard to them from any source of information open to me. A fragmentary record of them has been kept recently by the inspectors of exile transportation, but this record covers only a few years, and includes only " administratives," or persons banished by executive order for political "untrustworthiness." All the rest are classed, both in the reports of the inspectors and in the books of the *prikáz*, as either hard-labor convicts or penal colonists, and in these classes there is no means of distinguishing state criminals from common felons. There can be no doubt, however, that the number of political offenders is much smaller than it is generally supposed to be. From the annual reports of Colonel Vinokúrof, inspector of exile transportation for Western Siberia, it appears that the number of politicals banished by administrative process from 1879 to 1884 is as follows:

1879	145
1880	112
1881	108
1882	88
1883	156
1884	140
6 years	749

This is at an average rate of 125 per annum. If twenty-five more per annum be added for politicals sent to Siberia as hard-labor convicts and penal colonists, and not included in the above table, the whole number deported will make a little less than one per cent. of the total number of exiles; which is probably an approximation to the truth. This estimate, however, does not include Polish insurgents, and it may not hold good for years anterior to 1879. First and last, about 100,000 Poles have been banished, and first and last, a great many thousands of political conspirators. My estimate relates only to the years between 1879 and 1885.

THE TIUMÉN FORWARDING PRISON.

As a general rule, exile to Siberia, under the severer sentences and for felony, involves first, deprivation of all civil rights; second, forfeiture of all property, which, upon the conviction of the criminal, descends to his heirs as if he were dead; and third, severance of all family relations, unless the criminal's family voluntarily accompanies him to his place of exile. If a prisoner's wife and children wish to go with him, they are allowed to do so, and are furnished by the Government with transportation; but if not, the authority of the criminal over his family ceases with his exile, and his wife is at liberty to marry again precisely as if he were dead.

Exiles of all classes are now brought from Kazán to Tiumén either in convict railway trains or in convict barges. The route is precisely the same one that we followed, viz., down the Vólga and up the Káma by steamer to Perm, and thence across the mountains of the Urál to Ekaterínburg and Tiumén by rail. At Tiumén all exiles go into the Tiumén forwarding prison, and lie there, on an average, about two weeks. They are then sent in convict barges down the Írtish and up the Ob to the city of Tomsk.

After our arrest in Perm for merely looking at the outside of a prison, we naturally felt some doubt as to the result of an application for leave to inspect the forwarding prison of Tiumén; but upon presenting my letters of introduction to Mr. Bóris Krásin, the *isprávnik* or chief police officer of the district, I was received with a cordiality that was as pleasant as it was unexpected. Mr. Krásin invited us to lunch, said that he had already been informed by private and official letters from St. Petersburg of our projected journey through Siberia, and that he would gladly be of service to us in any way possible. He granted without hesitation my request to be allowed to visit the forwarding prison, and promised to go thither with us on the following day. We would find the prison, he said, greatly overcrowded and in bad sanitary condition; but, such as it was, we should see it.

Mr. Krásin was unfortunately taken sick Monday, but, mindful of his promise, he sent us on Tuesday a note of introduction to the warden which he said would admit us to the prison; and about ten o'clock Wednesday morning, accompanied by Mr. Ignátof, a former member of the prison committee, we presented ourselves at the gate. The Tiumén forwarding prison is a rectangular three-story brick building, 75 feet in length by 40 or 50 in width, covered with white stucco and roofed with painted tin. It is situated in a large yard formed by a whitewashed brick wall 12 or 15 feet in height, at each corner of which stands a black-and-white zig-zag-barred sentry-box, and along each face of which paces a sentry carrying a loaded Berdan rifle with fixed bayonet. Against this wall, on the right-hand side of the gate, is a small building used as a prison office, and in front of it stands a post surmounted by a small A-shaped roof under which hangs a bell. A dozen or more girls and old women were sitting on the ground in front of the prison with baskets full of black rye-bread, cold meat, boiled eggs, milk, and fish-pies for sale to the imprisoned exiles. The Tiumén prison was originally built to hold 550 prisoners, but was subsequently enlarged by means of detached barracks so that it could accommodate 850. On the day of our visit, as we were informed by a small blackboard hanging beside the office door, it contained 1741. As we approached the entrance we were stopped by an armed sentry, who, upon being informed that we desired admittance, shouted through a square port-hole in the heavy gate, " Star-she-e-e !" (the usual call for the officer of the day). A corporal or sergeant, with a saber at his side and a Colt's revolver in a holster on his hip, answered the summons, carried our note to the warden, and in a moment we were admitted to the prison yard. Fifty or sixty exiles and convicts were walking aimlessly back and forth in front of the main prison building, or sitting idly in groups here and there on the ground. They were all dressed from head to foot in a costume of gray, consisting of a visorless Scotch cap, a shirt and trousers of coarse homespun linen, and a long gray overcoat with one or two diamond-shaped patches of black or yellow cloth sewn upon the back between the shoulders. Nearly all of them wore leg-fetters, and the air was filled with a

THE COURT-YARD OF THE TIUMÉN PRISON.

peculiar clinking of chains which suggested the continuous jingling of innumerable bunches of keys.

The first *kámera* or cell that we entered was situated in a one-story log barrack standing against the wall on the left of the gate, and built evidently to receive the overflow from the crowded main building. The room was about 35 feet in length by 25 in width and 12 feet high; its walls of hewn logs were covered with dirty whitewash; its rough plank floor was black with dried mud and hard-trodden filth; and it was lighted by three grated windows looking out into the prison yard. Down the center of the room, and occupying about half its width, ran the sleeping-bench—a wooden platform 12 feet wide and 30 feet long, supported at a height of 2 feet from the floor by stout posts. Each longitudinal half of this low platform sloped a little, roof-wise, from the center, so that when the prisoners slept upon it in two closely packed transverse rows, their heads in the middle were a few inches higher than their feet at the edges. These sleeping-platforms are known as *nári*, and a Siberian prison cell contains no other furniture except a large wooden tub for excrement. The prisoners have neither pillows, blankets, nor bed-clothing, and must lie on these hard plank *nári* with no covering but their overcoats. As we entered the cell, the convicts, with a sudden jingling of chains, sprang to their feet, removed their caps, and stood silently in a dense throng around the *nári*. "Zdrástvuitye rebiáta!" [How do you do, boys?] said the warden. "Zdrávie zheláiem váshe vuisóki blaga-ródie" [We wish you health, your high nobility], shouted a hundred voices in a hoarse chorus. "The prison," said the warden, "is terribly overcrowded. This cell, for example, is only 35 feet long by 25 wide, and has air space for 35, or at most 40 men. How many men slept here last night?" he inquired, turning to the prisoners.

"A hundred and sixty, your high nobility," shouted half a dozen hoarse voices.

"You see how it is," said the warden, again addressing me. "This cell contains more than four times the number of prisoners that it was intended to hold, and the same condition of things exists throughout the prison." I looked around the cell. There was practically no ventilation whatever, and the air was so poisoned and foul that I could hardly force myself to breathe it. We visited successively in the yard six *kámeras* or cells essentially like the first, and found in every one of them three or four times the number of prisoners for which it was intended, and five or six times the number for which it had adequate air space. In most of the cells there was not room enough on the sleeping-platforms for all of the convicts, and scores of men slept every night on the foul, muddy floors, under the *nári*, and in the gangways between them and the walls. Three or four pale, dejected, and apparently sick prisoners crawled out from under the sleeping-platform in one of the cells as we entered.

From the log barracks in the prison yard we went into the main building, which contained the kitchen, the prison workshops, and the hospital, as well as a large number of *kámeras*, and which was in much worse sanitary condition than the barracks. It was, in fact, a building through which Mr. Ignátof—a former member of the prison committee—declined to accompany us. On each side of the dark, damp, and dirty corridors were heavy wooden doors, opening into cells which varied in size from 8 feet by 10 to 10 by 15, and contained from half a dozen to thirty prisoners. They were furnished with *nári*, like those in the cells that we had already inspected; their windows were small and heavily grated, and no provision whatever had been made for ventilation. In one of these cells were eight or ten *dvoryáne*, or "nobles," who seemed to be educated men, and in whose presence the warden removed his hat. Whether any of them were "politicals" or not I do not know; but in this part of the prison the politicals were usually confined. The air in

MAKING UP AN EXILE PARTY IN THE TIUMÉN PRISON.

the corridors and cells, particularly in the second story, was indescribably and unimaginably foul. Every cubic foot of it had apparently been respired over and over again until it did not contain an atom of oxygen; it was laden with fever germs from the unventilated hospital wards, fetid odors from diseased human lungs and unclean human bodies, and the stench arising from unemptied excrement buckets at the ends of the corridors. I breathed as little as I possibly could, but every respiration seemed to pollute me to the very soul, and I became faint from nausea and lack of oxygen. It was like trying to breathe in an underground hospital-drain. The *smatrítel*, or warden, noticing perhaps that my face had grown suddenly pale, offered me his cigarette case, and said : " You are not accustomed to prison air. Light a cigarette : it will afford some relief, and we will get some wine or *vódka* presently in the dispensary." I acted upon this suggestion and we continued our investigations. The prison workshops, to which we were next taken, consisted of two small cells in the second story, neither of them more than eight feet square, and neither of them designed for the use to which it had been put. In one, three or four convicts were engaged in cobbling shoes, and in the other an attempt was being made to do a small amount of carpenter's work. The workmen, however, had neither proper tools nor suitable appliances, and it seemed preposterous to call the small cells which they occupied " workshops."

We then went to the prison kitchen, a dark, dirty room in the basement of the main building, where three or four half-naked men were baking black rye-bread in loaves about as large as milk-pans, and boiling soup in huge iron kettles on a sort of brick range. I tasted some of the soup in a greasy wooden bowl which a convict hastily cleaned for me with a wad of dirty flax, and found it nutritious and good. The bread was rather sour and heavy, but not worse than that prepared and eaten by Russian peasants generally. The daily ration of the prisoners consisted of two and a half pounds of this black bread, about six ounces of boiled meat, and two or three ounces of coarsely ground barley or oats, with a bowl of *kvas* morning and evening for drink.[1]

After we had examined the workshops, the kitchen, and most of the *kámeras* in the first and second stories, the *smatrítel* turned to me and said, "Do you wish to go through the hospital wards?" "Certainly," I replied; "we wish to see everything that there is to be seen in the prison." The warden shrugged his shoulders, as if he could not understand a curiosity which was strong enough to take travelers into a Siberian prison hospital; but, without making any remarks, he led the way up another flight of stone steps to the third story, which was given up entirely to the sick. The hospital wards, which numbered five or six, were larger and lighter than any of the cells that we had previously examined in the main building, but they were wholly unventilated, no disinfectants apparently were used in them, and the air was polluted to the last possible degree. It did not seem to me that a well man could live there a week without becoming infected with disease, and that a sick man should ever recover in that awful atmosphere was inconceivable. In each ward were twelve or fifteen small iron bedsteads, set with their heads to the walls round three sides of the room, and separated one from another by about five feet of space. Each bedstead was furnished with a thin mattress consisting of a coarse gray bed-tick filled with straw, a single pillow, and either a gray blanket or a ragged quilt. Mr. Frost thought that some of the beds were supplied with coarse gray linen sheets and pillow-cases, but I did not notice anything of the kind. Over the head of each bedstead was a small blackboard, bearing in Russian and Latin

[1] According to the report of the inspector of exile transportation for 1884, the cost to the Government for the food furnished each prisoner in the Tiumén forwarding prison is 3½ cents a day (7 *kopéks*). Prisoners belonging to the privileged classes (including politicals) receive food that costs the Government 5 cents a day per man. Of course the quality of a daily ration that costs only 3½ cents cannot be very high.

characters the name of the prisoner's disease and the date of his admission to the hospital. The most common disorders seemed to be scurvy, typhus fever, typhoid fever, acute bronchitis, rheumatism, and syphilis. Prisoners suffering from malignant typhus fever were isolated in a single ward; but with this exception no attempt apparently had been made to group the patients in classes according to the nature of their diseases. Women were separated from the men, and that was all. Never before in my life had I seen faces so white, haggard, and ghastly as those that lay on the gray pillows in these hospital cells. The patients, both men and women, seemed to be not only desperately sick, but hopeless and heart-broken. I could not wonder at it. As I breathed that heavy, stifling atmosphere, poisoned with the breaths of syphilitic and fever-stricken patients, loaded and saturated with the odor of excrement, disease germs, exhalations from unclean human bodies, and foulness inconceivable, it seemed to me that over the hospital doors should be written, "All hope abandon, ye who enter here." [1]

After we had gone through the women's lying-in ward and the ward occupied by patients suffering from malignant typhus fever, I told the *smatrítel* that I had seen enough; all I wanted was to get out of doors where I could once more breathe. He conducted us to the dispensary on the ground floor, offered us alcoholic stimulants, and suggested that we allow ourselves to be sprayed with carbolic acid and water. We probably had not been in the prison long enough, he said, to take any infection; but we were unaccustomed to prison air, the hospital was in bad condition, we had visited the malignant typhus fever ward, and he thought the measure that he suggested was nothing more than a proper precaution. We of course assented, and were copiously sprayed from head to foot with

[1] The cost of the maintenance of each patient in the hospital of the Tiumén forwarding prison in 1884, including food, medicines, etc., was 27 cents a day. The dead were buried at an expense of $1.57 each. [Report of inspector of exile transportation for 1884.]

dilute carbolic acid, which, after the foulness of the prison atmosphere, seemed to us almost as refreshing as spirits of cologne.

At last, having finished our inspection of the main building, we came out into the prison yard, where I drew a long, deep breath of pure air with the delicious sense of relief that a half-drowned man must feel when he comes to the surface of the water.

"How many prisoners," I asked the warden, "usually die in that hospital in the course of the year?"

"About 300," he replied. "We have an epidemic of typhus almost every fall. What else could you expect when buildings that are barely adequate for the accommodation of 800 persons are made to hold 1800? A prison so overcrowded cannot be kept clean, and as for the air in the cells, you know now what it is like. In the fall it is sometimes much worse. During the summer the windows can be left open, and some ventilation can be secured in that way; but when the weather becomes cold and stormy the windows must be closed, and then there is no ventilation at all. We suffer from it as well as the prisoners. My assistant has only recently recovered from an attack of typhus fever which kept him in bed for six weeks, and he caught the disease in the prison. The local authorities here have again and again urged the Government to make adequate provision for the large number of exiles crowded into this prison during the season of navigation, but thus far nothing has been done beyond the building of two log barracks."

The warden spoke naturally and frankly, as if the facts that he gave me were known to everybody in Tiumén, and as if there was no use in trying to conceal them even from a foreign traveler when the latter had been through the prison and the prison hospital.

From the main prison building we went to the women's prison, which was situated on the other side of the road in

COURT-YARD OF THE WOMEN'S PRISON, TIUMÉN.

a court-yard formed by a high stockade of closely set and sharpened logs. It did not differ much in external appearance from the men's barracks inside the prison-wall, which we had already examined. The *kámeras* varied in size from 10 feet by 12 to 30 feet by 45, and contained from three to forty women each. They were all clean and well lighted, the floors and sleeping-platforms had been scrubbed to a snowy whiteness, strips of coarse carpet had been laid down here and there in the gangways between the *nári*, and one cell even had potted plants in the window. The women, like the men, were obliged to sleep in rows on the hard platforms without pillows or blankets, but their cells were not so overcrowded as were those of the men, and the air was infinitely purer. Most of the women seemed to belong to the peasant class; many of them were accompanied by children, and I saw very few hard or vicious faces.

From the women's prison we went to the prison for exiled families, another stockaded log barrack about 75 feet in length which had no cell partitions and which contained nearly 300 men, women, and children. Here again the sleeping-platforms were overcrowded; the air was heavy and foul; dozens of children were crying from hunger or wretchedness; and the men and women looked tired, sleepless, and dejected. None of the women in this barrack were criminals. All were voluntarily going into banishment with their criminal husbands, and most of them were destined for points in Western Siberia.

About one o'clock in the afternoon, after having made as thorough an examination as possible of all the prison buildings, Mr. Frost and I went with Mr. Ignátof to lunch. Knowing that our host was the contractor for the transportation of exiles eastward by barge, and that he had been a prominent member of the Tiumén prison committee, I asked him if the Government in St. Petersburg was aware of the condition of the Tiumén forwarding prison, and of the sickness and misery in which it resulted. He replied in the affirmative. The local authorities, the prison committee, and the inspector of exile transportation for Western Siberia had reported upon the condition of the Tiumén prison, he said, every year; but the case of that prison was by no means an exceptional one. New prisons were needed all over European Russia, as well as Siberia, and the Government did not yet feel able financially to make sweeping prison reforms, nor to spend perhaps ten million rubles in the erection of new prison buildings. The condition of the Tiumén prison was, he admitted, extremely bad, and he himself had resigned his place as a member of the prison committee because the Government would not authorize the erection of a new building for use as a hospital. The prison committee had strongly recommended it, and when the Government disapproved the recommendation, he resigned.

In the foregoing pages I have tried to describe the Tiumén forwarding prison as it appears to the senses; I will now describe it as it appears in the official records.

Colonel Vinokúrof, inspector of exile transportation for Western Siberia, in his annual report for 1884 refers to it as follows:

The Tiumén forwarding prison and the two wooden buildings of the former *étape*, taken together, have not cubic air space enough to accommodate more than 550 persons. To these accommodations of the prison proper there may be added, in summer, two cold barracks [not warmed in any way], one in the prison yard and one outside. In each of them may be put 150 persons.

It thus officially appears that the Tiumén forwarding prison, including the log buildings that once constituted the *étape* and two unwarmed wooden barracks, cannot properly be made to hold more than 850 prisoners. From the table quoted below it may be seen how many prisoners these buildings actually did hold during the exile season from May

1 to October 1, 1884. The figures are from the report of
Colonel Vinokúrof above cited.

1884. The prison population was	In May, Days.	In June, Days.	In July, Days.	In August, Days.	In Sept., Days.	Total, Days.
300					2	2
350					2	2
400					7	7
450					7	7
500					3	3
550					2	2
600	6		1	1	3	11
650		1	1		1	3
700	1	1	1	2		5
750		3	4	4		11
800		3	1	2	2	8
850	1	4	3	4	1	13
900	1	1	4	5		11
950	1	3	1			5
1000	1	2	3	6		12
1050	1	4	4	1		10
1100	3	3	4	5		15
1150	1	1	1			3
1200	2	2	2			6
1250	4			1		5
1300	3	1	1			5
1350	2					2
1450	2					2
1500	2					2
1650	1					1
	32[1]	29[1]	31	31	30	153

From this table it appears that the prison began to be
overcrowded in May, almost as soon as the great annual
flood of exiles began to pour into it from European Russia.
It was crowded beyond its normal capacity 24 days in May,
17 days in June, 20 days in July, and 18 days in August;
and at the time of the greatest congestion, just before the
opening of the season of navigation on the river Ob, it held
almost twice the number of prisoners for which it was intended.

[1] Error in original report. One day has been put into May that belongs in June.

The natural result of such overcrowding as this, in old buildings, not properly warmed, ventilated, or drained, is an extremely high death-rate. The following table of sickness and mortality is from the annual report of the inspector of exile transportation for the year 1885.

HOSPITAL RECORD OF TIUMÉN FORWARDING PRISON.

1885. Month.	Average daily number of prisoners.	Average daily number in hospital.	Percent.	Number of deaths.
January	705.2	88.3	12.5	14
February	668.4	62.6	9.3	9
March	670	50	7.4	3
April	823.1	58.5	7.1	2
May	1200	60.6	5	10
June	1278.6	78.2	6.1	18
July	963.5	78	7.8	51
August	431.3	49	3.2[1]	20
September	346.6	34.3	9.9	15
October	682.8	48	7	8
November	964	71.6	7.4	12
December	709	89.8	12.6	20

Average daily number of prisoners for the year, 786. Total number of deaths, 182. Death rate, 23.1 per cent.

The significance of the figures in the foregoing table will become apparent if the reader will take into consideration the fact that the average death-rate in English towns is from 1.9 to 2.5 per cent. Even in the most benighted and unheathful parts of Siberia, where there are no physicians, where the peasants are densely ignorant, and where no attention whatever is paid to the laws of health, the death-rate rarely exceeds 6 per cent. In the Tiumén forwarding prison in 1885 it was 23.1 per cent. Nor was the year 1885 an exceptional year in the sense of being worse than usual.

[1] Error in original report. Should be 11.3.

On the contrary, that year, regarded from the point of view of vital statistics, seems to have been a better one than usual. Below will be found another table, also taken from the annual report of the inspector of exile transportation, containing statistics of sickness and death in the same prison for the year 1884.

HOSPITAL RECORD OF TIUMÉN FORWARDING PRISON.

1884. Month.	Average daily number of prisoners.	Average daily number in hospital.	Percent.	Deaths.
January	552.3	64.3	11.8	13
February	543.4	62.7	11.5	3
March	553	50	9	4
April	575.8	37	6.4	5
May	1105	48	4.3	7
June	989.5	53.2	5.4	26
July	978	58.8	6	39
August	938	68.2	7.3	48
September	521	43	8	16
October	472	58.4	12.3	9
November	771	75	9.8	11
December	899	129	14.3	38

Average daily number of prisoners for the year, 741. Total number of deaths, 219. Death rate, 29.5 per cent.

Such an annual death-rate as this is not to be found, I believe, outside the Russian empire, in all the civilized world. In the prisons of France the average death-rate is about 3.8 per cent., in the prisons of Austria 3.5 per cent., in the prisons of Belgium and Denmark 1.8 per cent., in the prisons of the United States 1.7 to 2 per cent., and in the prisons of England 1.4 per cent. In the Tiumén forwarding prison the average death-rate was 29.5 per cent., or almost 300 per thousand.

But the mortality in the Tiumén prison has been, at times, even greater than this.   Below will be found a table that I have compiled from the annual reports of the inspectors of exile transportation for the eleven-year period from the 1st of January, 1876, to the 1st of January, 1887.[1]

DEATH-RATE IN TIUMÉN FORWARDING PRISON

FOR ELEVEN-YEAR PERIOD FROM 1876 TO 1886 INCLUSIVE.

Year.	Whole number of prisoners for year.	Average daily number of prisoners.	Whole number of deaths.	Percentage of deaths.
1876	20,482	813	284	34.9
1877	19,042	756	279	36.9
1878	19,972	793	329	41.4
1879	20,174	801	354	44.1
1880	19,975	793	256	32.2
1881	19,063	757	219	29.9
1882	18,580	738	175	23.7
1883	22,010	874	311	35.5
1884	21,014	834	224[2]	26.8
1885	19,250	764	182	23.8
1886	19,016	755	254	33.6

From the above table it appears that, in the course of the eleven-year period from 1876 to 1886 inclusive, the death-rate in the Tiumén forwarding prison ranged from 23.7 per cent. to 44.1 per cent.; and that in seven years out of the eleven it was higher than 30 per cent. This would completely annihilate a fixed population in from two and a half to four years.   The record of our convict camps, and the

[1] The average daily number of prisoners is computed from the total annual number upon the basis of 14½ days' detention for every prisoner. This is not absolutely correct, but the error, as may be seen by comparison with the foregoing tables, is not great enough to make any material difference.

[2] As regards this number there is a discrepancy in the original report which I am unable to rectify. In one table it is given as 219, in the other 224.

history of our leased-convict system in North Carolina, Tennessee, Mississippi, and Louisiana — shocking and shameful as that record is—cannot parallel this rate of mortality. According to Mr. Cable, whose researches in the field of leased-convict labor are well known, the annual death-rate amongst leased convicts working on railroads in North Carolina in 1879 was a little less than 11.5 per cent.—a death-rate, he remarks, higher than that of the city of New Orleans during the great epidemic of yellow fever in 1853. And yet this rate is only a quarter as high as the death-rate in the Tiumén forwarding prison that very same year of 1879.

It has been said to me repeatedly, since the publication of my magazine articles upon this subject, that " there are prisons in America as bad as any that you have described in Russia." This remark has been made to me even by American prison officials. I should like to know in what part of the United States such prisons are situated. Some American prisons, I know, are bad enough, and I have no desire to excuse or palliate their evils; but when an American says that they are as bad as the Tiumén forwarding prison, he does not know, or does not appreciate, the state of affairs in the latter.

In the year 1885 Dr. P. D. Sims, chairman of the prison committee of the Tennessee State Board of Health, made a report to the president of that board upon the condition of the convicts in the Tennessee State prisons under the so-called "lease system." In this report he showed that among the prisoners in the branch prisons at Coal Creek and Tracy City the death-rate ranged from 10 to 14 per cent. per annum, or from 105 to 147 per annum per thousand. After quoting the statistics in detail he said:

Before these figures humanity stands aghast and our boasted civilization must hide her face in shame. We are appalled at their enormity. We fain would throw over them the mantle of eternal oblivion and forever hide them from the gaze of the civilized world; but we must not. They are our own published records, made by ourselves for ourselves. The once proud State of Tennessee, chivalrous and public-spirited, stands to-day before the world a self-convicted murderer; and her victims are her own sons and daughters. Prison mortality should run from 8 to 25 per thousand per annum, whereas ours has reached the startling height of 147 per thousand per annum. If by a humane and well-regulated penal system prison mortality is reduced to an average of 15 per thousand per annum, then the system that shows a mortality of 147 per thousand is responsible for the murder of 132 per annum of every thousand in its charge.[1]

I would ask the gentlemen who think that some American prisons are as bad as any that I have described, to compare the Coal Creek and Tracy City statistics with the records of Tiumén. Dr. Sims declares that "before a death-rate of 147 per thousand per annum humanity stands aghast." What, then, must be said of a death-rate that ranges from 230 per thousand to 440 per thousand? Between 1876 and 1887 there was not a single year in which the death-rate in the Tiumén forwarding prison was not more than double that in the Tennessee prisons, and in 1878 and 1879 it was more than three times the Tennessee rate. If, to adopt the metaphor of the Chattanooga surgeon, "Civilization hides her face in shame" at a death-rate of 147 per thousand, by what gesture or attitude shall she express her humiliation when shown in Russia a death-rate of 440 per thousand?

It may be said that the cases are not parallel, for the reason that the population of the Tiumén forwarding prison is composed largely of young children, who, by reason of their tender age, are more susceptible to disease and more likely to die than the mature convicts in Tennessee. This may be a good and sufficient explanation of a part of the difference between a death-rate of 147 and a death-rate of

[1] Report of Dr. P. D. Sims, chairman of the prison committee of the Tennessee State Board of Health, dated Chat- tanooga, January 6, 1885. *Nashville Weekly Banner*, January 29, 1885.

440; but it is by no means a good defense against the charge of inhumanity. If it be cruel and shameful to kill grown criminals by subjecting them to murderous sanitary conditions, how much more cruel and shameful it is to put to death in that way innocent children, whose only crime is their helpless dependence upon exiled parents.

Readers who are familiar with the constant relation that exists between a high death-rate on the one hand, and over-crowding, filth, foul air, bad food, and bad sanitary conditions generally on the other, will not, I think, regard my description of the Tiumén forwarding prison as exaggerated, when they read it in the light of an officially admitted death-rate ranging from 23 to 44 per cent. — a death-rate which, to adopt the words of Mr. Cable, "exceeds that of any pestilence that ever fell on Europe in the Middle Ages."

CHAPTER V

THE town of Tiumén, and the province of Tobólsk in which it is situated, have much more commercial importance than is generally supposed. Siberian cold and Siberian desolation have been so much talked and written about, and have been brought so forcibly to the attention of the world by the terrible experience of De Long and the survivors of the *Jeannette*, that nine readers out of ten, in forming a conception of the country, give undue prominence to its arctic side and its winter aspect. When, in conversation since my return, I have happened to refer to Siberian tobacco, Siberian orchids, or Siberian camels, my remarks have even been received with smiles of incredulity. I do not know any better way to overthrow the erroneous popular conception of Siberia than to assail it with facts and statistics, even at the risk of being wearisome. I will therefore say, briefly, that the province of Tobólsk, which is the part of Siberia with which a traveler from Europe first becomes acquainted, extends from the coast of the arctic ocean to the sun-scorched steppes of Semipalátinsk and Akmolínsk, and from the mountains of the Urál to the boundary line of Yeniséisk and Tomsk. It has an area of 590,000 square miles and includes 27,000,000 acres of arable land. It contains 8 towns of from 3000 to 20,000 inhabitants, and its total population exceeds 1,200,000. In the last year for which I was able to get statistics the province produced 30,044,880 bushels of grain and 3,778,230 bushels of potatoes,

and contained 2,647,000 head of live stock. It sends annually
to European Russia enormous quantities of raw products,
such as hides, tallow, bristles, furs, birds' skins, flax, and
hemp; it forwards more than 2,000,000 pounds of butter to

TIUMÉN LABORERS WAITING FOR EMPLOYMENT.

Constantinople by way of Rastóf, on the Don; and there is
held within its limits, at Irbít, a commercial fair whose transactions amount annually to 35,000,000 rubles ($17,500,000).
The manufacturing industries of the province, although still
in their infancy, furnish employment to 6252 persons and

put annually upon the market goods to the value of 8,517,000 *rúbles*. Besides the workmen employed in the regular manufacturing establishments, the urban population includes 27,000 mechanics and skilled laborers. Cottage industries are carried on extensively throughout the province, and produce annually, among other things, 50,000 rugs and carpets; 1,500,000 fathoms of fish netting; 2,140,000 yards of linen cloth; 50,000 barrels; 70,000 *telégas* and sleighs; leather manufactures to the value of 2,500,000 *rúbles;* and quantities of dressed furs, stockings, mittens, belts, scarfs, laces, and ornamented towels and sheets. The quantity of fish caught annually along the Ob and its tributaries is estimated at 8000 tons, and salt to the amount of 3000 tons is used in curing it. Tiumén, which is the most important town in the province, stands on a navigable branch of the vast Ob river system, through which it has steam communication with the greater part of Western Siberia, from Semipalátinsk and Tomsk to the shores of the arctic ocean. Fifty-eight steamers ply on the Ob and its tributaries, most of them between Tomsk and Tiumén, and through the latter city is transported annually merchandise to the value of thirty or forty million *rúbles*. Sixteen million *rúbles'* worth of Siberian products are brought every year to the Nízhni Nóvgorod fair, and in exchange for this mass of raw material European Russia sends annually to Siberia nearly 300,000 tons of manufactured goods.

It cannot, I think, be contended that a country which furnishes such statistics as these is an arctic desert or an uninhabited waste.

On the next day after our arrival in Tiumén the weather furnished us with convincing evidence of the fact that the Siberian summer climate, although sometimes as mild and delightful as that of California, is fickle and untrustworthy. During the night the wind changed suddenly to the northeast, and a furious storm of cold, driving rain swept down across the *tundras* from the coast of the arctic ocean, turning

the unpaved and unsewered streets of the city to lakes of
liquid mud, and making it practically impossible to go out
of doors. We succeeded, with the aid of a *droshky*, in getting to the post-office and back, and devoted the remainder
of the day to reading, and to writing letters. On Saturday,
during lulls in the storm, we walked and rode about the city,
but saw little to reward us for our trouble. The muddy,
unpaved streets did not differ much in appearance from the
streets of the villages through which we had passed, except

that some of them
had plank sidewalks,
and the unpainted
log houses with high,
steep, pyramidal
roofs were larger and
more   pretentious.
There was the same
absence of trees,
shrubbery, front

THE "REAL SCHULE."

yards and front doors which we had noticed in all of the
Siberian villages ; and but for the white-walled and green-
domed churches, which gave it a certain air of picturesqueness, the town would have been commonplace and
uninteresting.

The only letter of introduction we had to deliver in Tiumén was from a Russian gentleman in St. Petersburg to
Mr. Slovtsóf, director of the *reálnoi uchílishche*, an institution that is known in Germany as a "real schule."
Saturday afternoon, the storm having broken, we presented
this letter and were received by Mr. Slovtsóf with great
cordiality. The educational institution over which he pre-
sides is a scientific and technical school similar in plan to
the Institute of Technology in Boston. It occupies the
largest and finest edifice in the city — a substantial two-
story structure of white-stuccoed brick, nearly twice as large
as the Executive Mansion in Washington. This building was

erected and equipped at a cost of $85,000 by one of Tiu-
mén's wealthy and public-spirited merchants, and was then
presented to the city as a gift. One would hardly expect
to find such a school in European Russia, to say nothing
of Siberia, and indeed one might look far without finding
such a school even in the United States. It has a mechanical department, with a steam engine, lathes, and tools of
all kinds; a department of physics, with fine apparatus,
including even the Bell, Edison, and Dolbear telephones
and the phonograph; a chemical laboratory, with a more
complete equipment than I have ever seen, except in the
Boston Institute of Technology; a department of art and
mechanical drawing; a good library, and an excellent museum — the latter containing, among other things, 900
species of wild flowers collected in the vicinity of the city.
It is, in short, a school that would be in the highest degree
creditable to any city of similar size in the United States.

From Mr. Slovtsóf we obtained the address of Mr.
Jacob R. Wardropper, a Scotch gentleman who had
for twenty years or more been engaged in business in
Siberia; and feeling sure that Mr.
Wardropper would be glad to see
any one from the western world,
we ventured to call upon him
without the formality of an introduction. We were received by
the whole family with the most
warm-hearted hospitality, and their
house was made almost a home to
us during the remainder of our
stay in the city.

"VOLUNTARY EXILES."
(DOBROVÓLNI.)

On the morning after our first visit to the Tiumén forwarding prison we had an opportunity of seeing the departure of a marching exile party. We went to the prison
merely for the purpose of getting a sketch or a photograph
of it, but happened to be just in time to see a party of 360

men, women, and children set out on foot for Yalútorfsk. Our attention was first attracted by a great crowd of people standing in the street outside the prison wall. As we drew nearer, the crowd resolved itself into a hundred or more women and children in bright-colored calico gowns, with kerchiefs over their heads, and about 250 men dressed in the gray exile costume, all standing close together in a dense throng, surrounded by a cordon of soldiers. In the street near them were fifteen or twenty one-horse *telégas*, or small four-wheeled wagons, some piled high with the gray bags in which exiles carry their spare clothing and personal property, and some filled with men, women, and children, who, by reason of age, weakness, or infirmity, could not walk. It seemed surprising to me that anybody should be able to walk after a week's confinement in that prison. The air was filled with a continuous hum of voices as the exiles talked eagerly with one another, and occasionally we could hear the wail of a sick child from one of the *telégas*, or a faint jingle of chains as some of the men, tired of standing, changed their positions or threw themselves on the ground. The officer in charge of the party, a heavily built man with yellowish side-whiskers, light-blue eyes, and a hard, unsympathetic face, stood near the *telégas*, surrounded by women and children, who were begging him to let them ride.

"Please put my little girl in a wagon," said one pale-faced woman, as I approached the group. "She is n't ten years old and she has a lame ankle; she can never walk thirty *versts*."

"What 's the matter with her ankle?" inquired the officer impatiently, looking down at the child's thin bare feet and legs.

"I don't know; she says it hurts her," replied the mother. "Please let her ride, for God's sake!"

"She can't ride, I tell you — there 's no room," said the officer, still more impatiently. "I don't believe there 's

A MARCHING EXILE PARTY.

anything the matter with her ankle, and anybody can see that she 's more than twelve years old." [1]

"Stupái!" [Move on!], he said sternly to the child; "you can pick flowers better if you walk."

The mother and the child shrank away without a word, and the officer, to escape further importunities, shouted the order to " Form ranks!" The hum of conversation suddenly ceased; there was a jingling of chains as the prisoners who had been lying on the ground sprang to their feet; the soldiers of the guard shouldered their rifles; the exiles crossed themselves devoutly, bowing in the direction of the prison chapel; and at the word " March!" the whole column was instantly in motion. Three or four Cossacks, in dark-green uniforms and with rifles over their shoulders, took the lead; a dense but disorderly throng of men and women followed, marching between thin, broken lines of soldiers; next came the *telégas* with the old, the sick, and the small children; then a rear-guard of half a dozen Cossacks; and finally four or five wagons piled high with gray bags. Although the road was soft and muddy, in five minutes the party was out of sight. The last sounds I heard were the jingling of chains and the shouts of the Cossacks to the children to keep within the lines. These exiles were nearly all persons banished by Russian communes, and were destined for towns and villages in the southern part of the province of Tobólsk.[2]

Having witnessed the departure of one of the marching parties, we went down Saturday afternoon to the steamer-landing to see the embarkment of 700 exiles for Tomsk. Criminals destined for points in Eastern Siberia are transported from Tiumén to Tomsk in convict barges, furnished for the purpose by a wealthy firm of contractors, and towed

[1] All children twelve years of age and upward, without regard to sex, are expected to march if well. Children less than twelve years of age are carried in rude one-horse carts.

[2] I shall describe fully in a later chapter the life of marching exile parties on the road. I did not have a favorable opportunity to study it until I reached Tomsk.

back and forth by their passenger steamers. The contractors, at the time of our journey to Siberia, were Kurbátof and Ignátof, steamboat proprietors of Tiumén. The convict barges are three in number, and during the season of navigation, which lasts from May until October, they make, on an average, six round trips each, or eighteen trips altogether. In 1884, the first barge left Tiumén on the 27th of May and the last one reached Tomsk on the 4th of October. The voyage between the two cities occupies from seven to ten days according to the season of the year and the stage of the water. In 1884, the shortest voyage was seven days and six hours, and the longest ten days and nine hours. The number of convicts and exiles transported by these barges from Tiumén to Tomsk in the five years from 1880 to 1884 inclusive was reported by the inspector of exile transportation as follows.

Year.	Received in Tiumén.	Delivered in Tomsk.
1880	10,243	10,269
1881	10,757	10,462
1882	10,630	10,245
1883	10,726	11,049
1884	10,229	10,692
Totals	52,585	52,717[1]

The contract for the transportation of exiles from Tiumén to Tomsk, which was made with Kurbátof & Ignátof in 1882, provides that the contractors shall furnish three barges large enough to accommodate 600 prisoners each, and that such barges shall make eighteen trips between terminal points in the course of every season of navigation. The contract, therefore, requires the transportation of 10,800 exiles per annum. The average number actually carried in the five years covered by the foregoing table was 10,543 per annum, and at that rate the average barge-load

---

[1] A few were taken or left every year at Tobólsk and other way places.

would be 586 persons. Owing, however, to circumstances beyond the control of the contractors and the local authorities in Tiumén, it becomes necessary, at certain times, to despatch the barges only half loaded, and at other times to crowd them to the very point of suffocation. In 1884, for example, the barge-loads ranged from 334 to 797. The

A CONVICT BARGE.

FIG. 1.　PLAN OF CAGE-DECK.

A, Men's cage; B, Women's cage; C, Hospital cells and dispensary; D, Officers' quarters and cells for privileged class; E, Cook's galley.

FIG. 2.　PLAN OF LOWER-DECK.

F, Cabin for hard-labor convicts (men); G, Cabin for exiles and penal colonists (men); H, Women's cabin; a, b, Nares, or sleeping-platforms.

FIG. 3.　TRANSVERSE SECTION OF BARGE.

D D, Deck-houses; G, Sleeping-cabin; a, b, Cross-section of sleeping-platforms.

latter number was probably more than twice as great as could be comfortably accommodated in a vessel of such form and dimensions.

The convict barge which lay at the Tiumén steamboat-landing on Saturday, June 27th, and which we were permitted to inspect, did not differ much in general appearance from an ordinary ocean steamer, except that it drew less water and had no rigging. The black iron hull was about 220 feet in length by 30 in width, pierced by a horizontal line of small rectangular port-holes which opened into the sleeping-cabins on the lower deck. The upper deck supported two large yellow deck-houses about 75 feet apart, one of which contained three or four hospital wards and a dispensary, and the other, quarters for the officers of the convoy and a few cells for exiles belonging to the noble or privileged class. The space between the deck-houses was roofed over and inclosed on each side by a coarse network of heavy iron wire, so as to make a cage 30 feet wide and 75 feet long, where the prisoners could walk and breathe the fresh air. This cage, which is known to the common-criminal exiles as the " chicken-coop," was divided by a network partition into two compartments of unequal size, the smaller of which was intended for the women and children and the larger for the men. Companion-ladders

AN EXILE PARTY ABOUT TO EMBARK.

led down into the sleeping cabins, of which there were three or four, varying in length from 30 to 60 feet, with a uniform width of 30 feet and a height of about 7. One of these cabins was occupied by the women and children, and the others were given up to the men. Through the center of each cabin ran longitudinally two tiers of double sleeping-platforms, precisely like those in the Tiumén prison *kámeras*, upon which the exiles lay athwart-ship in four closely packed rows, with their heads together over the line of the keel. Along each side of the barge ran two more tiers of *nári*, upon which the prisoners lay lengthwise head to feet, in rows four or five wide. A reference to the plan and section of the barge will, I think, render this description of the interior of the sleeping-cabins fairly intelligible. The vessel had been thoroughly cleaned and disinfected after its return from a previous trip to Tomsk, and the air in the cabins was pure and sweet.

The barge lay at a floating landing-stage of the type with which we had become familiar on the rivers Vólga and Káma, and access to it was gained by means of a zigzag wooden bridge sloping down to it from the high bank of the river. When we reached the landing, a dense throng of exiles, about one-third of whom were women, were standing on the bank waiting to embark. They were surrounded by a cordon of soldiers, as usual, and non-commissioned officers were stationed at intervals of twenty or thirty feet on the bridge leading down to the landing-stage. I persuaded Colonel Vinokúrof, inspector of exile transportation for Western Siberia, to delay the embarkment a little, in order that we might take photographs of the exiles and the barge. As soon as this had been accomplished the order was given to "Let them go on board," and the prisoners, shouldering their gray bags, walked one by one down the sloping bridge to the landing-stage. More than three-fourths of the men were in leg-fetters, and for an hour there was a continuous clinking of chains as the prisoners passed me on their way to the barge. The exiles, although uniformly clad in gray, presented, from an ethnological point of view, an extraordinary diversity of types, having been collected evidently from all parts of the vast empire. There were fierce, wild-looking mountaineers from Daghestán and Circassia, condemned to penal servitude for murders of blood-revenge; there were Tatárs from the lower Vólga, who had been sunburned until they were almost as black as negroes; Turks from the Crimea, whose scarlet fezzes contrasted strangely with their gray convict overcoats; crafty-looking Jews from Podólia, going into exile for smuggling; and finally, common peasants in great numbers from all parts of European Russia. The faces of the prisoners generally were not as hard, vicious, and depraved as the faces of

EXILES GOING ON BOARD THE BARGE.

criminals in America. Many of them were pleasant and
good-humored, some were fairly intelligent, and even the
worst seemed to me stupid and brutish rather than savage

MEN'S CAGE, CONVICT BARGE — EXILES BUYING FOOD.

or malignant. At last all were on board; the sliding doors
of the network cages were closed and secured with heavy
padlocks, and a regular Russian bazar opened on the landing-stage. Male and female peddlers to the number of

forty or fifty were allowed to come down to the side of the barge to sell provisions to the prisoners, most of whom seemed to be in possession of money. In one place might be seen a half-grown girl passing hard-boiled eggs one by one through the interstices of the network; in another, a gray-haired old woman was pouring milk through a tin tube into a tea-pot held by a convict on the inside of the cage; .and all along the barge men were buying or bargaining for loaves of black rye-bread, salted cucumbers, pretzels, and fish turnovers. The peddlers seemed to have perfect trust in the convicts, and often passed in food to them before they had received pay for it. The soldiers of the guard, who were good-looking, fresh-faced young fellows, facilitated the buying and selling as far as possible by handing in the provisions and handing out the money, or by opening the sliding doors for the admission of such bulky articles as loaves of bread, which could not be passed through the network.

While we stood looking at this scene of busy traffic, a long-haired Russian priest in a black gown and a broad-brimmed felt hat crossed the landing-stage and entered one of the deck-houses, followed by an acolyte bearing his robes and a prayer-book. In a few moments, having donned his ecclesiastical vestments, he entered the women's cage, with a smoking censer in one hand and an open book in the other, and began a *molében*, or service of prayer. The women all joined devoutly in the supplications, bowing, crossing themselves, kneeling, and even pressing their foreheads to the deck. The priest hurried through the service, however, in a perfunctory manner, swung the censer back and forth a few times so as to fill the compartment with fragrant smoke, and then went into the men's cage. There much less interest seemed to be taken in the services. The convicts and soldiers removed their caps, but only a few joined in the prayer, and buying and selling went on without interruption all along the side of the barge. The deep-voiced chanting of

the priest mingling with the high-pitched rattle of chains, the
chaffering of peddlers, and the shouting of orders to soldiers
on the roof of the cage produced a most strange and incon-

INSIDE THE WOMEN'S CAGE, CONVICT BARGE.

gruous effect. Finally, the service ended, the priest took off
his vestments, wished the commanding officer of the convoy
a pleasant voyage, and returned to the city, while Mr. Frost
and I walked back and forth on the landing-stage studying
the faces of the prisoners. With few exceptions the latter

seemed cheerful and happy, and in all parts of the cage we could hear laughter, joking, and animated conversation. Mr. Frost finally began making sketches in his note-book of some of the more striking of the convict types on the other side of the network. This soon attracted the attention of the prisoners, and amidst great laughter and merriment they began dragging forward and arranging, in what they regarded as artistic poses, the convicts whom they thought most worthy of an artist's pencil. Having selected a subject,

CONVICT TYPES.

they would place him in all sorts of studiously careless and negligent attitudes, comb and arrange the long hair on the unshaven side of his head, try the effect of a red fez or an embroidered Tatár cap, and then shout suggestions and directions to the artist. This arranging of figures and groups for Mr. Frost to draw seemed to afford them great amusement, and was accompanied with as much joking and laughter as if they were school-boys off for a picnic, instead of criminals bound for the mines.

At last, just after sunset, a steamer made fast to the barge, the order was given to cast off the lines, the exiles all crowded against the network to take a parting look at Tiumén, and the great black-and-yellow floating prison moved slowly out into the stream and began its long voyage to Tomsk.

CHAPTER VI

THE traveler who desires to go from Tiumén to Eastern Siberia has a choice of three widely different routes; namely, first, the northern or river route down the Írtish and up the Ob by steamer to Tomsk; second, the middle or winter route, which follows the great Siberian post road through Omsk, Káinsk, and Kolіván; and third, the southern or steppe route, via Omsk, Pavlodár, Semipalátinsk, and Barnaül. Each of these routes has some advantage not possessed by either of the others. The middle route, for example, is the shortest, but it is also the most traveled and the best known. The northern route is less familiar, and in summer is more comfortable and convenient; but it takes one through an uninteresting, thinly inhabited, sub-arctic region.

I decided, after careful consideration, to proceed from Tiumén to Tomsk through the steppes of the Írtish by way of Omsk, Pavlodár, Semipalátinsk, Ust-Kamenogórsk, and Barnaül. This route would take us through the best agricultural part of the provinces of Tobólsk and Tomsk, as well as the districts most thickly settled by exiles; it would enable us to see something of the Mohammedan city of Semipalátinsk and of the great nomadic and pastoral tribe of natives known as the Kírghis; and finally it would afford us an opportunity to explore a part of the Russian Altái — a high, picturesque, mountainous region on the Mongolian frontier, which had been described to me by Russian army officers, in terms of enthusiastic admiration, as "the Siberian Switzerland." I had, moreover, another reason for wishing to keep as far away as possible from the regular through routes of travel. I supposed when we left St. Petersburg that we should be obliged to go from Tiumén to Tomsk either by steamer or over the great Siberian road. The Minister of the Interior understood that such would be our course, and he caused letters to be written to all the local officials along these routes, apprising them of our coming and furnishing them with such instructions concerning us as the circumstances seemed to require. What these instructions were I could never ascertain; but they anticipated us at every important point on the great Siberian road from Tiumén to the capital of the Trans-Baikál. In Eastern Siberia the local authorities knew all about us months before we arrived. I first became aware of

ENLARGED MAP OF ROUTE FROM TIUMÉN TO SEMIPALÁTINSK.

these letters and this system of official surveillance at Tiumén; and as they seemed likely to interfere seriously with my plans,—particularly in the field of political exile,—I determined to escape or elude them as far as possible, by leaving the regular through route and going into a region where the authorities had not presumably been forewarned of our coming. I had reason afterward to congratulate myself upon the exercise of sound judgment in making this decision. The détour to the southward brought us not only into the part of Siberia where the political exiles enjoy most freedom, and where it is easiest to make their acquaintance, but into a province which was then governed by a liberal and humane man.

On the morning of Tuesday, June 30, having made our farewell calls, purchased a *tárantás*, and provided ourselves with a *padarózhnaya*, or order for horses, we left Tiumén for Semipalátinsk by the regular Government post. The Imperial Russian Post is now perhaps the most extensive and perfectly organized horse-express service in the world. From the southern end of the peninsula of Kamchátka to the most remote village in Finland, from the frozen, wind-swept shores of the arctic ocean to the hot, sandy deserts of Central Asia, the whole empire is one vast network of post routes. You may pack your portmanteau in Nízhni Nóvgorod, get a *padarózhnaya* from the postal department, and start for Petropávlovsk, Kamchátka, seven thousand miles away, with the full assurance that throughout the whole of that immense distance there will be horses, rein-deer, or dogs ready and waiting to carry you on, night and day, to your destination. It must, however, be borne in mind that the Russian post route is a very different thing from the old English post route, and that the Russian horse express differs widely, not only from our own west-ern "pony express," but from the horse expresses of most other countries. The characteristic feature of the west European and American systems is the stage-coach or dili-gence, which leaves certain places at certain stated hours, or, in other words, runs upon a prearranged time schedule. It is precisely this feature that the Russian system does not have. There are, generally speaking, no stage-coach lines in Russia; the vehicles that carry the mails do not carry passengers, and, away from the railroads, there is no such thing as traveling upon a fixed time schedule. You are never obliged, therefore, to wait for a public convey-ance which leaves at a certain stated hour, and then go through to your destination in that conveyance, stopping

when it stops and starting when it starts, without regard
to your own health, comfort, or convenience.   On the contrary, you may ride in your own sleigh or carriage, and
have it drawn by post horses.   You may travel at the rate
of 175 miles in twenty-four hours, or twenty-four miles in
175 hours, just as you feel inclined.   You may stop when
you like, where you like, and for as long a time as you like,
and when you are ready to move on you have only to
order out your horses and get
into your ve- hicle. It makes
no difference  in what part
of the empire you may hap-
pen to be, nor to what part
you may wish to go.   Send

OUR TÁRANTÁS.

your *padarózhnaya* to the nearest post station, and in twenty
minutes you will be riding away at the rate of ten miles an
hour, with your postal order in your pocket and a hundred
relays of fresh horses distributed at intervals along your
route.

The established rate of payment for transportation over
the post routes of Western Siberia seems to an American
absurdly low.   It amounts, including the compensation of
the driver, to $1\frac{1}{8}$ cent per mile for every horse, or $3\frac{3}{8}$ cents
per mile for the usual *tróika*, or team of three.   In other
words, two persons can travel in their own carriage with a
team of three horses a distance of twenty miles for 68 cents,
or 34 cents each.   I used to feel almost ashamed sometimes
to wake up a driver at a post station, in the middle of a
stormy night, compel him to harness three horses and drive
us twenty miles over a dark, miry, and perhaps dangerous
road, and then offer him for this service the pitiful sum of
68 cents.   Trifling and inadequate, however, as such compensation may seem, it is large enough to tempt into this field
of enterprise hundreds of peasant farmers who compete
with the Government post by furnishing what are known as
vólni or " free " horses, for the transportation of travelers

from one village to another.   As these free horses are generally better fed and in better condition than the overdriven animals at the post stations, it is often advantageous to employ them; and your driver, as you approach a village, will almost always turn around and inquire whether he shall take you to the Government post station or to the house of a " friend."   Traveling with *drushkí*, or " friends," costs no more than traveling by post, and it enables one to see much more of the domestic life of the Siberian peasants than one could see by stopping and changing horses only at regular post stations.

The first part of our journey from Tiumén to Omsk was comparatively uneventful and uninteresting.   The road ran across a great marshy plain, full of swampy lakes, and covered with a scattered growth of willow and alder bushes, small birch-trees, and scrubby firs and pines, which in every direction limited the vision and hid the horizon line.   All this part of the province of Tobólsk seems to have been, within a comparatively recent geological period, the bottom of a great inland sea which united the Caspian and the Sea of Aral with the arctic ocean, along the line of the shallow depression through which now flow the rivers Írtish and Ob. Everywhere between Tiumén and Omsk we saw evidences, in the shape of sand-banks, salt-marshes, beds of clay, and swampy lakes, to show that we were traveling over a partly dried up sea bottom.

About a hundred versts from Tiumén, just beyond the village of Zavódo-ukófskaya, we stopped for two hours early in the evening at the residence and estate of a wealthy Siberian manufacturer named Kolmakóf, to whom I had a letter of introduction from a Russian friend.   I was surprised to find in this remote part of the world so many evidences of comfort, taste, and luxury as were to be seen in and about Mr. Kolmakóf's house.   The house itself was only a two-story building of logs, but it was large and comfortably furnished, and its windows looked out over an artificial lake, and a beautiful garden, with winding walks, rustic arbors, long lines of currant and raspberry bushes, and beds of flowering plants. At one end of this garden was a spacious conservatory, filled with geraniums, verbenas, hydrangeas, cactuses, orange and lemon trees, pine-apples, and all sorts of tropical and semi-tropical shrubs, and near at hand was a large hot-house full of cucumbers and ripening cantaloupes. In the middle of the garden stood a square building, sixty feet long by forty or fifty feet wide, which was composed almost entirely of glass, which had no floor except the earth, and which served, Mr. Kolmakóf said, as a sort of winter garden and a place of recreation during cold or stormy weather. In this miniature Crystal Palace stood a perfect grove of bananas and young palms, through which ran winding walks bordered by beds of flowers, with here and there amidst the greenery a comfortable lounging-place or rustic seat. The trees, flowers, and shrubs were not planted in tubs or pots, but grew directly out of the earthen floor of the greenhouse, so that the effect was almost precisely that of a semi-tropical garden enclosed in glass.

"Who would have thought," said Mr. Frost, as he threw himself into one of the rustic seats beside a bed of blossoming verbenas, "that we should come to Siberia to sit under palm-trees and in the shade of bananas?"

After a walk through the spacious wooded park which adjoined the garden, we returned to the house, and were served with a lunch or cold supper consisting of caviar, pickled mushrooms, salmon, cold boiled fowl, white bread, sweet cakes, and wild strawberries, with *vódka*, two or three kinds of wine, and tea.

It had grown quite dark when, about eleven o'clock, the horses that we had ordered in the neighboring village arrived, and, bidding our courteous host good-by, we climbed into the *tárantás* and set out for a long, dark, and dreary night's ride. The road, which had never been good, was in worse condition than usual, owing to recent and heavy rains.

Our driver urged four powerful horses over it at break-neck speed, and we were so jounced, jolted, and shaken that it was utterly impossible to get any sleep, and difficult enough merely to keep our seats in the vehicle. Early in the morning, sleepy, jaded, and exhausted, we reached the village of Nóvo Zaímskaya, entered the little log-house of our driver's "friend," threw ourselves on the bare floor, where half a dozen members of the friend's family were already lying, and for two or three hours lost consciousness of our aching spinal columns in the heavy, dreamless slumber of physical exhaustion.

Throughout the next day and the following night we traveled, without rest, and of course without sleep, over a terribly bad steppe road, and at six o'clock Thursday morning arrived in a pelting rain-storm at the circuit town of Ishím. No one who has not experienced it can fully realize the actual physical suffering that is involved in posting night and day at high speed over bad Siberian roads. We made the 200 miles between Tiumén and Ishím in about thirty-five hours of actual travel, with only four hours of sleep, and were so jolted and shaken that every bone in our bodies ached, and it was with difficulty that we could climb into and out of our mud-bespattered *tárantás* at the post stations.

It had been our intention to make a short stop at Ishím, but the bad weather discouraged us, and, after drinking tea at a peasant's house on the bank of the Ishím River, we resumed our journey. As we rode out of the town through a thin forest of birch-trees, we began to notice large numbers of men, women, and children plodding along on foot through the mud in the same direction that we were going. Most of them were common *muzhíks* with trousers inside their boots and shirt-flaps outside their trousers, or sunburned peasant women in red and blue gowns, with white kerchiefs over their heads; but there were also a few pedestrians in the conventional dress of the civilized world, who manifestly belonged to the higher classes, and who even carried umbrellas.

About four miles from the town we saw ahead a great crowd of men and women marching towards us in a dense, tumultuous throng, carrying big three-armed crosses, white and colored banners, and huge glass lanterns mounted on long black staves.

"What is that?" I inquired of the driver.

"The Mother of God is coming home," he replied, with reverent gravity.

As they came nearer I could see that the throng was densest in the middle of the muddy road, under what seemed to be a large gilt-framed picture which was borne high in air at the end of a long, stout wooden pole. The lower end of this pole rested in a socket in the middle of a square framework which had handles on all four sides, and which was carried by six bareheaded peasants. The massive frame of the portrait was made either of gold or of silver gilt, since it was manifestly very heavy, and half a dozen men steadied, by means of guy ropes, the standard which supported it, as the bearers, with their faces bathed in perspiration, staggered along under their burden. In front of the picture marched a bareheaded, long-haired priest with a book in his hands, and on each side were four or five black-robed deacons and acolytes, carrying embroidered silken banners, large three-armed gilt crosses, and peculiar church lanterns, which looked like portable street gas-posts with candles burning in them. The priest, the deacons, and all the bareheaded men around the picture were singing in unison a deep, hoarse, monotonous chant as they splashed along through the mud, and the hundreds of men and women who surged around the standard that supported the portrait were constantly crossing themselves, and joining at intervals in the chanted psalm or prayer. Scores of peasant women had taken off their shoes and stockings and slung them over their shoulders, and were wading with bare feet and legs through the black, semi-liquid mire, and neither men nor women seemed to pay the slightest attention to the rain, which beat upon their unprotected heads and trickled in little rivulets down their hard, sunburned faces. The crowd numbered, I should think, four or five hundred persons, more than half of whom were women, and as it approached the town it was constantly receiving accessions from the groups of pedestrians that we had overtaken and passed.

Since entering Siberia I had not seen such a strange and medieval picture as that presented by the black-robed priest and acolytes, the embroidered banners, the lighted lanterns, the gilded crosses, and the great throng of bareheaded and bare-legged peasants, tramping along the black, muddy road through the forest in the driving rain, singing a solemn ecclesiastical chant. I could almost imagine that we had been carried back to the eleventh century and were witnessing the passage of a detachment of Christian villagers who had been stirred up and excited by the eloquence of Peter the Hermit, and were marching with crosses, banners, and chanting to join the great host of the crusaders.

When the last stragglers in the rear of the procession had passed, and the hoarse, monotonous chant had died away in the distance, I turned to Mr. Frost and said, "What do you suppose is the meaning of all that?"

"I have n't the least idea," he replied. "It is evidently a church procession, but what it has been doing out here in the woods I can't imagine."

By dint of persistent questioning I finally succeeded in eliciting from our driver an intelligible explanation of the phenomenon. There was, it appeared, in one of the churches of Ishím, a very old *ikón*, or portrait of "the Mother of God," which was reputed to have supernatural powers and to answer the prayers of faithful believers. In order that the country people who were unable to come to Ishím might have an opportunity to pray to this miracle-working image, and to share in the blessings supposed to be conferred by its mere presence, it was carried once a year,

RETURN OF THE MIRACLE-WORKING IKÓN.

or once in two years, through all the principal villages of the Ishím *ókrug*, or district. Special services in its honor were held in the village churches, and hundreds of peasants accompanied it as it was borne with solemn pomp and ceremony from place to place. It had been on such a tour when we saw it, and was on its way back to the church in Ishím, where it belonged, and our driver had stated the fact in the simplest and most direct way when he said, " The Mother of God is coming home."

Rain fell at intervals throughout the day Thursday, but we pushed on over a muddy steppe road in the direction of Tiukalínsk, changing horses at the post stations of Boróf-skaya, Tushnalóbova, Abátskaya, and Kamishénka, and stopping for the night at a peasant's house in the village of Orlóva. In the sixty hours which had elapsed since our departure from Tiumén we had traveled 280 miles, with only four hours of sleep, and we were so much exhausted that we could not go any farther without rest. The weather during the night finally cleared up, and when we resumed our journey on the following morning the sun was shining brightly in an almost unclouded sky, and the air was fresh, invigorating, and filled with fragrant odors.

Although the road continued bad, the country as we proceeded southward and eastward steadily improved in appearance, and before noon we were riding across a beautiful, fertile, and partly cultivated prairie, which extended in every direction as far as the eye could reach, with nothing to break the horizon line except an occasional clump of small birch-trees or a dark-green thicket of willow and alder bushes. The steppe was bright with flowers, and here and there appeared extensive tracts of black, newly plowed land, or vast fields of waving grain, which showed that the country was inhabited; but there was not a fence, nor a barn, nor a house to be seen in any direction, and I could not help wondering where the village was to which these cultivated fields belonged. My curiosity was soon to be sat-

isfied.   In a few moments our driver gathered up his muddy
rope reins, braced himself securely in his seat, threw out
behind and above his head the long, heavy lash of his short-
handled *knut*, and bringing it down with stinging force
across the backs of his four horses shouted, in a high fal-
setto and a deep bass, "Heekh-ya-a-a!"   The whole team
instantly broke into a frantic, tearing gallop, which made
me involuntarily hold my breath, until it was suddenly
jounced out of me by a terrific jolt as the *tárantás*, going
at the rate of fifteen miles an hour, dropped into a deep
rut and rebounded with tremendous force, throwing me
violently out of my seat, and making my head and back
throb with the shock of the unexpected concussion.   I
needed no further evidence that we were approaching a
village.   A Siberian team never fully shows what it can
do until it is within half a mile of its destination, and then
it suddenly becomes a living tornado of energy.   I shouted
to the driver, "Pastói! Tíshei!" [Hold on! Don't go so
fast!] but it was of no use.   Both driver and horses knew
that this was the final spurt, and exerted themselves to the
utmost, the horses laying back their ears and tearing ahead
as if pursued by a prairie fire, while the driver lashed them
fiercely with his heavy *knut* to an accompaniment of shrill,
wild cries, whoops, whistles, and shouts of "Ya-a-a-va!"
"Ay durak!" "Noo-oo-oo!" (with a falling inflection) "Heekh-
ya-a-a!"   All that we could do was to shut our eyes, trust
in Providence, and hold on.   The *tárantás* was pelted with
a perfect storm of mud from the flying hoofs of four gal-
loping horses, and if, putting out my head, I opened my
mouth to expostulate with the driver, I ran great risk of
having it effectually closed by a teacupful of tenacious
black mire, thrown like a semi-liquid ball from the catapult of a horse's hoof.   In a moment we saw, barring the
way ahead, a long wattled fence extending for a mile or
more to the right and left, with a narrow gate at the point
where it intersected the road.   It was the fence which

inclosed the pasture ground of the village that we were approaching. As we dashed, with a wild whoop from our driver, through the open gateway, we noticed beside it a

HUTS OF VILLAGE GATE-KEEPERS.

curious half-underground hut, roofed partly with bushes and partly with sods, out of which, as we passed, came the village gate-keeper—a dirty, forlorn-looking old man with inflamed eyes and a long white beard, who reminded me of Rip Van Winkle after his twenty years' sleep. While he was in the act of bowing and touching the weather-beaten remains of what was once a hat, we whirled past and lost sight of him, with a feeling of regret that we could not stop and take a photograph of such a wild, neglected picturesque embodiment of poverty and wretchedness clothed in rags. Just inside the gate stood an unpainted sign-post, upon the board of which had been neatly inscribed in black letters the words

VILLAGE OF KRUTAYA.
Distance from St. Petersburg, 2992 versts.
Distance from Moscow, 2526 versts.
Houses, 42. Male souls, 97.

Between the gate and the village there was a grassy common about half a mile wide, upon which were grazing hundreds of cattle and sheep. Here and there stood a huge, picturesque windmill, consisting of a small gable-roofed house with four enormous wind-vanes mounted on a pivot at the apex of a pyramid of cross-piled logs. Beyond the windmills appeared the village, a small collection of gray, weather-beaten log-houses, some with roofs of boards, some with a roofing of ragged birch-bark held in place by tightly lashed poles, some thatched with straw, and some the flat roofs of which had been overlaid with black earth from the steppe and supported a thrifty steppe flora of weeds, buttercups, and wild mustard. Through this cluster of gray log-houses ran one central street, which had neither walks nor gutters, and which, from side to side and from end to end, was a shallow lake of black, liquid mud. Into this wide street we dashed at a tearing gallop; and the splattering of the horses' hoofs in the mud, the rumble of the *tárantás*, and the wild cries of our driver brought the whole population to the windows to see whether it was the governor-general or a special courier of the Tsar who came at such a furious pace into the quiet settlement. Presently our driver pulled up his reeking, panting horses before the court-yard gate of one of his friends and

shouted, "Davái loshedéi!" [Bring out the horses!] Then
from all parts of the village came, splashing and "thlup-
ping" through the mud, idlers and old men to see who had

A VILLAGE GATE-KEEPER.

arrived and to watch the changing of teams. Strange,
picturesque figures the old men were, with their wrinkled
faces, matted, neglected hair, and long, stringy, gray beards.
Some were bareheaded, some barefooted, some wore tat-
tered sheepskin *shúbas* and top-boots, and some had on

long-tailed butternut coats, girt about the waist with straps
or dirty colored sashes.   While they assembled in a group
around the *tárantás*, our driver climbed down from his high
seat and began to unharness his horses.   The owner of the
house in front of which we had stopped soon made his
appearance, and inquired whether we wished to drink tea
or to go on at once.   I replied that we desired to go on at
once.   "Andre!" he shouted to one of his sons, "ride to
the pasture and drive in the horses."   Andre sprang on a
barebacked horse which another boy brought out of the
court-yard and galloped away to the village common.   In
the mean time the assembled crowd of idlers watched our
movements, commented upon our "new-fashioned" *tárantás*, and tried to ascertain from our driver who we were
and where were going.   Failing to get from that source
any precise information, one of them, a bareheaded, gray-
haired old man, said to me, "Barin!   Permit us to ask—
where is God taking you to?"   I replied that we were going
to Omsk and Semipalátinsk.   "A-a-ah!" murmured the
crowd with gratified curiosity.

" Where do you condescend to come from ? " inquired the
old man, pursuing the investigation.

" From America," I replied.

" A-a-ah!" breathed the crowd again.

" Is that a Russian town ? " persisted the old man.

" America is n't a town," shouted a bright-faced boy on
the outskirts of the crowd.   " It 's a country.   All the world,"
he continued mechanically, as if reciting from a school-book,
" is divided into five parts, Europe, Asia, Africa, America,
and Australia.   Russia occupies two-thirds of Europe and
one-half of Asia."   Beyond this even the school-boy's geographical knowledge did not extend, and it was evident that
none of the old inhabitants of the village had even so much
as heard of America.   A young man, however, who had happened to be in Omsk when the bodies of the dead members
of the *Jeannette* arctic expedition were carried through that

city, undertook to enlighten the crowd upon the subject of
the Americans, who, he said, " were the wisest people that
God had ever created, and the only people that had ever
sailed into the great Icy Sea." One of the old inhabitants
contended that Russian navigators had also penetrated the
Icy Sea, and that although they might not be so " wise" as
the Americans, they were quite as good sailors in icy waters.
This gave rise to an animated discussion of polar exploration,
in the midst of which the young fellow who had been sent
after the horses came back with whistle and whoop, driving
the animals before him into the court-yard, where they were
soon harnessed, and were then brought out and fastened
with long rope traces to the *tárantás*. Our new driver
mounted the box, inquired whether we were ready, and
gathering up his rope reins shouted "Noo-oo!" to his horses;
and with a measured jangle of bells from the arch over the
thill-horse's back, and a " splash-spatter-splash" of hoofs in
the mud, we rolled out of the settlement.

Such, with trifling variations in detail, was the regular
routine of arrival and departure in all of the steppe villages where we changed horses between Tiumén and Omsk.
The greater number of these villages were dreary, forlorn-
looking places, containing neither yards, walks, trees, grass-
plots, nor shrubbery, and presenting to the eye nothing but
two parallel lines of gray, dilapidated log-houses and tumble-
down court-yard walls rising directly out of the long pool
of jet-black mud that formed the solitary street.

It is with a feeling of intense pleasure and relief that one
leaves such a village and rides out upon the wide, clean,
breezy steppe where the air is filled with the fragrance of
clover and the singing of birds, and where the eye is constantly delighted with great sweeps of smooth, velvety turf,
or vast undulating expanses of high steppe grass sprinkled
in the foreground with millions of wild roses, white mar-
guerites, delicate five-angled harebells, and dark-red tiger-
lilies. Between the village of Krutáya and Kalmakóva, on

Friday, we rode across a steppe that was literally a great ocean of flowers. One could pick twenty different species and a hundred specimens within the area of a single square yard. Here and there we deserted the miry road and drove for miles across the smooth, grassy plain, crushing flowers by the score at every revolution of our carriage-wheels. In the middle of the steppe I had our driver stop and wait for me while I alighted and walked away into the flowery solitude to enjoy the stillness, the perfumed air, and the sea of verdure through which ran the long, sinuous black line

A STEPPE VILLAGE.

of the muddy highway. On my left, beyond the road, was a wide, shallow depression six or eight miles across, rising on the opposite side in a long, gradual sweep to a dark blue line of birch forest which formed the horizon. This depression was one smooth expanse of close, green turf dotted with grazing cattle and sheep, and broken here and there by a silvery pool or lake. Around me, upon the higher ground, the steppe was carpeted with flowers, among which I noticed splendid orange asters two inches in diameter, spotted tiger-lilies with strongly reflexed petals, white clover, daisies, harebells, spirea, astragalus, melilotus, and a peculiar flower growing in long, slender, curved spikes which suggested

flights of miniature carmine sky-rockets sent up by the
fairies of the steppe. The air was still and warm, and had
a strange, sweet fragrance which I can liken only to the
taste of wild honey. There were no sounds to break the
stillness of the great plain except the drowsy hum of bees,
the regular measured "Kate-did-Kate-did" of a few katydids
in the grass near me, and the wailing cry of a steppe hawk
hovering over the nest of some field-mice. It was a delight
simply to lie on the grass amidst the flowers and see, hear,
and breathe.

We traveled all day Friday over flowery steppes and
through little log villages like those that I have tried to
describe, stopping occasionally to make a sketch, collect
flowers, or talk with the peasants about the exile system.
Now and then we met a solitary traveler in a muddy *tárantás* on his way to Tiumén, or passed a troop of exiles in
gray overcoats plodding along through the mud, surrounded
by a cordon of soldiers; but as we were off the great
through line of travel, we saw few vehicles except the *telégas* of peasants going back and forth between the villages
and the outlying fields.

The part of the province of Tobólsk through which we
traveled from Tiumén to Omsk is much more productive
and prosperous than a careless observer would suppose it to
be from the appearance of most of its villages. The four
ókrugs, or "circles," [1] of Tiumén, Yalútorfsk, Ishím, and
Tiukalínsk, through which our road lay, have an aggregate
population of 650,000 and contain about 4,000,000 acres of

---

[1] An *ókrug*, or circle, bears something like the same relation to a province that an American county does to
a state, except that it is proportion-
ately much larger. The province of
Tobólsk, with an area of 590,000 square
miles, has only ten *ókrugs*, so that the
average area of these subdivisions is
about that of the State of Michigan.
If all of the territory north of the Ohio
River and the Potomac and east of the
Mississippi were one State, and each
of the existing States were a county,
such State and counties would bear to
each other and to the United States
something like the same relation which
the province and *ókrugs* of Tobólsk
bear to each other and to Siberia. The
highest administrative officer in a Siberian province is the governor, who
is represented in every *ókrug* by an
isprávnik.

cultivated land. The peasants in these circles own 1,500,000 head of live stock, and produce perhaps two-thirds of the 30,000,000 bushels of grain raised annually in the province. There are held every year in the four circles 220 town and village fairs or local markets, to which the peasants bring great quantities of products for sale. The transactions of these fairs in the circle of Yalútorfsk, for example, amount annually to $2,000,000; in the circle of Ishím to $3,500,000; and in the whole province to about $14,000,000. From these statistics, and from such inquiries and observations as we were able to make along the road, it seemed to me that if the province of Tobólsk were honestly and intelligently governed, and were freed from the heavy burden of criminal exile, it would in a comparatively short time become one of the most prosperous and flourishing parts of the empire.

We drank tea Friday afternoon at the circuit town of Tiukalínsk, and after a short rest resumed our journey with four "free" horses. The road was still muddy and bad, and as we skirted the edge of the great marshy steppe of Barába between Tiukalínsk and Bekísheva, we were so tormented by huge gray mosquitos that we were obliged to put on thick gloves, cover our heads with calico hoods and horse-hair netting, and defend ourselves constantly with leafy branches. Between the mosquitos and the jolting we had another hard, sleepless night; but fortunately it was the last one, and at half-past ten o'clock on the morning of Saturday, July 4th, our *tárantás* rolled into the streets of Omsk. Both we and our vehicle were so spattered and plastered with black steppe mud that no one who had seen us set out from Tiumén would have recognized us. We had been four days and nights on the road, and had made in that time a journey of 420 miles, with only eleven hours of sleep.

CHAPTER VII

THE GREAT KÍRGHIS STEPPE

OMSK, which is a city of about 30,000 inhabitants, is the capital of the *óblast* of Akmolínsk, and the seat of government of the steppe territories.[1] It is an administrative rather than a commercial or a manufacturing town, and its population is largely composed of officials and clerks employed in the various Government bureaus and departments. It has a few noticeable public buildings, among which are the enormous white "cadet school," the house of the governor-general, the police station,—a rather picturesque log building, surmounted by a fire-alarm tower,— and the *krépast*, or fortress. The streets of the city are wide and unpaved; the dwelling-houses are made generally of logs; there is the usual number of white-walled churches and cathedrals with green, blue, or golden domes; and every building that would attract a traveler's attention belongs to the Government. If I were asked to characterize Omsk in a few words, I should describe it as a city of 30,000 inhabitants, in which the largest building is a military academy and the most picturesque building a police station; in which there is neither a newspaper nor a public library, and in which one-half the population wears

---

[1] The larger administrative divisions of the Russian empire are of two kinds and are known as *gubérnie* [governments] and *óblasti* [territories]. As the English word "government" already has more than one meaning, I shall use "province" in this work to denote the organized political division called in Russia a *gubérnia*, and "territory" to designate the comparatively unorganized division known as an *óblast*. The distinction between them is very much like that between our states and territories.

the Tsar's uniform and makes a business of governing the other half. The nature of the relations between the latter half and the former may be inferred from the fact that an intelligent and reputable citizen of this *chinóvnik*-dominated city, who had been kind and useful to us, said to me, when he bade me good-by, "Mr. Kennan, if you find

POLICE STATION AND FIRE TOWER IN OMSK.

it necessary to speak of me by name in your book, please don't speak of me favorably."

"For Heaven's sake, why not?" I inquired.

"Because," he replied, "I don't think your book will be altogether pleasing to the Government; and if I am mentioned favorably in it, I shall be harried by the officials here more than I am now. My request may seem to you absurd, but it is the only favor I have to ask."[1]

[1] This was said to me upon our return from Eastern Siberia in the following winter, and was called out by an account which I had given to Mr. X—— of our experience and the results of our observations. I should

We found in Omsk very little that was either interesting or instructive. The city was the place of exile of a well-known and talented Russian author named Petropávlovski, but as we were not aware of the fact we missed an opportunity to make the acquaintance of a man whose wide and thorough knowledge of Russian life, as well as of the exile system, might have been in the highest degree useful to us.[1] The only letter of introduction that I had to deliver in Omsk was a brief note from the editor of a newspaper in St. Petersburg to Colonel Paivtsóf, president of the West Siberian branch of the Imperial Geographical Society. The latter received me very cordially, gave me some useful information with regard to the comparative merits of different routes from Semipalátinsk to Tomsk, and went with me to see the little museum connected with the Geographical Society, which, apparently, was the only evidence of culture that the city afforded. Mr. Frost, meanwhile, made explorations in the neighborhood; discovered and sketched a wretched suburb north of the river Om, which seemed to be inhabited chiefly by poor, common criminal exiles, and made the drawing of the police station that is reproduced on page 141. I tried to find the *ostróg*[2] where the gifted Russian novelist Dostoyéfski spent so many years of penal servitude and where, according to the testimony of his

be glad to give some illustrations of the "harrying" to which Mr. X—— referred, if I could do so without disclosing his identity.

[1] Mr. Petropávlovski has written a great deal for the *Atéchestvenia Zapíski* and other Russian magazines under the pen-name of "Karónin," and a volume of his collected stories was published in Moscow in 1890. His field as a writer is the Russian village and the everyday life of the Russian peasant, and he has shown in that field not only great accuracy of observation and faithfulness of portrayal, but a sympathetic comprehension of all the sufferings that the common people are forced to endure

as one of the results of a bad system of government. I do not know for what specific reason he was banished to Siberia, but I presume that his writings were regarded by the censor as "pernicious in tendency."

[2] The word *ostróg* meant originally a stockaded entrenchment and was applied to the rude forts built by the Cossacks as they marched eastward into Siberia three centuries ago. The custom of confining criminals in these forts finally gave to *ostróg* the meaning of "prison," and up to the present century nearly all of the prisons in Siberia were known as *ostrógs*.

fellow prisoners, he was twice flogged[1]; but I was told that it had long before been torn down.

I did not wonder that the Government should have

THE EXILE SUBURB—OMSK.

wished to tear down walls that had witnessed such scenes of misery and cruelty as those described in Dostoyéfski's

[1] A touching account of this part of Dostoyéfski's life, by a convict named Rozhnófski who occupied the same cell with him in the Omsk *ostróg*, has recently been published in the Tiflis newspaper *Kavkáz*. Rozhnófski says that Dostoyéfski was flogged the first time for making complaint, in behalf of the other prisoners, of a lump of filth found in their soup. His second punishment was for saving a fellow-prisoner from drowning when the major in command of the *ostróg* had ordered him not to do so. The flogging in each case was so brutally severe that the sufferer had to be taken to the hospital, and after the second "execution," Rozhnófski says, the convicts generally regarded Dostoyéfski as dead. When he reappeared among them, after lying six weeks in the hospital, they gave him the nickname *pokóinik* [the deceased]. For further particulars of Dostoyéfski's trial, condemnation, and life in penal servitude see *Atéchestvenia Zapíski* [Annals of the Fatherland], Feb. 1881, and March, 1882.

"Notes from a House of the Dead." There was one other building in Omsk that we desired to inspect, namely, the prison that had taken the place of the old *ostróg;* but we were treated with such contemptuous discourtesy by the governor of the territory when we called upon him and asked

A KÍRGHIS ENCAMPMENT.

permission to examine it, that we could only retire without even having taken seats in his High Excellency's office.

On Wednesday, July 8th, having fully recovered from the fatigue of our journey from Tiumén, we left Omsk with three post horses and a Cossack driver for Semipalátinsk. The road between the two cities runs everywhere along the right bank of the Írtish through a line of log villages which do not differ essentially in appearance from those north of Omsk, but which are inhabited almost exclusively by Cossacks. Whenever the Russian Government desires to strengthen a weak frontier line so as to prevent the incursions of hostile or predatory natives, it forcibly colonizes along that line a few hundred or a few thousand families of armed Cossacks. During the last century it formed in this way the "armed line of the Térek," to protect southeastern Russia from the raids of the Caucasian mountaineers, and a similar armed line along the Írtish, to hold in check the Kírghis. The danger that was apprehended from these half-wild tribes long ago passed away, but the descendants of the Cossack colonists still remain in the places to which their parents or their grandparents were transported. They have all the hardy virtues of pioneers and frontiersmen, are ingenious, versatile, and full of resources, and adapt themselves quickly to almost any environment. There are thirty or forty settlements of such Cossacks along the line of the Írtish between Omsk and Semipalátinsk, and as many more between Semipalátinsk and the Altái.

Almost immediately after leaving Omsk we noticed a great change in the appearance of the country. The steppe, which in the province of Tobólsk had been covered either with fresh green grass or with a carpet of flowers, here became more bare and arid, and its vegetation was evidently withering and drying up under the fierce heat of the midsummer sun. Flowers were still abundant in low places along the river, and we crossed now and then wide areas of grass that was still green, but the prevailing color of the high steppe was a sort of old-gold—a color like that of ripe wheat. The clumps of white-stemmed birch trees, that had diversified and given a park-like character to the scenery north of Omsk, became less and less frequent; cultivated fields disappeared altogether, and the steppe assumed more and more the aspect of a Central Asiatic desert.

A few stations beyond Omsk, we saw and visited for the first time an *aül* [encampment] of the wandering Kírghis, a pastoral tribe of natives who roam with their flocks and herds over the plains of southwestern Siberia from the

Caspian Sea to the mountains of the Altái, and who make up more than three-fourths of the population of the steppe territories. The *aül* consisted of only three or four small *kibítkas*, or circular tents of gray felt, pitched close together at a distance from the road in the midst of the great ocean-like expanse of dry, yellowish grass which stretched away in every direction to the horizon. There was no path leading to or from the encampment, and the little gray tents, standing alone on that boundless plain, seemed to be almost as much isolated, and as far removed from all civilized human interests, as if they were so many frail skin coracles floating in the watery solitude of the Pacific.

It was evident from the commotion caused by our approach that the encampment had not often been visited. The swarthy, half-naked children, who had been playing out on the grass, fled in affright to the shelter of the tents as they saw our *tárantás* coming towards them across the steppe; women rushed out to take a startled look at us and then disappeared; and even the men, who gathered in a group to meet us, appeared to be surprised and a little alarmed by our visit. A few words in Kírghis, however, from our Cossack driver reassured them, and upon the invitation of an old man in a red-and-yellow skull-cap, who seemed to be the patriarch of the band, we entered one of the *kibítkas*. It was a circular tent about fifteen feet in diameter and eight feet high, made by covering a dome-shaped framework of smoke-blackened poles with large overlapping sheets of heavy gray felt. The slightly curved rafters which formed the roof radiated like the spokes of a wheel from a large wooden ring in the center of the dome, and were supported around the circumference of the tent by a skeleton wall of wooden lattice-work in which there was a hinged door. The ring in the center of the dome outlined the aperture left for the escape of smoke and the admission of air, and directly under this aperture a fire was smoldering on the ground inside a circle of flat stones, upon which

INTERIOR OF A KÍRGHIS KIBÍTKA.

stood a few pots, kettles, and other domestic utensils. The furniture of the tent was very scanty, and consisted of a narrow, unpainted bedstead opposite the door, two or three cheap Russian trunks of wood painted blue and decorated with strips of tin, and a table about four feet in diameter and eight inches high, intended evidently to be used by persons who habitually squatted on the ground. Upon the table were a few dirty wooden bowls and spoons and an antique metal pitcher, while here and there, hanging against the lattice wall, were buckets of birch bark, a harness or two, a flint-lock rifle, a red-white-and-golden saddle of wood with silver-inlaid stirrups, and a pair of carpet saddle-bags.

The first duty that hospitality requires of a Kírghis host is the presentation of *kúmis* to his guests, and we had no sooner taken seats on a sheet of gray felt beside the fire than one of the women went to the *kúmis* churn,—a large, black, greasy bag of horse-hide hanging against the lattice wall,—worked a wooden churn-dasher up and down in it vigorously for a moment, and then poured out of it into a greasy wooden bowl fully a quart of the great national Kírghis beverage for me. It did not taste as much like sour milk and soda-water as I expected that it would. On the contrary, it had rather a pleasant flavor; and if it had been a little cleaner and cooler, it would have made an agreeable and refreshing drink. I tried to please the old Kírghis patriarch and to show my appreciation of Kírghis hospitality by drinking the whole bowlful; but I underestimated the quantity of *kúmis* that it is necessary to imbibe in order to show one's host that one does n't dislike it and that one is satisfied with one's entertainment. I had no sooner finished one quart bowlful than the old patriarch brought me another; and when I told him that a single quart was all that I permitted myself to take at one time, and suggested that he reserve the second bowlful for my comrade, Mr. Frost, he looked so pained and grieved that in order to restore his serenity I had to go to the *tárantás*, get my banjo, and sing

" There is a Tavern in the Town." Mr. Frost, meanwhile, had shirked his duty and his *kúmis* by pretending that he could not drink and draw simultaneously, and that he wanted to make a likeness of the patriarch's six-year-old son. This seemed to be a very adroit scheme on Mr. Frost's part, but it did not work as well as he had expected. No sooner had he begun to make the sketch than the boy's mother, taking alarm at the peculiar, searching way in which the artist looked at his subject, and imagining perhaps that her offspring was being mesmerized, paralyzed, or bewitched, swooped down upon the ragged little urchin, and kissing him passionately, as if she had almost lost him forever, carried him away and hid him. This untoward incident cast such a gloom over the subsequent proceedings that after singing four verses of " Solomon Levi," in a vain attempt to restore public confidence in Mr. Frost, I put away my banjo and we took our departure. I should like to know what traditions are now current in that part of the Kírghis steppe with regard to the two plausible but designing gia-ours who went about visiting the *aüls* of the faithful, one of them singing unholy songs to the accompaniment of a strange stringed instrument, while the other cast an " evil eye " upon the children, and tried to get possession of their souls by making likenesses of their bodies.

Day after day we traveled swiftly southward over a good road through the great Kírghis steppe, stopping now and then to pick snowy pond-lilies in some reed-fringed pool, or to visit an *aül* and drink *kúmis* with the hospitable nomads in their gray felt tents. Sometimes the road ran down into the shallow valley of the Írtish, through undulating seas of goldenrod and long wild grass, whose wind-swept waves seemed to break here and there in foaming crests of snowy spirea; sometimes it made a long détour into the high, arid steppe back from the river, where the vegetation had been parched to a dull uniform yellow by weeks of hot sunshine; and sometimes it ran suddenly into a low, moist

oasis around a blue steppe lake, where we found ourselves
in a beautiful natural flower-garden crowded with rose-
bushes, hollyhocks, asters, daisies, fringed pinks, rosemary,
flowering pea, and splendid dark-blue spikes of aconite
standing shoulder high.

Animals and birds were much more plentiful than they
had been in the province of Tobólsk, and were, moreover,
remarkably tame. Magnificent eagles perched upon the
telegraph poles and did not fly away until we were almost
opposite them; slate-colored steppe quails with tufted heads
ran fearlessly along the very edge of the road as we passed,
and even the timid little jerboa that the Cossacks call *tar-
bogán* stopped every now and then to look at us as it hopped
away into the dry grass.

As we went farther and farther from Omsk the steppe
became more and more sea-like in its appearance, until,
shortly after we passed the post-station of Piatorízhskaya
Thursday afternoon, it looked like a great yellow ocean
extending in every direction to the smooth horizon line.
Its peculiar old-gold color was given to it apparently by
the prevailing species of grass which, as it gradually dried
up in the hot sunshine, turned from green through reddish-
brown to the color of dead-ripe wheat. In places where
the soil happened for any reason to be moist, as in the
vicinity of small brackish ponds and lakes, the grass was
still fresh and was sprinkled with flowers; but the steppe,
as a rule, presented the appearance of a boundless ocean of
wheat stubble, deepening here and there into the rich
orange of goldenrod.

Just before sunset we passed at a distance of two or
three hundred yards a lonely Kírghis cemetery, and, as we
had never before seen a burial-place of this nomadic tribe,
we stopped to examine it. It consisted of a few low, bare
mounds of various shapes and dimensions, and three or
four large, rectangular, fort-like structures of sun-dried
bricks. The high walls of the latter had raised corners.

and were pierced with square portholes through which, I presume, the bodies of the dead were carried into the inclosure for burial. Inside of each of these adobe forts were two or more grave-shaped hillocks, and at the head of every hillock stood a stick or pole with a small quantity of sheep's wool wrapped around it. There were no inscriptions or pictographs in or about these mortuary inclosures, and, apart from the wrappings of wool, I could discover nothing that seemed likely to have significance. The sun was just setting as we finished our inspection and resumed our jour-

A KÍRGHIS CEMETERY.

ney, and twenty minutes later, when I looked back at the lonely, abandoned cemetery, its orange-tinted walls made the only break in the vast, curving horizon line of the Sea of Grass.

The road everywhere between Omsk and Semipalátinsk was hard and dry, and so smooth that we were scarcely conscious of being jolted. We slept every night in our *tárantás* while going at the rate of eight miles an hour, and if it had not been necessary to get out at the stations in order to show our *padarózhnaya* and see to the harnessing of fresh horses, we might have slept all night without waking.

Very soon after we began to travel at night in Western Siberia, our attention was attracted and our curiosity excited by the peculiar throbbing beat of an instrument that we took to be a watchman's rattle, and that we heard in every village through which we passed between sunset and dawn. It was not exactly like any sound that either of us had ever heard before, and we finally became very curious to see how it was made. It suggested, at times, the shaking of a billiard ball in a resonant wooden box; but the throbs were too clear-cut and regular to be made in that way, and I concluded at last that they must be produced by beating rapidly some sort of rude wooden drum. No night-watchman ever happened to come near us until we approached Pávlodár, a little town midway between Omsk and Semipalátinsk. About two o'clock that morning, while it was still very dark, we stopped to change horses at the post station of Chernoyárskaya. While a sleepy Kírghis hostler was harnessing fresh horses under the supervision of a large-bodied, sharp-tongued woman with a lantern in her hand and a lighted cigarette in her mouth, we were suddenly startled by the hollow staccato beat of a night-watchman's drum coming out of the darkness behind us and only a few feet away. "Now," I said to Mr. Frost, "I 'll see what that thing is," and springing from the *tárantás* I called the watchman and asked him to show me his *kolotúshka* [literally "hammerer"]. It proved to be the simplest sort of a noise-producing instrument. If the reader will take a wooden box about the size of a common brick, knock out the two narrow sides, attach a wooden spool to one end by means of a four-inch cord and fasten a clothes-brush handle to the other, he will have a fairly good imitation of a Siberian night-watchman's rattle. When this instrument is shaken vigorously and rhythmically from side to side, as if it were a heavy palm-leaf fan, the clapper, which is attached to the upper end and which is represented by the spool, swings back and forth, striking the box first on one side and then on the other, and producing a series of rapid staccato beats that can be heard on a still night at a distance of two miles.

After a little argument and persuasion the Chernoyár-skaya night-watchman consented to sell me his rattle, as a curiosity, for the sum of ten cents : but he soon had reason to regret the transaction. No sooner had he parted with the insignia of office than the sharp-tongued and misanthropic postmistress, who was leaning against the court-yard gate, and whose face I could just make out by the glow of her cigarette, opened upon him a hot fire of sarcastic and contemptuous remarks. "A fine night-watchman you are!" she said with scornful irony. "What are you good for now? There was nothing of you before but your breeches and your rattle—and now you've sold your rattle!"

"I can make another to-morrow," replied the night-watchman in a deprecating tone.

"Make another!" retorted the postmistress contemptuously. "There's no use in making another if you don't shake it oftener than you have to-night. Where have you been all night anyhow—drunk again with the priest?"

"Yei Bókhu mátushka! [Before God, my little mother] I have n't taken a drop on my tongue to-night!" protested the night-watchman solemnly. "Of course you don't hear my rattle when you're asleep—God forgive you for what you say!" and the watchman, as if to appease the woman's wrath, began to help the Kírghis hostler harness the horses —but it was of no use.

"What are you trying to do now?" inquired the postmistress fiercely—"harness those horses up goose-fashion?[1] "Nyet brátushka" [No, my little brother], you may walk goose-fashion with the priest when you and he go on a spree, but you can't harness my horses goose-fashion. Go curl up in the sand somewhere until the Kabák[2] opens or the priest gets up. Now that you've sold the best part of yourself for twenty *kopéks* you're of no use to anybody. A night-*wa-a-tch*man! that SELLS his *r-r-attle!!* and harnesses a *tróika* GOOSE-fashion!!!" she concluded with immeasurable and

1 Tandem.   2 Dram-shop.

inexpressible contempt.   A moment passed—two minutes
—but there was no reply.   The discomfited night-watchman
had slunk away into the darkness.

After we had passed the little Cossack town of Pavlodár
on Friday, the weather, which had been warm ever since

AN OASIS IN THE KÍRGHIS STEPPE.

our departure from Omsk, became intensely hot, the thermometer indicating ninety-one degrees Fahrenheit at 1 p. m.
As we sat, without coats or waistcoats, under the sizzling
leather roof of our *tárantás*, fanning ourselves with our hats,
panting for breath, fighting huge green-eyed horseflies,
and looking out over an illimitable waste of dead grass

which wavered and trembled in the fierce glare of the tropical sunshine, we found it almost impossible to believe that we were in Siberia.

Many of the Cossack villages along this part of our route were situated down under the high, steep bank of the Írtish at the very water's edge, where the soil was moist enough to support a luxuriant vegetation. As a result of such favorable situation, these villages were generally shaded by trees and surrounded by well-kept vegetable and flower gardens. After a ride of twenty miles over an arid steppe in the hot, blinding sunshine of a July afternoon, it was indescribably pleasant and refreshing to come down into one of these little oases of greenery, where a narrow arm of the Írtish flowed tranquilly under the checkered shade of leafy trees; where the gardens of the Cossack housewives were full of potato, cucumber, and melon vines, the cool, fresh green of which made an effective setting for glowing beds of scarlet poppies; and where women and girls with tucked-up skirts were washing clothes on a little platform projecting into the river, while half-naked children waded and splashed in the clear, cool water around them.

We made the last stretches of our journey to Semipalá-tinsk in the night. The steppe over which we approached the city was more naked and sterile than any that we had crossed, and seemed in the faint twilight to be merely a desert of sun-baked earth and short, dead grass, with here and there a ragged bush or a long, ripple-marked dune of loose, drifting sand. I fell asleep soon after midnight, and when I awoke at half-past two o'clock Sunday morning day was just breaking, and we were passing a large white building with lighted lanterns hung against its walls, which I recognized as a city prison. It was the *tiurémni zámok*, or "prison castle" of Semipalátinsk. In a few moments we entered a long, wide, lonely street, bordered by un-painted log-houses, whose board window-shutters were all closed, and whose steep, pyramidal roofs loomed high and black in the first gray light of dawn. The street was full of soft, drifted sand, in which the hoofs of our horses fell noiselessly, and through which our *tárantás* moved with as

WASHING CLOTHES IN THE ÍRTISH.

little jar as if it were a gondola floating along a watery street in Venice. There was something strangely weird and impressive in this noiseless night ride through the heart of a ghostly and apparently deserted city, in the streets of which were the drifted sands of the desert, and where there was not a sound to indicate the presence of life save the faint, distant throbbing of a watchman's rattle, like the rapid, far-away beating of a wooden drum. We stopped at last in front of a two-story building of brick, covered with white stucco, which our driver said was the hotel *Sibír*. After pounding vigorously for five minutes on the front door, we were admitted by a sleepy waiter, who showed us to a hot, musty room in the second story, where we finished our broken night's sleep on the floor.

The city of Semipalátinsk, which has a population of about 15,000 Russians, Kírghis, and Tatárs, is situated on the right bank of the river Írtish, 480 miles southeast of Omsk and about 900 miles from Tiumén. It is the seat of government of the territory of Semipalátinsk, and is commercially a place of some importance, owing to the fact that it stands on one of the caravan routes to Tashkénd and Central Asia, and commands a large part of the trade of the Kírghis steppe. The country tributary to it is a pastoral rather than an agricultural region, and of its 547,000 inhabitants 497,000 are nomads, who live in 111,000 *kibítkas* or felt tents, and own more than 3,000,000 head of live stock, including 70,000 camels. The province produces annually, among other things, 45,000 pounds of honey, 370,000 pounds of tobacco, 100,000 bushels of potatoes, and more than 12,000,000 bushels of grain. There are held every year within the limits of the territory eleven commercial fairs, the transactions of which amount in the aggregate to about $1,000,000. Forty or fifty caravans leave the city of Semipalátinsk every year for various points in Mongolia and Central Asia, carrying Russian goods to the value of from $150,000 to $200,000.

It is hardly necessary, I suppose, to call the attention of persons who think that all of Siberia is an arctic waste to the fact that honey and tobacco are not arctic products, and that the camel is not a beast of burden used by Eskimos on wastes of snow. If Mr. Frost and I had supposed the climate of southwestern Siberia to be arctic in its character, our minds would have been dispossessed of that erroneous idea in less than twelve hours after our arrival in Semipalátinsk. When we set out for a walk through the city about one o'clock Sunday afternoon, the thermometer indicated eighty-nine degrees Fahrenheit in the shade, with a north wind, and the inhabitants seemed to regard it as rather a cool and pleasant summer day. After wading around in the deep sand under a blazing sun for an hour and a half, we were more than ready to seek the shelter of the hotel and call for refrigerating drinks. The city of Semipalátinsk fully deserves the nickname that has been given to it by the Russian officers there stationed, viz., "The Devil's Sand-box." From almost any interior point of view it presents a peculiar gray, dreary appearance, owing partly to the complete absence of trees and grass, partly to the ashy, weather-beaten aspect of its unpainted log-houses, and partly to the loose, drifting sand with which its streets are filled. We did not see in our walk of an hour and a half a single tree, bush, or blade of grass, and we waded a large part of the time through soft, dry sand which was more than ankle-deep, and which in places had been drifted, like snow, to a depth of four or five feet against the walls of the gray log-houses. The whole city made upon me the impression of a Mohammedan town built in the middle of a north African desert. This impression was deepened by the Tatár mosques here and there with their brown, candle-extinguisher minarets; by the groups of long-bearded, white-turbaned mullas who stood around them; and by the appearance in the street now and then of a huge double-humped Bactrian camel, ridden into the city by a swarthy, sheepskin-hooded Kírghis from the steppes.

Monday morning I called upon General Tseklínski, the governor of the territory, presented my letters from the Russian Minister of the Interior and the Minister of Foreign

A STREET IN SEMIPALÁTINSK.

Affairs, and was gratified to find that he had apparently received no private instructions with regard to us and knew nothing whatever about us. He welcomed me courteously, granted me permission to inspect the Semipalátinsk prison, said he would send the chief of the police to take us to the mosques and show us about the city, and promised to have prepared for us an open letter of introduction to all the subordinate officials in the Semipalátinsk territory.

From the house of the governor I went, upon his recommendation, to the public library, an unpretending log-house in the middle of the town, where I found a small anthropological museum, a comfortable little reading-room supplied with all the Russian newspapers and magazines, and a well-chosen collection of about one thousand books, among which I was somewhat surprised to find the works of Spencer, Buckle, Lewes, Mill, Taine, Lubbock, Tylor, Huxley, Darwin, Lyell, Tyndall, Alfred Russell Wallace, Mackenzie Wallace, and Sir Henry Maine, as well as the novels and stories of Scott, Dickens, Marryat, George Eliot, George Macdonald, Anthony Trollope, Justin McCarthy, Erckmann-Chatrian, Edgar Allan Poe, and Bret Harte. The library was particularly strong in the departments of science and political economy, and the collection of books, as a whole, was in the highest degree creditable to the intelligence and taste of the people who made and used it. It gave me a better opinion of Semipalátinsk than anything that I had thus far seen or heard.[1]

---

[1] Most of the works of the scientific authors above named were expurgated Russian editions. Almost every chapter of Lecky's "History of Rationalism" had been defaced by the censor, and in a hasty examination of it I found gaps where from ten to sixty pages had been cut out bodily. Even in this mutilated form, and in the remote Siberian town of Semipalátinsk, the book was such an object of terror to a cowardly Government, that it had been quarantined by order of the Tsar, and could not be issued to a reader without special permission from the Minister of the Interior. A similar taboo had been placed upon the works of Spencer, Mill, Lewes, Lubbock, Huxley, and Lyell, notwithstanding the fact that the censor had cut out of them everything that seemed to him to have a " dangerous" or "demoralizing" tendency. I subsequently ascertained that these volumes, with more than 100 others, had been put into the *index expurgatorius*, and that every public librarian in the empire had been forbidden to issue them to readers. A complete list of the books thus placed under the ban will be found in Appendix B.

A CAMEL TEAM CROSSING THE FORD.

From the library I strolled eastward along the bank of the Írtish to the pendulum ferry by which communication is maintained between Semipalátinsk and a Kírghis suburb on the other side of the river. The ferry-boat starts from a wooded island in mid-stream, which is reached either by crossing a foot-bridge, or by fording the shallow channel that separates it from the Semipalátinsk shore. Just ahead of me were several Kírghis with three or four double-humped camels, one of which was harnessed to a Russian *teléga*. Upon reaching the ford the Kírghis released the draught camel from the *teléga*, lashed the empty vehicle, wheels upwards, upon the back of the grunting, groaning animal, and made him wade with it across the stream. A Bactrian camel, with his two loose, drooping humps, his long neck, and his preposterously conceited and disdainful expression of countenance, is always a ridiculous beast, but he never looks so absurdly comical as when crossing a stream with a four-wheeled wagon lashed bottom upward on his back. The shore of the Írtish opposite Semipalátinsk is nothing more than the edge of a great desert-like steppe which stretches away to the southward beyond the limits of vision. I reached there just in time to see the unloading of a caravan of camels which had arrived from Tashkénd with silks, rugs, and other Central Asiatic goods for the Semipalátinsk market.

Late in the afternoon I retraced my steps to the hotel, where I found Mr. Frost, who had been sketching all day in the Tatár or eastern end of the town. The evening was hot and sultry, and we sat until eleven o'clock without coats or waistcoats, beside windows thrown wide open to catch every breath of air, listening to the unfamiliar noises of the Tatár city. It was the last night of the great Mohammedan fast of Ramazan, and the whole population seemed to be astir until long after midnight. From every part of the town came to us on the still night air the quick staccato throbbing of watchmen's rattles, which sounded like the rapid beating of wooden drums, and suggested some pagan ceremony in central Africa or the Fiji Islands. Now and then the rattles became quiet, and then the stillness was broken by the long-

A KÍRGHIS HORSEMAN IN GALA DRESS.

drawn, wailing cries of the muezzins from the minarets of the Tatár mosques.

Tuesday morning when we awoke we found the streets full of Tatárs and Kírghis in gala dress, celebrating the first

of the three holidays that follow the Mohammedan Lent.
About noon the chief of police came to our hotel, by direction of the governor, to make our acquaintance and to show
us about the city, and under his guidance we spent two or
three hours in examining the great Tatár mosque and
making ceremonious calls upon mullas and Tatár officials.
He then asked us if we would not like to see a Tatár and
Kírghis wrestling match. We replied, of course, in the
affirmative, and were driven at once in his *droshky* to an
open sandy common at the eastern end of the city, where
we found a great crowd assembled and where the wrestling
had already begun. The dense throng of spectators—mostly
Kírghis and Tatárs—was arranged in concentric circles
around an open space twenty-five or thirty feet in diameter.
The inner circle was formed by two or three lines of men,
squatting on their heels; then came three or four lines of
standing men, and behind the latter was a close circle of
horsemen sitting in their saddles, and representing the
gallery. The chief of police made a way for us through
the crowd to the inner circle, where we took orchestra seats
in the sand under a blazing sun and in a cloud of fine dust
raised by the wrestlers. The crowd, as we soon discovered,
was divided into two hostile camps, consisting respectively
of Kírghis and Tatárs. Ours was the Kírghis side, and
opposite us were the Tatárs. There were four masters of
ceremonies, who were dressed in long green *khaláts*, and
carried rattan wands. The two Tatár officials would select
a champion in their corner, throw a sash over his head, pull
him out into the arena, and then challenge the Kírghis officials
to match him. The latter would soon find a man about
equal to the Tatár champion in size and weight, and then
the two contestants would prepare for the struggle. The
first bout after we arrived was between a good-looking,
smooth-faced young Kírghis, who wore a blue skull-cap and
a red sash, and an athletic, heavily built Tatár, in a yellow
skull-cap and a green sash. They eyed each other warily

A WRESTLING MATCH.

for a moment, and then clinched fiercely, each grasping with one hand his adversary's sash, while he endeavored with the other to get an advantageous hold of wrist, arm, or shoulder. Their heads were pressed closely together, their bodies were bent almost into right angles at their waists, and their feet were kept well back to avoid trips. Presently both secured sash and shoulder holds, and in a bent position backed each other around the arena, the Kírghis watching for an opportunity to trip and the Tatár striving to close in. The veins stood out like whipcords on their foreheads and necks, and their swarthy faces dripped with perspiration as they struggled and manœuvered in the scorching sunshine, but neither of them seemed to be able to find an opening in the other's guard or to get any decided advantage. At last, however, the Tatár backed away suddenly, pulling the Kírghis violently towards him; and as the latter stepped forward to recover his balance, he was dexterously tripped by a powerful side-blow of the Tatár's leg and foot. The trip did not throw him to the ground, but it did throw him off his guard; and, before he could recover himself, the Tatár broke the sash and shoulder hold, rushed in fiercely, caught him around the body, and, with a hip-lock and a tremendous heave, threw him over his head. The unfortunate Kírghis fell with such violence that the blood streamed from his nose and mouth and he seemed partly stunned; but he was able to get up without assistance and walked in a dazed way to his corner, amidst a roar of shouts and triumphant cries from the Tatár side.

As the excitement increased new champions offered themselves, and in a moment two more contestants were locked in a desperate struggle, amidst a babel of exclamations, suggestions, taunts, and yells of encouragement or defiance from their respective supporters. The hot air was filled with a dusty haze of fine sand, which was extremely irritating to the eyes; our faces and hands burned as if they were being slowly blistered by the torrid sunshine; and the odors of horses, of perspiration, and of greasy old sheepskins, from the closely packed mass of animals and men about us, became so overpowering that we could scarcely breathe; but there was so much excitement and novelty in the scene, that we managed to hold out through twelve or fifteen bouts. Two police officers were present to maintain order and prevent fights, but their interference was not needed. The wrestling was invariably good-humored, and the vanquished retired without any manifestations of ill-feeling, and often with laughter at their own discomfiture. The Kírghis were generally overmatched. The Tatárs, although perhaps no stronger, were quicker and more dexterous than their nomadic adversaries, and won on an average two falls out of every three. About five o'clock, although the wrestling still continued, we made our way out of the crowd and returned to the hotel, to bathe our burning faces and, if possible, get cool.

CHAPTER VIII

OUR FIRST MEETING WITH POLITICAL EXILES

OUR first meeting with political exiles in Siberia was brought about by a fortunate accident, and, strangely enough, through the instrumentality of the Government. Among the many officers whose acquaintance we made in Semipalátinsk was an educated and intelligent gentleman named Pávlovski, who had long held an important position in the Russian service, and who was introduced to us as a man whose wide and accurate knowledge of Siberia, especially of the steppe territories, might render him valuable to us, both as an adviser and as a source of trustworthy information. Although Mr. Pávlovski impressed me from the first as a cultivated, humane, and liberal man, I naturally hesitated to apply to him for information concerning the political exiles. The advice given me in St. Petersburg had led me to believe that the Government would regard with disapprobation any attempt on the part of a foreign traveler to investigate a certain class of political questions or to form the acquaintance of a certain class of political offenders; and I expected, therefore, to have to make all such investigations and acquaintances stealthily and by underground methods. I was not at that time aware of the fact that Russian officials and political exiles are often secretly in sympathy, and it would never have occurred to me to seek the aid of the one class in making the acquaintance of the other. In all of my early conversations with Mr. Pávlovski, therefore, I studiously avoided the subject of political exile, and gave him, I think, no reason whatever to suppose that I knew anything about the Russian revolutionary movement, or felt any particular interest in the exiled revolutionists.

In the course of a talk one afternoon about America, Mr. Pávlovski, turning the conversation abruptly, said to me, "Mr. Kennan, have you ever paid any attention to the movement of young people into Siberia?"

I did not at first see the drift nor catch the significance of this inquiry, and replied, in a qualified negative, that I had not, but that perhaps I did not fully understand the meaning of his question.

"I mean," he said, "that large numbers of educated young men and women are now coming into Siberia from European Russia; I thought perhaps the movement might have attracted your attention."

The earnest, significant way in which he looked at me while making this remark, as if he were experimenting upon me or sounding me, led me to conjecture that the young people to whom he referred were the political exiles. I did not forget, however, that I was dealing with a Russian officer; and I replied guardedly that I had heard something about this movement, but knew nothing of it from personal observation.

"It seems to me," he said, looking at me with the same watchful intentness, "that it is a remarkable social phenomenon, and one that would naturally attract a foreign traveler's attention."

I replied that I was interested, of course, in all the social phenomena of Russia, and that I should undoubtedly feel a deep interest in the one to which he referred if I knew more about it.

"Some of the people who are now coming to Siberia," he continued, "are young men and women of high attainments — men with a university training and women of remarkable character."

"Yes," I replied, "so I have heard; and I should think that they might perhaps be interesting people to know."

"They are," he assented. "They are men and women who, under other circumstances, might render valuable services to their country; I am surprised that you have not become interested in them."

In this manner Mr. Pávlovski and I continued to fence cautiously for five minutes, each trying to ascertain the views of the other, without fully disclosing his own views concerning the unnamed, but clearly understood, subject of political exile. Mr. Pávlovski's words and manner seemed to indicate that he himself regarded with great interest and respect the "young people now coming to Siberia"; but that he did not dare make a frank avowal of such sentiments until he should feel assured of my discretion, trustworthiness, and sympathy. I, on my side, was equally cautious, fearing that the uncalled-for introduction of this topic by a Russian official might be intended to entrap me into an admission that the investigation of political exile was the real object of our Siberian journey. The adoption of a quasi-friendly attitude by an officer of the Government towards the exiled enemies of that Government seemed to me an extraordinary and unprecedented phenomenon, and I naturally regarded it with some suspicion.

At last, tired of this conversational beating around the bush, I said frankly, "Mr. Pávlovski, are you talking about the political exiles? Are they the young people to whom you refer?"

"Yes," he replied; "I thought you understood. It seems to me that the banishment to Siberia of a large part of the youth of Russia is a phenomenon that deserves a traveler's attention."

"Of course," I said, "I am interested in it, but how am I to find out anything about it? I don't know where to look for political exiles, nor how to get acquainted with them; and I am told that the Government does not regard with favor intercourse between foreign travelers and politicals."

"Politicals are easy enough to find," rejoined Mr. Pávlovski. "The country is full of them, and [with a shrug of the shoulders] there is nothing, so far as I know, to prevent you from making their acquaintance if you feel so disposed. There are thirty or forty of them here in Semipalátinsk, and they walk about the streets like other people: why should n't you happen to meet them?"

Having once broken the ice of reserve and restraint, Mr. Pávlovski and I made rapid advances towards mutual confidence. I soon became convinced that he was not making a pretense of sympathy with the politicals in order to lead me into a trap; and he apparently became satisfied that I had judgment and tact enough not to get him into trouble by talking to other people about his opinions and actions. Then everything went smoothly. I told him frankly what my impressions were with regard to the character of nihilists generally, and asked him whether, as a matter of fact, they were not wrong-headed fanatics and wild social theorists, who would be likely to make trouble in any state.

"On the contrary," he replied, "I find them to be quiet, orderly, reasonable human beings. We certainly have no trouble with them here. Governor Tseklínski treats them with great kindness and consideration; and, so far as I know, they are good citizens."

In the course of further conversation, Mr. Pávlovski said that there were in Semipalátinsk, he believed, about forty political exiles, including four or five women. They had all been banished without judicial trial, upon mere executive orders, signed by the Minister of the Interior and approved by the Tsar. Their terms of exile varied from two to five years; and at the expiration of such terms, if their behavior meanwhile had been satisfactory to the local Siberian authorities, they would be permitted to return, at their own expense, to their homes. A few of them had found employment in Semipalátinsk and were supporting themselves; others received money from relatives or friends; and the remainder were supported — or rather kept from actual starvation — by a Government allowance, which amounted to six rubles ($3.00) a month for exiles belonging to the noble or privileged class, and two rubles and seventy *kopéks* ($1.35) a month for non-privileged exiles.

"Of course," said Mr. Pávlovski, "such sums are wholly inadequate for their support. Nine *kopéks* [four and a half cents] a day won't keep a man in bread, to say nothing of providing him with shelter; and if the more fortunate ones who get employment or receive money from their relatives did not help the others, there would be much more suffering than there is. Most of them are educated men and women, and Governor Tseklínski, who appreciates the hardships of their situation, allows them to give private lessons, although, according to the letter of the law, teaching is an occupation in which political exiles are forbidden to engage. Besides giving lessons, the women sew and embroider, and earn a little money in that way. They are allowed to write and receive letters, as well as to have unobjectionable books and periodicals; and although they are nominally under police surveillance, they enjoy a good deal of personal freedom."

"What is the nature of the crimes for which these young people were banished?" I inquired. "Were they conspirators? Did they take part in plots to assassinate the Tsar?"

"Oh, no!" said Mr. Pávlovski with a smile; "they were only *neblagonadiozhni* [untrustworthy]. Some of them belonged to forbidden societies, some imported or were in possession of forbidden books, some had friendly relations with other more dangerous offenders, and some were connected with disorders in the higher schools and the universities. The greater part of them are administrative exiles — that is, persons whom the Government, for various reasons, has thought it expedient to remove from their homes and put under police surveillance in a part of the empire where they can do no harm. The real conspirators and revolutionists — the men and women who have actually been engaged in criminal activity — are sent to more remote parts of Siberia and into penal servitude. Banishment to the steppe territories is regarded as a very light punishment; and, as a rule, only administrative exiles are sent here."

In reply to further questions with regard to the character of these political exiles, Mr. Pávlovski said, "I don't know anything to their discredit; they behave themselves well enough here. If you are really interested in them, I can, perhaps, help you to an acquaintance with some of them, and then you can draw your own conclusions as to their character."

Of course I assured Mr. Pávlovski that an introduction to the politicals would give me more pleasure than any other favor he could confer upon me. He thereupon suggested that we should go at once to see a young political exile named Lobonófski, who was engaged in painting a drop-curtain for the little town theater.

"He is something of an artist," said Mr. Pávlovski, "and has a few Siberian sketches. You are making and collecting such sketches: of course you want to see them."

"Certainly," I replied with acquiescent diplomacy. "Sketches are my hobby, and I am a connoisseur in drop-curtains. Even although the artist be a nihilist and an exile, I must see his pictures."

Mr. Pávlovski's *dróshky* was at the door, and we drove at once to the house where Mr. Lobonófski was at work.

I find it extremely difficult now, after a whole year of intimate association with political exiles, to recall the impressions that I had of them before I made the acquaintance of the exile colony in Semipalátinsk. I know that I was prejudiced against them, and that I expected them to be wholly unlike the rational, cultivated men and women whom one meets in civilized society; but I cannot, by any exercise of will, bring back the unreal, fantastic conception of them that I had when I crossed the Siberian frontier. As nearly as I can now remember, I regarded the people whom I called nihilists as sullen, and more or less incomprehensible "cranks," with some education, a great deal of fanatical courage, and a limitless capacity for self-sacrifice, but with the most visionary ideas of government and social organization, and with only the faintest trace of what an American would call "hard common-sense." I did not expect to have any more ideas in common with them than I should have in common with an anarchist like Louis Lingg; and although I intended to give their case against the Government a fair hearing, I believed that the result would be a confirmation of the judgment I had already formed. Even after all that Mr. Pávlovski had said to me, I think I more than half expected to find in the drop-curtain artist a long-haired, wild-eyed being who would pour forth an incoherent recital of wrongs and outrages, denounce all governmental restraint as brutal tyranny, and expect me to approve of the assassination of Alexander II.

The log house occupied by Mr. Lobonófski as a work-shop was not otherwise tenanted, and we entered it without announcement. As Mr. Pávlovski threw open the door, I saw, standing before a large square sheet of canvas which covered one whole side of the room, a blond young man, apparently about thirty years of age, dressed from head to foot in a suit of cool brown linen, holding in one hand an artist's brush, and in the other a plate or palette covered with freshly mixed colors. His strongly built figure was erect and well-proportioned; his bearing was that of a cultivated gentleman; and he made upon me, from the first, a pleasant and favorable impression. He seemed, in fact, to be an excellent specimen of the blond type of Russian young manhood. His eyes were clear and blue; his thick, light-brown hair was ill cut, and rumpled a little in a boyish way over the high forehead; the full blond beard gave manliness and dignity to his well-shaped head, and his frank, open, good-tempered face, flushed a little with heat and wet with perspiration, seemed to me to be the face of a warmhearted and impulsive but, at the same time, strong and well-balanced man. It was, at any rate, a face strangely out of harmony with all my preconceived ideas of a nihilist.

Mr. Pávlovski introduced me to the young artist as an American traveler, who was interested in Siberian scenery, who had heard of his sketches, and who would like very much to see some of them. Mr. Lobonófski greeted me quietly but cordially, and at once brought out the sketches —apologizing, however, for their imperfections, and asking us to remember that they had been made in prison, on coarse writing-paper, and that the out-door views were limited to landscapes that could be seen from prison and *étape* windows. The sketches were evidently the work of an untrained hand, and were mostly representations of prison and *étape* interiors, portraits of political exiles, and such bits of towns and villages as could be seen from the windows of the various cells that the artist had occupied in the course of his journey to Siberia. They all had, however, a certain rude force and fidelity, and one of them served as material for the sketch illustrating the Tiumén prison-yard on page 85.

My conversation with Mr. Lobonófski at this interview did not touch political questions, and was confined, for the most part, to topics suggested by the sketches. He described his journey to Siberia just as he would have described it if he had made it voluntarily, and, but for an occasional reference to a prison or an *étape*, there was nothing in the recital to remind one that he was a nihilist and an exile. His manner was quiet, modest, and frank; he followed any conversational lead with ready tact, and although I watched him closely I could not detect the slightest indication of eccentricity or " crankiness." He must have felt conscious that I was secretly regarding him with critical curiosity,— looking at him, in fact, as one looks for the first time at an extraordinary type of criminal,— but he did not manifest the least awkwardness, embarrassment, or self-consciousness. He was simply a quiet, well-bred, self-possessed gentleman.

When we took our leave, after half an hour's conversation, Mr. Lobonófski cordially invited me to bring Mr. Frost to see him that evening at his house, and said that he would have a few of his friends there to meet us. I thanked him and promised that we would come.

" Well," said Mr. Pávlovski, as the door closed behind us, " what do you think of the political exile ? "

" He makes a very favorable impression upon me," I replied. "Are they all like him ? "

" No, not precisely like him; but they are not bad people. There is another interesting political in the city whom you ought to see—a young man named Leántief. He is employed in the office of Mr. Makovétski, a justice of the peace here, and is engaged with the latter in making anthropological researches among the Kírghis. I believe they are now collecting material for a monograph upon Kírghis customary law.[1] Why should n't you call upon Mr. Makovétski ? I have no doubt that he would introduce Mr. Leántief to you, and I am sure that you would find them both to be intelligent and cultivated men."

This seemed to me a good suggestion; and as soon as Mr. Pávlovski had left me I paid a visit to Mr. Makovétski, ostensibly for the purpose of asking permission to sketch some of the Kírghis implements and utensils in the town library, of which he was one of the directors. Mr. Makovétski seemed pleased to learn that I was interested in their little library, granted me permission to sketch the

[1] This monograph has since been published in the "Proceedings of the West Siberian Branch of the Imperial Geographical Society."

specimens of Kírghis handiwork there exhibited, and finally introduced me to his writing-clerk, Mr. Leántief, who, he said, had made a special study of the Kírghis, and could give me any desired information concerning the natives of that tribe.

Mr. Leántief was a good-looking young fellow, apparently about twenty-five years of age, rather below the medium height, with light-brown hair and beard, intelligent gray eyes, a slightly aquiline nose, and a firm, well-rounded chin. His head and face were suggestive of studious and scientific tastes, and if I had met him in Washington and had been asked to guess his profession from his appearance, I should have said that he was probably a young scientist connected with the United States Geological Survey, the Smithsonian Institution, or the National Museum. He was, as I subsequently learned, the son of an army officer who at one time commanded the Cossack garrison in this same city of Semipalátinsk. As a boy he was enrolled in the corps of imperial pages, and began his education in the large school established by the Government for the training of such pages in the Russian capital. At the age of eighteen or nineteen he entered the St. Petersburg University, and in the fourth year of his student life was arrested and exiled by "administrative process" to Western Siberia for five years, upon the charge of having had secret communication with political prisoners in the fortress of Petropávlovsk.

Although Mr. Leántief's bearing was somewhat more formal and reserved than that of Mr. Lobonófski, and his attitude toward me one of cool, observant criticism, rather than of friendly confidence, he impressed me very favorably; and when, after half an hour's conversation, I returned to my hotel, I was forced to admit to myself that if all nihilists were like the two whom I had met in Semipalátinsk, I should have to modify my opinions with regard to them. In point of intelligence and education Mr. Lobonófski and

Mr. Leántief seemed to me to compare favorably with any young men of my acquaintance.

At eight o'clock that evening Mr. Frost and I knocked at Mr. Lobonófski's door, and were promptly admitted and cordially welcomed. We found him living in a small log house not far from our hotel. The apartment into which we were shown, and which served in the double capacity of sitting-room and bed-room, was very small—not larger, I think, than ten feet in width by fourteen feet in length. Its log walls and board ceiling were covered with dingy whitewash, and its floor of rough unmatched planks was bare. Against a rude, unpainted partition to the right of the door stood a small single bedstead of stained wood, covered with neat but rather scanty bed-clothing, and in the corner beyond it was a triangular table, upon which were lying, among other books, Herbert Spencer's "Essays: Moral, Political, and Esthetic," and the same author's "Principles of Psychology." The opposite corner of the room was occupied by a what-not, or étagère, of domestic manufacture, upon the shelves of which were a few more books, a well-filled herbarium, of coarse brown wrapping-paper, an opera-glass, and an English New Testament. Between two small deeply set windows opening into the court-yard stood a large, unpainted wooden table, without a cloth, upon which was lying, open, the book that Mr. Lobonófski had been reading when we entered—a French translation of Balfour Stewart's "Conservation of Energy." There was no other furniture in the apartment except three or four unpainted wooden chairs. Everything was scrupulously neat and clean; but the room looked like the home of a man too poor to afford anything more than the barest essentials of life.

After Mr. Lobonófski had made a few preliminary inquiries with regard to the object of our journey to Siberia, and had expressed the pleasure which he said it afforded him to meet and welcome Americans in his own house, he turned to me with a smile and said, "I suppose, Mr. Kennan, you have heard terrible stories in America about the Russian nihilists?"

"Yes," I replied; "we seldom hear of them except in connection with a plot to blow up something or to kill somebody, and I must confess that I have had a bad opinion of them. The very word 'nihilist' is understood in America to mean a person who does not believe in anything and who advocates the destruction of all existing institutions."

"'Nihilist' is an old nickname," he said; "and it is no longer applicable to the Russian revolutionary party, if, indeed, it was ever applicable. I don't think you will find among the political exiles in Siberia any 'nihilists,' in the sense in which you use the word. Of course there are, in what may be called the anti-Government class, people who hold all sorts of political opinions. There are a few who believe in the so-called policy of 'terror'—who regard themselves as justified in resorting even to political assassination as a means of overthrowing the Government; but even the terrorists do not propose to destroy all existing institutions. Every one of them, I think, would lay down his arms, if the Tsar would grant to Russia a constitutional form of government and guarantee free speech, a free press, and freedom from arbitrary arrest, imprisonment, and exile. Have you ever seen the letter sent by the Russian revolutionists to Alexander III. upon his accession to the throne?"

"No," I replied; "I have heard of it, but have never seen it."

"It sets forth," he said, "the aims and objects of the revolutionary party, and contains a distinct promise that if the Tsar will grant freedom of speech and summon a national assembly the revolutionists will abstain from all further violence, and will agree not to oppose any form of government which such assembly may sanction.[1] You can hardly say that people who express a willingness to enter

1 See appendix C.

into such an agreement as this are in favor of the destruction
of all existing institutions.   I suppose you know," he continued, "that when your President Garfield was assassinated,
the columns of ' The Will of the People ' [the organ of the
Russian revolutionists in Geneva] were bordered with black
as a token of grief and sympathy, and that the paper contained an eloquent editorial condemning political assassination as wholly unjustifiable in a country where there are open
courts and a free press, and where the officers of the government are chosen by a free vote of the people ? "

" No," I replied; " I was not aware of it."

" It is true," he rejoined.   " Of course at that time Garfield's murder was regarded as a political crime, and as
such it was condemned in Russia, even by the most extreme
terrorists."

Our conversation was interrupted at this point by the
entrance of three young men and a lady, who were introduced to us as Mr. Lobonófski's exiled friends.   In the
appearance of the young men there was nothing particularly striking or noticeable.   One of them seemed to be
a bright university student, twenty-four or twenty-five
years of age, and the other two looked like educated peasants or artisans, whose typically Russian faces were rather
heavy, impassive, and gloomy, and whose manner was
lacking in animation and responsiveness.   Life and exile
seemed to have gone hard with them, and to have left
them depressed and embittered.   The lady, whose name
was Madame Dicheskúla, represented apparently a different social class, and had a more buoyant and sunny disposition.   She was about thirty years of age, tall and straight,
with a well-proportioned but somewhat spare figure, thick,
short brown hair falling in a soft mass about the nape of
her neck, and a bright, intelligent, mobile face, which I
thought must once have been extremely pretty.   It had become, however, a little too thin and worn, and her com-
plexion had been freckled and roughened by exposure to

wind and weather and by the hardships of prison and *étape* life. She was neatly and becomingly dressed in a Scotch plaid gown of soft dark serge, with little ruffles of white lace at her throat and wrists; and when her face lighted up in animated conversation, she seemed to me to be a very attractive and interesting woman. In her demeanor there was not a suggestion of the boldness, hardness, and eccentricity that I had expected to find in women exiled to Siberia for political crime. She talked rapidly and well; laughed merrily at times over reminiscences of her journey to Siberia; apologized for the unwomanly shortness of her hair, which, she said, had all been cut off in prison; and related with a keen sense of humor her adventures while crossing the Kírghis steppe from Akmolá to Semipalátinsk. That her natural buoyancy of disposition was tempered by deep feeling was evident from the way in which she described some of the incidents of her Siberian experience. She seemed greatly touched, for example, by the kindness shown to her party by the peasants of Kamishlóva, a village through which they passed on their way from Ekaterínburg to Tiumén. They happened to arrive there on Trinity Sunday, and were surprised to find that the villagers, as a manifestation of sympathy with the political exiles, had thoroughly scoured out and freshened up the old village *étape*, and had decorated its gloomy cells with leafy branches and fresh wild-flowers. It seemed to me that tears came to her eyes as she expressed her deep and grateful appreciation of this act of thoughtfulness and good-will on the part of the Kamishlóva peasants.

About nine o'clock Mr. Lobonófski brought in a steaming *sámovar*, Madàme Dicheskúla made tea, and throughout the remainder of the evening we sat all around the big pine table as if we had been acquainted for months instead of hours, talking about the Russian revolutionary movement, the exile system, literature, art, science, and American politics. The cool, reasonable way in which these exiles discussed public affairs, problems of government, and their personal experience impressed me very favorably. There was none of the bitterness of feeling and extravagance of statement that I had anticipated, and I did not notice in their conversation the least tendency to exaggerate or even to dwell upon their own sufferings as a means of exciting our sympathy. Madame Dicheskúla, for instance, had been robbed of most of her clothing and personal effects by the police at the time of her arrest; had spent more than a year in solitary confinement in the Moscow forwarding prison; had then been banished, without trial, to a dreary settlement in the Siberian province of Akmolínsk; and, finally, had been brought across the great Kírghis steppe in winter to the city of Semipalátinsk. In all this experience there must have been a great deal of intense personal suffering; but she did not lay half as much stress upon it in conversation as she did upon the decoration of the old *étape* with leafy branches and flowers by the people of Kamishlóva, as an expression of sympathy with her and her exiled friends. About eleven o'clock, after a most pleasant and interesting evening, we bade them all good-night and returned to our hotel.

On the following morning Mr. Lobonófski, Madame Dicheskúla, Mr. Frost, and I took *dróshkies* and drove down the right bank of the Írtish a mile or two, to a small grove of poplars and aspens near the water's edge, where six or eight political exiles were spending the summer in camp. A large Kírghis *yurt* of felt, and two or three smaller cotton tents, had been pitched on the grass under the trees, and in them were living two or three young women and four or five young men, who had taken this means of escaping from the heat, glare, and sand of the verdureless city. Two of the women were mere girls, seventeen or eighteen years of age, who looked as if they ought to be pursuing their education in a high school or a female seminary, and why they had been exiled to Siberia I could not imagine.

It did not seem to me possible that they could be regarded in any country, or under any circumstances, as a dangerous menace to social order or to the stability of the Government. As I shook hands with them and noticed their shy, embarrassed behavior, and the quick flushes of color which came to their cheeks when I spoke to them, I experienced for the first time something like a feeling of contempt for the Russian Government. "If I were the Tsar," I said to Mr. Frost, "and had an army of soldiers and police at my back, and if, nevertheless, I felt so afraid of timid, half-grown school-girls that I could n't sleep in peaceful security until I had banished them to Siberia, I think I should abdicate in favor of some stronger and more courageous man." The idea that a powerful Government like that of Russia could not protect itself against seminary girls and Sunday-school teachers without tearing them from their families, and isolating them in the middle of a great Asiatic desert, seemed to me not only ludicrous, but absolutely preposterous.

We spent in the pleasant shady camp of these political exiles nearly the whole of the long, hot summer day. Mr. Frost made sketches of the picturesquely grouped tents, while I talked with the young men, read Irving aloud to one of them who was studying English, answered questions about America, and asked questions in turn about Siberia and Russia. Before the day ended we were upon as cordial and friendly a footing with the whole party as if we had known them for a month.

Late in the afternoon we returned to the city, and in the evening went to the house of Mr. Leántief, where most of the political exiles whom we had not yet seen had been invited to meet us. The room into which we were ushered was much larger and better furnished than that in which Mr. Lobonófski lived; but nothing in it particularly attracted my attention except a portrait of Herbert Spencer, which hung on the wall over Mr. Leántief's desk. There

were twelve or fifteen exiles present, including Mr. Lobonófski, Madame Dicheskúla, Dr. Bogomólets,—a young surgeon whose wife was in penal servitude at the mines of
Kará,—and the two Prisédski sisters, to whom reference
was made in my article upon the "Prison Life of the Russian Revolutionists," in *The Century Magazine* for December, 1887. The general conversation which followed our
introduction to the assembled company was bright, animated, and informal. Mr. Leántief, in reply to questions
from me, related the history of the Semipalátinsk library,
and said that it had not only been a great boon to the
political exiles, but had noticeably stimulated the intellectual life of the city. "Even the Kírghis," he said, "occasionally avail themselves of its privileges. I know a learned
old Kírghis here, named Ibrahim Konobai, who not only
goes to the library, but reads such authors as Buckle, Mill,
and Draper."

"You don't mean to say," exclaimed a young university
student, "that there is any old Kírghis in Semipalátinsk
who actually reads Mill and Draper!"

"Yes, I do," replied Mr. Leántief, coolly. "The very first
time I met him he astonished me by asking me to explain
to him the difference between induction and deduction.
Some time afterward I found out that he was really making
a study of English philosophy, and had read Russian translations of all the authors that I have named."

"Do you suppose that he understood what he read?"
inquired the university student.

"I spent two whole evenings in examining him upon
Draper's 'Intellectual Development of Europe,'" replied Mr.
Leántief; "and I must say that he seemed to have a very
fair comprehension of it."

"I notice," I said, "that a large number of books in the
library—particularly the works of the English scientists—
have been withdrawn from public use, although all of them
seem once to have passed the censor. How does it happen

that books are at one time allowed and at another time prohibited ? "

" Our censorship is very capricious," replied one of the exiles. " How would you explain the fact that such a book as Adam Smith's ' Wealth of Nations ' is prohibited, while Darwin's ' Origin of Species ' and ' Descent of Man ' are allowed ? The latter are certainly more dangerous than the former."

" It has been suggested," said another, " that the list of prohibited books was made up by putting together, without examination, the titles of all books found by the police in the quarters of persons arrested for political offenses. The ' Wealth of Nations ' happened to be found in some unfortunate revolutionist's house, therefore the ' Wealth of Nations ' must be a dangerous book."

" When I was arrested," said Mr. Lobonófski, " the police seized and took away even a French history that I had borrowed from the public library. In looking hastily through it they noticed here and there the word 'revolution,' and that was enough. I tried to make them understand that a French history must, of course, treat of the French Revolution, but it was of no use. They also carried off, under the impression that it was an infernal machine, a rude imitation of a steam-engine which my little brother had made for amusement out of some bits of wood and metal and the tubes of an old opera-glass." Amidst general laughter, a number of the exiles related humorous anecdotes illustrating the methods of the Russian police, and then the conversation drifted into other channels.

As an evidence of the intelligence and culture of these political exiles, and of the wide range of their interests and sympathies, it seems to me worth while to say that their conversation showed more than a superficial acquaintance with the best English and American literature, as well as a fairly accurate knowledge of American institutions and history. Among the authors referred to, discussed, or quoted by them that evening were Shakspere, Mill, Spencer, Buckle, Balfour Stewart, Heine, Hegel, Lange, Irving, Cooper, Longfellow, Bret Harte, and Harriet Beecher Stowe. They knew the name and something of the record of our newly elected President, discussed intelligently his civil-service reform policy and asked pertinent questions with regard to its working, and manifested generally an acquaintance with American affairs that one does not expect to find anywhere on the other side of the Atlantic, and least of all in Siberia.

After a plain but substantial supper, with delicious overland tea, the exiles sang for us in chorus some of the plaintive popular melodies of Russia, and Mr. Frost and I tried, in turn, to give them an idea of our college songs, our war songs, and the music of the American negroes. It must have been nearly midnight when we reluctantly bade them all good-by and returned to the Hotel Sibir.

It is impossible, of course, to give even the substance of the long conversations concerning the Russian Government and the Russian revolutionary movement which I had with the political exiles in Semipalátinsk. All that I aim to do at present is to describe, as fairly and accurately as possible, the impression that these exiles made upon me. If I may judge others by myself, American readers have had an idea that the people who are called nihilists stand apart from the rest of mankind in a class by themselves, and that there is in their character something fierce, gloomy, abnormal, and, to a sane mind, incomprehensible, which alienates from them, and which should alienate from them, the sympathies of the civilized world. If the political exiles in Semipalátinsk be taken as fair representatives of the class thus judged, the idea seems to me to be a wholly mistaken one. I found them to be bright, intelligent, well-informed men and women, with warm affections, quick sympathies, generous impulses, and high standards of honor and duty. They are, as Mr. Pávlovski said to me, "men and women who, under other circumstances, might render valuable services to their country." If, instead of thus serving their country, they are living in exile, it is not because they are lacking in the virtue and the patriotism that are essential to good citizenship, but because the Government, which assumes the right to think and act for the Russian people, is out of harmony with the spirit of the time.

CHAPTER IX

BRIDLE PATHS OF THE ALTÁI

O N Saturday, July 18th, after having inspected the city
prison, obtained as much information as possible concerning the exile system, and made farewell calls upon our
friends, we provided ourselves with a new *padarózhnaya*
and left Semipalátinsk with three post-horses for the mountains of the Altái. The wild alpine region that we hoped
to explore lies along the frontier of Mongolia, about 350
miles east of Semipalátinsk and nearly 600 miles due south
from Tomsk. The German travelers Finsch and Brehm
went to the edge of it in 1876, but the high snowy peaks of
the Katúnski and Chúiski Alps, east of the Altái Station,
had never been seen by a foreigner, and had been visited
by very few Russians.

For nearly two hundred versts, after leaving Semipalátinsk, we rode up the right bank of the Írtish, through a
great rolling steppe of dry, yellowish grass. Here and there,
where this steppe was irrigated by small streams running
into the Írtish, it supported a luxuriant vegetation, the little
transverse valleys being filled with wild roses, hollyhocks,
goldenrod, wild currant and gooseberry bushes, and splendid spikes, five feet in height, of dark-blue aconite; but in
most places the great plain was sun-scorched and bare. The
Cossack villages through which we passed did not differ
materially from those between Semipalátinsk and Omsk,
except that their log houses were newer and in better repair,
and their inhabitants seemed to be wealthier and more

prosperous. The Russian love of crude color became again
apparent in the dresses of the women and girls; and on

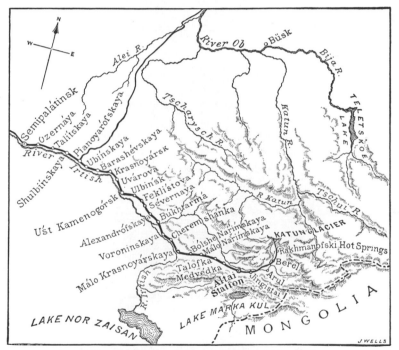

MAP OF ROUTE FROM SEMIPALÁTINSK TO THE ALTÁI.

Sunday, when all of the Cossacks were in holiday attire, the
streets of these villages were bright with the red, blue, and
yellow costumes of the young men and women, who sat in

rows upon benches in the shade of the houses, talking, flirting, and eating melon seeds, or, after the sun had gone down, danced in the streets to the music of fiddles and triangular guitars.

COSSACK PEASANT GIRL SPINNING.

The farther we went up the Irtish the hotter became the weather and the more barren the steppe, until it was easy to imagine that we were in an Arabian or a north African desert. The thermometer ranged day after day from 90° to 103° in the shade; the atmosphere was suffocating; every leaf and every blade of grass, as far as the eye could reach, had been absolutely burned dead by the fierce sunshine; great whirling columns of sand, 100 to 150 feet in height, swept slowly and majestically across the sun-scorched plain; and we could trace the progress of a single mounted Kírghis five miles away by the cloud of dust that his horse's hoofs raised from the steppe. I suffered intensely from heat and thirst, and had to protect myself from the fierce sunshine by swathing my body in four thicknesses of blanket and putting a big down pillow over my legs. I could not hold my hand in that sunshine five minutes without pain, and wrapping my body in four thicknesses of heavy woolen blanketing gave me at once a sensation of coolness. Mine was the southern or sunny side of the *tárantás*, and I finally became so exhausted with the fierce heat, and had such a strange feeling of faintness, nausea, and suffocation, that I asked Mr. Frost to change sides with me, and give me a brief respite. He wrapped himself up in a blanket, put a pillow over his legs, and managed to endure it until evening. Familiar as I supposed myself to be with Siberia, I little thought, when I crossed the frontier, that I should find in it a North African desert, with whirling sand-columns, and sunshine from which I should be obliged to protect my limbs with blankets. I laughed at a Russian officer in Omsk who told me that the heat in the valley of the Írtish was often so intense as to cause nausea and fainting, and who advised me not to travel between eleven o'clock in the morning and three in the afternoon when the day was cloudless and hot. The idea of having a sunstroke in Siberia, and the suggestion not to travel there in the middle of the day, seemed to me so preposterous that I could not restrain a smile of amusement. He assured me, however, that he was talking seriously, and said that he had seen soldiers unconscious for hours after a fit of nausea and fainting, brought on by marching in the sunshine. He did not know sunstroke by name, and seemed to think that the

symptoms which he described were peculiar effects of the
Írtish valley heat, but it was evidently sunstroke that he
had seen.

At the station of Voronínskaya, in the middle of this
parched desert, we were overtaken by a furious hot sand-

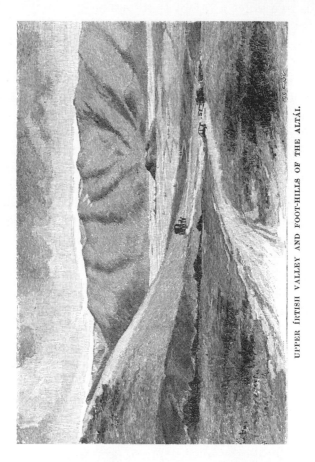

UPPER ÍRTISH VALLEY AND FOOT-HILLS OF THE ALTÁI.

storm from the southwest, with a temperature of 103° in
the shade. The sand and fine hot dust were carried to a
height of a hundred feet, and drifted past us in dense, suffocating clouds, hiding everything from sight and making
it almost impossible to breathe. Although we were riding

with the storm, and not against it, I literally gasped for breath for more than two hours; and when we arrived at the station of Cheremshánka, it would have been hard to tell, from an inspection of our faces, whether we were Kírghis or Americans — black men or white. I drank nearly a quart of cold milk, and even that did not fully assuage my fierce thirst. Mr. Frost, after washing the dust out of his eyes and drinking seven tumblers of milk, revived sufficiently to say, " If anybody thinks that it does n't get hot in Siberia, just refer him to me ! "

At the station of Málo Krasnoyárskaya we left the Írtish to the right and saw it no more. Late that afternoon we reached the first foot-hills of the great mountain range of the Altái, and began the long, gradual climb to the Altái Station. Before dark on the following day we were riding through cool, elevated alpine meadows, where the fresh green grass was intermingled with bluebells, fragrant spirea, gentians, and delicate fringed pinks, and where the mountain tops over our heads were white, a thousand feet down, with freshly fallen snow. The change from the torrid African desert of the Írtish to this superb Siberian Switzerland was so sudden and so extraordinary as to be almost bewildering. I could not help asking myself every fifteen minutes, " Did I only dream of that dreary, sun-scorched steppe yesterday, with its sandspouts, its mountains of furnace slag, its fierce heat, and its whitening bones, or is it really possible that I can have come from that to this in twenty-four hours ? " To my steppe-wearied eyes, the scenery, as we approached the Altái Station, was indescribably beautiful. On our left was a range of low mountains, the smooth slopes of which were checkered with purple cloud shadows and tinted here and there by vast areas of flowers; on our right, rising almost from the road, was a splendid chain of bold, grandly sculptured peaks from seven thousand to nine thousand feet in height, crowned with one thousand feet of fresh, brilliantly white snow, and belted with a broad zone of evergreen forest; beneath lay a beautiful, park-like valley, through which ran the road, under the shade of scattered larches, across clear, rushing mountain streams which came tumbling down in cascades from the melting snows above, and over grassy meadows sprinkled with wild pansies, gentians, fringed pinks, and ripening strawberries. After three thousand miles of almost unbroken plain, or steppe, this scene

THE ALTÁI STATION.

made upon me a profound impression. We reached the Altái Station about six o'clock in the cool of a beautiful, calm, midsummer afternoon. I shall never forget the enthusiastic delight that I felt as I rode up out of a wooded valley fragrant with wild-flowers, past a picturesque cluster of colored Kírghis tents, across two hundred yards of smooth, elevated meadow, and then, stopping at the entrance to the village, turned back and looked at the mountains. Never, I thought, had I seen an alpine picture that could for a moment bear comparison with it. I have seen the most beautiful scenery in the mountains of the Sierra Nevada, of Nicaragua, of Kamchátka, of the Caucasus, and of the Russian Altái, and it is my deliberate opinion that for varied beauty, picturesqueness, and effectiveness that mountain landscape is absolutely unsurpassed. If there exist anywhere a more superbly situated village, I am ready to cross three oceans to see it.

The Altái Station, or, as the Kírghis call it, "Kotón Karagháï," is situated at a height of about thirty-five hundred feet in the upper part of the fertile alpine valley known as the valley of the Búkhtarmá. The village stands upon a small, flat terrace or plateau two or three miles square, which is bounded on the north by rolling, flowery foot-hills and on the south by a shallow wooded ravine through which flows an insignificant tributary of the Búkhtarmá River. The main street of the little hamlet runs parallel with the ravine, and on the opposite side of the latter rise abruptly three or four grandly sculptured peaks, whose steep slopes are clothed to a height of two or three thousand feet with larch forests, and above that are generally white, even in midsummer, with fresh-fallen snow. The village itself is a mere Cossack picket of seventy or eighty log houses, with wide, clean streets, and with a quaint log church at one end; but to a traveler just from the hot, arid plains of the Írtish even this insignificant Cossack station has its peculiar charm. In front of every house in the settlement is a little inclosure, or front yard, filled with young birches, silver-leafed aspens, and flowering shrubs, and through all of these yards, down each side of every street runs a tinkling, gurgling stream of clear, cold water from the melting snows on the mountains. The whole village, therefore, go where you will, is filled with the murmur of falling water; and how pleasant that sound is, you must travel for a month in the parched, dust-smothered, sun-scorched valley of the Írtish fully to understand. The little rushing streams seem to bring with them, as they tumble in rapids through the

settlement, the fresh, cool atmosphere of the high peaks
where they were born two hours before; and although your
thermometer may say that the day is hot and the air sultry, its statements are so persistently, so confidently, so
hilariously controverted by the joyous voice of the stream
under your window, with its half-expressed suggestions of
snow and glaciers and cooling spray, that your reason is

OUR HOUSE AT THE ALTÁI STATION.

silenced and your imagination accepts the story of the
snow-born brook.

The morning after our arrival at the Altái Station dawned
clear, cool, and bright, and after a good breakfast served by
the wife of the Cossack in whose house we had found
shelter, we went out to survey the village. Mr. Frost, who
was equipped with sketching-block and pencils, soon discovered a desirable point of view for a picture and, having
hired a burly Cossack to stand beside him in such a
position as to throw the shadow of his body across the
paper, and thus serve as a sun-umbrella, he went to work.
Meanwhile I strolled through the village and out past the
quaint log church in the direction of the village shops which,
with the Government storehouses, were situated on the

eastern side of the plateau.   Three or four hundred yards from the church, in the middle of the flowery plain, a company of Cossacks, dressed in dark-green uniforms and armed with Berdan rifles, were practising what seemed to be the Russian skirmish drill.   They had been divided into three squads, each of which, under the direction of an officer, was manœuvering against an imaginary enemy. Now they would rush forward at " double-quick," firing at will as they advanced, then they would suddenly close up, throw themselves at full length on the ground, and in that position deliver volley after volley until they were hidden in powder smoke, and finally the three squads would unite and charge fiercely in solid column, with the peculiar continuous Russian " oor-rah-ah-ah-ah-ah ! " which has been heard with anxiety and dread by the defenders of many a Turkish redoubt.

The shops of the Altái Station were only three or four in number, and I found in them few things that were either curious or interesting.   Perhaps, however, I should qualify this statement by limiting it to things purchasable.   The shops were full of Kírghis buyers and Kírghis horses, and in many respects they were interesting enough to satisfy the most exacting foreign traveler.   There is a certain amount of adventurous interest in the mere act of forcing one's way into a shop when the shop is full of Kírghis and the door is completely blocked up with the bodies of Kírghis saddle-horses.   Hitching-posts at the Altái Station are entirely unknown, and in the absence of such conveniences Kírghis horsemen are accustomed to lead their horses directly into the shops that they have occasion to visit and hold them there by the bridles while they themselves stand at the counter and examine goods.   As a result of this interesting custom you will often see four or five Kírghis horses whose heads and fore-legs are across the threshold of a shop door, while their hind-quarters are massed in a sort of reversed equine phalanx outside.   If you have not implicit confidence in the tempers of Kírghis mountain ponies, their bodies thus arranged constitute a most formidable barricade. By means of soothing and conciliatory measures I generally succeeded in separating two horses sufficiently so that I could squeeze through between them into the shop, but I rarely found there anything of local origin or manufacture to repay me for my trouble. Most of the goods that were shown to me were from European Russia, and were such as I had seen in scores of Siberian shops already. The mountain Kírghis, however, who were the chief consumers of these goods, were interesting enough to more than make up for the commonplace nature of the goods themselves. They were generally wilder-looking men than the steppe Kírghis whose acquaintance we had made in the territory of Semipalátinsk, and the wildness of their appearance was heightened, perhaps, to some extent, by their dress. This consisted of an under tunic or shirt of cotton cloth striped perpendicularly with red, straight trousers of butternut homespun thrust into top-boots, a *beshmét* or quilted dressing-gown of black, brown, or gray homespun girt about the waist with a narrow, silver-studded leather belt, and finally an extraordinary pointed hood of quilted cloth covering the whole head and neck, with long chin-laps hanging over the shoulders in front and a bunch of soft feathers dangling from the high, pointed crown. These hoods were almost invariably lined and trimmed with fur, and were made frequently of a peculiar kind of Russian cloth, in which the wavy markings of watered silk are imitated in green, yellow, and purple, so as to produce a sort of chromatic moire antique. It would be hard to imagine anything stranger or wilder in appearance than the rough-hewn, beardless, sun-scorched face of an old Kírghis, framed in one of these high, pointed hoods of green, yellow, and purple, and half concealed by the chin-laps and the shaggy fringe of bear-skin or wolf-skin that hangs like a neglected bang over the dark, fierce eyes.

I spent an hour or more that morning in the little shops of the Altái Station, making a pretense of looking at goods in order that I might have an opportunity to study the Kírghis. I was greatly interested in their forms of salutation, and particularly in their method of shaking or pressing hands, which I had never before seen. When two Kírghis acquaintances meet, after a period of separation, each of them holds out both his hands with thumbs uppermost, very much as he would hold out his arms to take a baby. One of them puts the palm of his right hand against the back of the other's left, and the back of his left hand against the palm of the other's right, and then both bring their hands together as if they were about to clap them. The result is a sandwiching of the two pairs of hands in such a manner that each person has between his two palms one hand of the other. The hands are pressed closely together in this way without motion while the acquaintances exchange salutations and inquiries with regard to health. This seemed to me to be a much more graceful and appropriate form of hand-greeting than the vise-like grip and the meaningless shake of the civilized world. The mere pumping of interlocked hands has neither grace nor significance, while the gentle pressure of a friend's hand between both one's own is a perfectly natural and suitable expression of affectionate regard. The only objection that I can see to it is that, for indiscriminate use, it partakes too much of the nature of a caress. In civilized society, therefore, it should be reserved for cases in which a hand-shake would be too formal and an embrace too familiar. Thus restricted, I offer it to the world as the first contribution of the Altái Kírghis to the polite ceremonies of social life.

Upon returning from the shops to the place where I had left Mr. Frost, I found him still at work upon his sketch, which had begun to assume the appearance of the illustration on page 194. Just before noon, at the suggestion of the Cossack *atamán* who came to our house to return our passports, I made a call of ceremony upon Captain Maiéfski, the *uyéizdni nachálnik* or chief administrative officer of the southern Altái district. I found him to be a pleasant, cultivated officer about thirty-five years of age, who had just returned from a trip on horseback through the high Altái, and who could give me the fullest and most accurate information with regard to scenery and routes. He welcomed me very cordially, introduced me to his wife,—a most agreeable and intelligent young woman,—and invited me to come with Mr. Frost that day to dinner. I accepted the invitation, both for myself and for my comrade, and we thus began an acquaintance that proved to be a very delightful and advantageous one for us, and that brought some novelty and variety, I hope, into the rather lonely and eventless lives of Captain and Mrs. Maiéfski.

We remained at the Altái Station three or four days, making excursions into the neighboring mountains with Captain Maiéfski and his wife, visiting and photographing the Kírghis who were encamped near the village, and collecting information with regard to the region lying farther to the northward and eastward which we hoped to explore. The mountains of the Altái occupy in southern Siberia an area more than three times as great as that of Switzerland. Only a small part of this vast wilderness of mountains has been actually settled by the Russians, and outside of the fertile valleys of such rivers as the Katún and the Búkhtarmá it is very imperfectly known, even to the hardy and daring Cossack pioneers. For this ignorance, however, there are several good reasons. In the first place, the southern part of the Russian Altái, including the valley of the Búkhtarmá and the high peaks of the Katúnski and Chúiski Alps, belonged, until very recently, to the empire of China. The Russians first appeared in the upper part of the Búkhtarmá valley in 1869, and the Altái Station was not founded until two years later. It was then nothing more than a Cossack observing-picket on the new Chinese frontier. In the second place, exploration of these wild mountain fastnesses has always been attended with great difficulty. In the high alpine valleys, and on the elevated plateaus of the main range, snow falls to a great depth in winter; the short summer begins late; the streams that rise among the colossal peaks of the Great Altái are generally torrents and flow through deep, rugged, almost impassable gorges until they descend to the level of the foot-hills; and the mountain walls that separate neighboring valleys are so high, rocky, and precipitous, that crossing them on horseback is difficult and dangerous, even when they are free from snow. There is only one practicable commercial route over the main range of the Altái between the Chúiski Alps and the right bank of the Írtish,—a distance of more than two hundred miles,—and this solitary route is a mere bridle-path, which crosses the desolate plateau of Ukéik and the precipitous water-shed of Úlan-dába at a height of 9260 feet. Of course in such a wilderness as this there was an ample field for enterprising explorers, but as our time was limited we decided, after a number of consultations with Captain Maiéfski, to content ourselves with an excursion to the peaks and glaciers of the Katúnski Alps.

The day of our departure happened to be Captain Maiéfski's namesday; and in order to celebrate it and at the same time to give us a pleasant "send-off," he invited a party of friends to go with us as far as the rapids of the Búkhtarmá river, about fifteen *versts* from the Station, and there have a picnic. When we started, therefore, we were accompanied by Captain Maiéfski and his wife and daughter, the Cossack *atamán* and his wife, a political exile named Zavalíshin and his wife, and three or four other officers and ladies. The party was escorted by ten or fifteen mounted Kírghis in bright-colored *beshméts* girt about the waist with silver-studded belts; and the cavalcade of uniformed officers, gaily dressed ladies, and hooded Kírghis presented a most novel and picturesque appearance, as it cantered away across the grassy plateau.

The day was warm and sunshiny, but clouds were drifting occasionally across the snow-clad peaks south of the village, diversifying their sides with moving areas of purple shadow and increasing the impression of great height that they made upon one. The road, which was dry, hard, and in good condition, crossed the little valley just above the village and then ran along the slopes of the southern mountains through an open, park-like forest of larch, poplar, and silver birch. Flowers were blossoming everywhere in almost incredible luxuriance and profusion. The sunny stretches of grass in the forest openings were embroidered with dark-blue gentians, wild pansies, forget-me-nots, and delicate fringed pinks; in moister, cooler places stood splendid ultramarine spikes, eight feet high, of aconite, and here and there, on the brink of the valley, were white drifts of spirea covering areas of from twenty to fifty square feet with dense masses of snowy bloom.

All along the road, where it ran through the open forest, we noticed ant-hills, four or five feet in height, swarming with large black ants. As we passed one of them Mrs. Maiéfski handed her white cambric handkerchief to a Kírghis horseman, and told him to throw it upon the hill and then give it to me. The handkerchief no sooner touched the hill than it was black with startled ants. After allowing them to run over it for three or four seconds the Kírghis, who had evidently seen this experiment tried before, caught it up dexterously by one corner, gave it a quick, sharp flirt to free it from the insects, and then handed it to me.

"Smell of it," said Mrs. Maiéfski. I obeyed, and was surprised to discover that, although perfectly dry to the touch, it affected the nostrils precisely as if it had been saturated with aromatic vinegar. It had acquired this odor in the few seconds that it had lain upon the ant-hill. I then tried the same experiment with my own handkerchief. After the ants had run over it for three minutes it was so impregnated with the strong, pungent vapor of formic acid that I could not bring it anywhere near my face without strangling. The odor, which is that of aromatic vinegar, is rather plea-

PICNIC GROUND, VALLEY OF THE BÚKHTARMÁ.

sant if not too strong, but in excess it affects the nostrils very much in the same way that ammonia affects them.

About twelve *versts* from the Altái Station we began to catch glimpses, now and then, of the pale-green glacier water of the Búkhtarmá, flowing through a deep wooded valley on our left and suggesting, in color and topographical environment, the water of the Niagara below the falls. Just beyond the sixteen-*verst* post we abandoned the road, and turning sharply to the left descended to the bank of the river. Captain Maiéfski had sent forward to the picnic ground early that morning two Kírghis tents,·a quantity of rugs and pillows, and his whole house-keeping outfit; and when we arrived a most luxurious camp was in complete readiness. The two tents—one of them white trimmed with scarlet and the other a deep Pompeiian red—had been pitched in a beautiful grassy nook beside the river; soft Bokharan rugs from a Kírghis *kibítka* had been lavishly used to line and carpet them; a polished *sámovár* was steaming and singing on the grass in the shade of a drooping birch, and columns of smoke and sparks were rising from two or three cheerful camp-fires. In less than ten minutes after our arrival the whole party was scattered up and down the bank of the river, every one engaged in the occupation that was to him most congenial. Captain Maiéfski and Mr. Frost, armed with long-handled nets, were rushing hither and thither in pursuit of brilliantly colored but erratic butterflies; the Cossack *atamán* was casting a hook and line into the river and landing every now and then a silvery fish; Mrs. Maiéfski was superintending the preparations for dinner, while Mr. Zavalíshin and I, having neither duty nor speciality, strolled aimlessly about the neighborhood, picking flowers, watching the Kírghis, and enjoying the picturesque effect of the dark-red tent against the background of green trees, the blue curling smoke of the camp-fires and the pale malachite coloring of the glacier-tinted stream.

After an excellently cooked and well-served dinner of soup, freshly caught fish, roast lamb, boiled mutton, cold chicken, pilau of rice with raisins, strawberries and confectionery, we spent a long and delightful afternoon in botanizing, fishing, rifle-shooting, catching butterflies, telling

riddles and singing songs.   It was, I think, the most pleasant
and successful picnic that I ever had the good fortune to
enjoy, and when, late in the afternoon, Mr. Frost and I bade
the party good-by, I am sure we both secretly wished that

COSSACK PICKET OF JINGISTÁI.

we could stay there in camp for a week instead of going to
the Katúnski Alps.

We spent that night at the little Cossack picket of Jingistái, which consisted of two newly built log houses situated
in the shallow, flower-carpeted valley of the Búkhtarmá,

about thirty *versts* from the Altái Station. The Cossack family that constituted the "picket" occupied only one of the houses, and we therefore bivouacked in the other. Our sleeping apartment contained no furniture of any kind, its windows were mere rectangular openings in the wall without sashes or glass, and we were forced to make our beds on the rough-hewn planks of the floor; but the room was filled with the faint, clean fragrance of pine shavings and spruce boards, the air that came in through the sashless windows was fresh from the flowery slopes of the hills, and we slept as soundly and awoke as much refreshed as if we had lain on couches of rose petals in the palace of the Tsar.

Tuesday, July 28th, we continued our ride up the valley of the Búkhtarmá in the general direction of the Katúnski Alps. The snowy range of the Great Altái could no longer be seen from the trail, and we did not catch a single glimpse that day of the group of colossal peaks at the source of the Katún; but the scenery through which we rode was, nevertheless, beautiful and picturesque. The high rolling foothills which formed the sides of the valley, and which concealed the peaks of the main range, were endlessly varied in outline and coloring; the valley itself was full of park-like openings and sunny glades where the soft green carpet of turf was sprinkled with violets, pansies, and forget-me-nots; and every *verst* or two a clear rushing stream came tumbling down across the trail from a melting snow-field in some deep shaded glen high up among the hills.

Early in the afternoon we reached a small Cossack village called Arúl, about thirty *versts* from Jingistái, and went to the house of the *atamán* to present our order for fresh horses. The *atamán's* son, a good-looking young fellow of twenty-two or three, soon made his appearance in full uniform, and said that his father, for whom we had inquired, was making hay on the mountain-side about twelve *versts* away, but that he would send for him if it was "shípka núzhni" [awful necessary]. We replied that we must have horses to continue our journey, and that if we could not get them without an order from the *atamán*, the *atamán* must be summoned. The young man, thereupon, saddled a horse and galloped away down the valley. While wait-

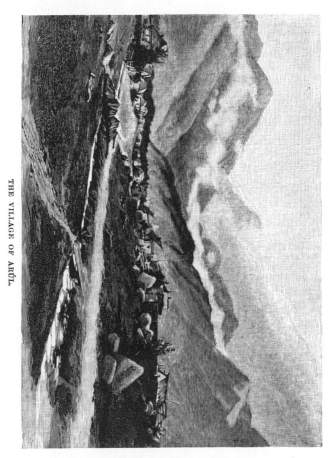

THE VILLAGE OF ARÚL.

ing for his return we refreshed ourselves with bread and tea, and Mr. Frost made the sketch of the village that is reproduced on this page. The *atamán* arrived in about an hour and a half. He proved to be an officer of intelligence and energy, and procured the necessary horses and a guide for us at once. The distance from Arúl to the Cossack village of Berél, where we expected to leave the valley of the Búkhtarmá, was only about twenty *versts*, and the road lay, as before, along the river. The foothills that bounded it were higher and steeper than in the part of the valley through which we had passed, and here and there, along their bases, were enormous masses of loose rocks and boulders which looked as if they might have been brought down into the valley by tremendous avalanches or landslides. About half-past four o'clock we crossed, on rude corduroy bridges, two or three turbid, milky arms of the Búkhtarmá River, and rode into the little hamlet of Berél—the most remote Russian settlement in that part of the Altái and the settlement where we expected to make our final arrangements for the long and difficult ride across the mountains to the Katúnski Alps.

The Cossack *atamán* at the Altái Station had given us a letter of introduction to one of his acquaintances in Berél— a peasant farmer named Bielaüsof —and we therefore went directly to the latter's house. He proved to be an intelligent man, fifty-five or sixty years of age, and an excellent type of the hardy Siberian pioneers who seek to escape from the burdensome restraints of government by migration to remote and unexplored regions. He was a nonconformist in religion, and had come to this wild corner of the Altái partly to enjoy freedom of religious worship and partly to find, if possible, the mythical *Bielovódye* or uninhabited land of peace and plenty which certain Russian dissenters believe to exist somewhere on the Mongolian frontier in the far East. He had not found the Siberian Eden which was the main object of his quest, but he had found the valley of the Búkhtarmá, and, tempted by its beauty and fertility, he had built a log house for himself at the intersection of the Búkhtarmá River and the Berél and in course of time had become prosperous and contented as a peasant farmer and a breeder of the *marál* or great Altái deer [Cervus elephas]. The horns of the *marál*, when at that stage of development known as "in the velvet," are believed by the Chinese to have peculiar medicinal properties, and are very highly prized. Chinese traders go in search of them to the remotest parts of the Altái and sometimes offer for them as much as four dollars a pound, or a hundred dollars for a single pair of large antlers. Bielaüsof had succeeded in capturing fifteen or twenty of these deer, and had shut them up in an extensive park, made by putting a nine-foot fence around a whole mountain so as to inclose a range almost as extensive as the animals would have had in a state of freedom. From the sale of the horns of the stags he derived every year an income of six or eight hundred dollars, which, with the proceeds of his farm, enabled him to live in more than ordinary comfort.

We spent in Berél only one night. Before we went to bed Tuesday evening we had engaged one of Bielaüsof's nephews to accompany us in the capacity of guide, had hired a second man to assist him in making camp, had procured the necessary number of horses, and were virtually ready to start. Wednesday morning at nine o'clock the whole population of Berél — about fifty souls — assembled in front of Bielaüsof's house to see the cavalcade get under way. Mikháiel, the guide, a stout, chubby-faced young fellow, with tangled masses of yellow hair falling over his shoulders, had arrayed himself in a traveling suit of extraordinary chromatic brilliancy, and was the admired of all beholders. His cotton shirt, which he wore outside his breeches like a tunic, was of a gory crimson, whose suggestions of bloodshed were relieved to some extent by a pattern of big yellow harps; his loose buckskin trousers were embroidered with bouquets of scarlet roses and huge orange sunflowers, and the brim of his antiquated chimney-pot hat had been turned up in piratical fashion on one side and fastened to the crown with round buttons of colored glass. His assistant, Nikolái, had on yellow buckskin trousers embroidered with Patagonian cactuses and a cot-

ton shirt of deep indigo blue. Our provisions, consisting
of tea, sugar, bread, two legs of mutton, and a little honey,

ASCENT OF THE MOUNTAIN FROM BERÉL.

were packed in capacious, antediluvian saddle-bags; our
brushes, soap, towels, sponges, and spare underclothing

were wrapped up in our blankets and securely lashed behind our saddles; and we sat on our pillows.   The horses that had been provided for our use did not look very promising at first sight, but I know that the good qualities of a Kírghis horse are not to be discovered by simple inspection, and I accepted Mikháiel's assurance that they were hardy, sure-footed, and accustomed to mountain paths.   About half-past nine o'clock everything was said to be ready, and climbing into our high, short-stirruped saddles we rode solemnly in single file out of the settlement.   There was a faint cheer from the more youthful half of the assembled crowd as we got under way, but Frost and I did not claim for ourselves, or for our horsemanship, any of the popular enthusiasm thus manifested.   We knew very well that it was inspired by the golden harps on the crimson tunic of the yellow-haired Mikháiel, and the Patagonian cactuses that blossomed all over the orange legs of the indigo-shirted Nikolái.

After having forded one of the milky channels of the Berél River we climbed slowly for two hours in short zigzags up a steep Kírghis trail that led to the summit of an immense mound-shaped foothill behind the village.   As we ascended, the whole magnificent amphitheater of snow-clad mountains at the head of the Búkhtarmá valley opened on our right, and a long line of sharp white peaks that we had not before seen appeared on the southern side of the Búkhtarmá along the boundary line of Mongolia.   Everywhere to the northward and eastward snowy mountains were piled on snowy mountains until there seemed to be no possibility of crossing or piercing the tremendous alpine barrier. On the summit of the mound-shaped foothill, two or three thousand feet above Berél, we found half a dozen Kírghis *kibítkas*, pitched here and there among immense glacial boulders and surrounded by flocks of Kírghis sheep and goats.   As the summer advances and the vegetation begins to dry up in the lower Altái valleys, the Kírghis are accus-

tomed to drive their flocks and herds to the crests of the
foothills where the grass is still fresh and green.   In the
latter part of July, therefore, they may be found encamped

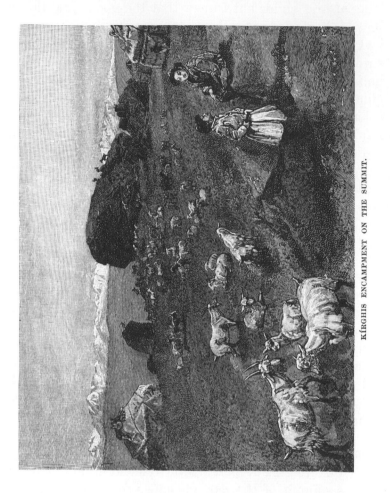

KÍRGHIS ENCAMPMENT ON THE SUMMIT.

high up in the mountains, and often in the most beautiful,
picturesque, and commanding situations.   From the *aül* of
the Berél Kírghis we could look out over a perfect ocean of
foothills and could trace the snowy range of the Great Altái
for a distance of a hundred miles.

After stopping for a few moments at the Kírghis encampment and making some inquiries with regard to the condition of the trail from there to the Rakmánofski hot springs, we tightened our saddle-girths and plunged into the wilderness of steep foothills and wild ravines that lies between the headwaters of the Búkhtarmá and the headwaters of the Katún. The northern slope of the mountain upon which the Kírghis encampment stood was much barer, bleaker, and more rocky than the slope that we had ascended. The yellow flowers that had given a sunny and cheerful glow to the latter suddenly disappeared, and their places were taken by a star-like purple blossom growing in long, slender spikes, and a very striking and showy species of dark-blue campanula. At the same time a new kind of shrub with silvery-gray leaves made its appearance, and grew so abundantly among the rocks as to change the whole tone of the landscape. I cannot remember to have seen in any other part of the world so sharp and sudden a transition from one aspect of nature to another under the very same atmospheric conditions. The northern exposure, the hoary, lichen-stained rocks, the dark-purple flowers, and the cool, silvery-gray foliage of the sage-like shrubs gave me the impression of a landscape seen by moonlight.

Soon after leaving the Kírghis encampment we crossed for the first time in Siberia the terminal moraine of an extinct glacier. It was an immense mass of loose rocks and boulders of all shapes and sizes thrown together in the wildest confusion, and extending far up and down one of the lateral ravines. At the point where we crossed it, it seemed to me to be at least an eighth of a mile wide, and it presented obstacles that brought out all the best qualities of our Kírghis horses. They made their way over the loose slabs and boulders with the judgment and agility of mountain sheep, rarely slipping, and, when they did slip, recovering their foothold without the least nervousness or excitement.

Late in the afternoon, after a very difficult and fatiguing journey of twenty-five or thirty *versts*, we rode two or three thousand feet down a slippery, break-neck descent into the

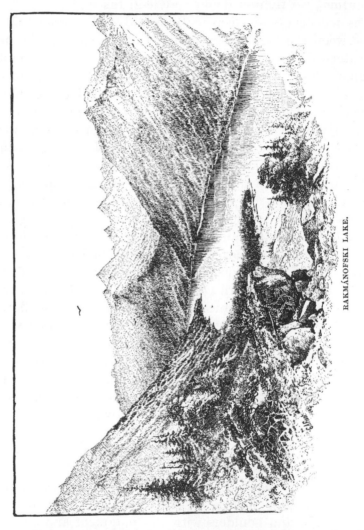

RAKMÁNOFSKI LAKE.

deep valley of the Rakmánofski hot springs, where, shut in by high mountains and framed in greenery and flowers, we found a beautiful alpine lake.　The medicinal properties of the water that flows from the Rakmánofski springs attract to this beautiful secluded valley every summer many Russians and Kírghis from the neighboring villages and encampments, and there have been erected for their accommodation two comfortable log buildings, and a small spring-house with three bathing-tanks. In the larger of the buildings, which had a well-built Russian oven, we stopped for the night. The ceiling and walls of the room that we occupied bore many names and inscriptions in French, Russian, and Tatár, among which I noticed "N. Yádrintsoff, 16 Aoute, 1880";[1] "Vlad. Banikof, VI 22, 1885"; and "M. T. Zheleiznikof, Semipalátinsk, 5 June, 1885." On the partition wall over the rude plank bench where Mr. Frost made his bed, some sufferer who, apparently, had come with weak faith to the springs in the hope of being cured had inscribed carefully in large, well-formed capital letters the words, "Lord, I believe, help thou mine unbelief."

The hot springs oozed out from under two or three piles of what seemed to be small glacial boulders, over which devout Russians had placed wooden crosses, and devout Kírghis had hung colored fragments from their shirts and trousers. The water from these springs was collected a short distance below in small vats or tanks in the spring-house, so that sufferers from rheumatism or cutaneous disease might be able to soak themselves in it under shelter. It was remarkably clear and bright in appearance, but had a peculiar soapy, slippery feeling, that suggested the presence of soda or borax. According to the Russian chemist Haller, who has made an analysis of it, it very closely resembles the water of the famous springs at Carlsbad. Its temperature in the tanks was 104° Fahrenheit.

When we awoke Thursday morning rain was falling heavily, and horseback travel in such a country was evidently out of the question. The storm continued, with an

---

[1] Mr. Yádrintsoff is the editor of the *Eastern Review* in Irkútsk and a well-known author, explorer, and anthropologist.

occasional brief intermission, for two days; but on the morning of the third the weather finally cleared up and, without waiting for the mountain slopes to become dry, we saddled our horses and went on.

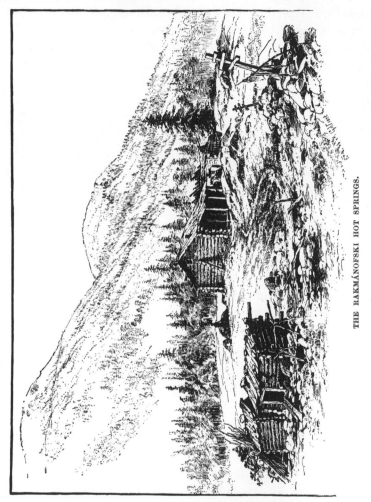

THE RAKMÁNOFSKI HOT SPRINGS.

The last sixty *versts* of our journey were made with great difficulty and much peril, our route lying across tremendous mountain ridges and deep valleys with almost precipitous sides, into which we descended by following the course of foaming mountain torrents, or clambering down the moraines of extinct glaciers, over great heaped-up masses of loose, broken rocks, through swamps, tangled jungles of laurel bushes and fallen trees, and down slopes so steep that it was almost impossible to throw one's body far enough back to keep one's balance in the saddle. Half the time our horses were sliding on all four feet, and dislodging stones which rolled or bounded for half a mile downward, until they were dashed to pieces over tremendous precipices. I was not wholly inexperienced in mountain travel, having ridden on horseback the whole length of the mountainous peninsula of Kamchátka, and crossed three times the great range of the Caucasus, once at a height of twelve thousand feet; but I must confess that during our descents into the valleys of the Rakmánofski, the Black Berél, the White Berél, and the Katún, my heart was in my mouth for hours at a time. On any other horses than those of the Kírghis such descents would have been utterly impossible. My horse fell with me once, but I was not hurt. The region through which we passed is a primeval wilderness, traversed only by the *Díko-kámenoi* Kírghis, or "Kírghis of the Wild Rocks," and abounding in game. We saw *maráls*, wolves, wild sheep, and many fresh trails made by bears in the long grass of the valley bottoms; we chased wild goats, and might have shot hundreds of partridges, grouse, ducks, geese, eagles, and cranes. The flora of the lower mountain valleys was extremely rich, varied, and luxuriant, comprising beautiful wild pansies of half a dozen varieties and colors, fringed pinks, spirea, two species of gentian, wild hollyhocks, daisies, forget-me-nots, alpine roses, trollius, wild poppies, and scores of other flowers that I had never before seen, many of them very large, brilliant, and showy. Among plants and fruits that with us are domesticated, but that in the Altái grow wild, I noticed rhubarb, celery, red currants, black currants, gooseberries, raspberries, strawberries, blackberries, wild cherries, crab-apples, and wild

apricots. Most of the berries were ripe, or nearly ripe, and
the wild currants were as large and abundant as in an
American garden. The scenery was extremely wild and

DESCENT INTO THE VALLEY OF THE WHITE BERÉL.

grand, surpassing, at times, anything that I had seen in
the Caucasus.

On Saturday, August 1st, we reached the foot of the last
great ridge, or water-shed, which separated us from the
main chain of the Katúnski Alps, and camped for the night

in a high mountain valley beside the White Berél, a milky stream which runs out from under a great glacier a few miles higher up. The air was clear and frosty, but we built a big camp-fire and managed to get through the night without much discomfort. Sunday morning we climbed about two thousand feet to the summit of the last ridge, and looked over into the wild valley of the Katún, out of which rise the "Katúnski Pillars," the highest peaks of the Russian

DISTANT VIEW OF THE KATÚNSKI ALPS.

Altái. I was prepared, to a certain extent, for grandeur of scenery, because I had already caught glimpses of these peaks two or three times, at distances varying from twenty-five to eighty miles; but the near view, from the heights above the Katún, so far surpassed all my anticipations that I was simply overawed. I hardly know how to describe it without using language that will seem exaggerated. The word that oftenest rises to my lips when I think of it is "tremendous." It was not beautiful, it was not picturesque; it was tremendous and overwhelming. The narrow valley, or gorge, of the Katún, which lay almost under our feet, was between 2000 and 3000 feet deep. On the other side of it rose, far above our heads, the wild, mighty chain of the Katúnski Alps, culminating just opposite us in two tremendous snowy peaks whose height I estimated at 15,000 feet.[1] They were white from base to summit, except where the snow was broken by great black precipices, or pierced by sharp, rocky spines, or aiguilles. Down the sides of these peaks, from vast fields of *névé* above, fell seven immense glaciers, the largest of them descending from the saddle between the twin summits in a series of ice falls for at least 4000 feet. The glacier on the extreme right had an almost perpendicular ice fall of 1200 or 1500 feet, and the glacier on the extreme left gave birth to a torrent which tumbled about 800 feet, with a hoarse roar, into the deep narrow gorge. The latter glacier was longitudinally divided by three moraines, which looked from our point of view like long, narrow, A-shaped dumps of furnace slag or fine coal dust, but which were in reality composed of black rocks, from the size of one's head to the size of a freight car, and extended four or five miles, with a width of 300 feet and a height of from 50 to 75 feet above the general level of the glacier. The extreme summits of the two highest peaks were more than half of the time hidden in clouds; but this rather added to than detracted from the wild grandeur of the scene, by giving mystery to the origin of the enormous glaciers, which at such times seemed to the imagination to be tumbling down from unknown heights in the sky through masses of rolling vapor. All the time there came up to us from the depths of the gorge the hoarse roar of the waterfall, and with it blended, now and then, the deeper thunder of the

[1] Captain Maiéfski's estimate of their height was 18,000 feet above the sea level. They have never been climbed nor measured, and I do not even know the height above the sea of the valley bottom from which they rise.

great glaciers, as masses of ice gave way and settled into
new positions in the ice falls. This thundering of the
glaciers continued for nearly a minute at a time, varying in
intensity, and resembling occasionally the sound of a distant

THE "KATÚNSKI PILLARS"—SOURCE OF THE KATÚN RIVER.

but heavy and rapid cannonade. No movement of the ice
in the falls was perceptible to the eye from the point at
which we stood, but the sullen, rumbling thunder was evidence enough of the mighty force of the agencies which
were at work before us.

After looking at the mountains for half an hour, we turned our attention to the valley of the Katún beneath us, with the view to ascertain whether it would be possible to get down into it and reach the foot of the main glacier, which gave birth to the Katún River. Mr. Frost declared the descent to be utterly impracticable, and almost lost patience with me because I insisted upon the guides trying it. "Anybody can see," he said, "that this slope ends in a big precipice; and even if we get our horses down there, we never can get them up again. It is foolish to think of such a thing." I had seen enough, however, of Kírghis horses to feel great confidence in their climbing abilities; and although the descent did look very dangerous, I was by no means satisfied that it was utterly impracticable. While we were discussing the question, our guide was making a bold and practical attempt to solve it. We could no longer see him from where we stood, but every now and then a stone or small boulder, dislodged by his horse's feet, would leap suddenly into sight 300 or 400 feet below us, and go crashing down the mountain side, clearing 200 feet at every bound, and finally dashing itself to pieces against the rocks at the bottom, with a noise like the distant rattling discharge of musketry. Our guide was evidently making progress. In a few moments he came into sight on a bold, rocky buttress about six hundred feet below us and shouted cheerfully, "Come on! This is nothing! You could get down here with a *teléga!*" Inasmuch as one could hardly look down there without getting dizzy, this was rather a hyperbolical statement of the possibilities of the case; but it had the effect of silencing Mr. Frost, who took his horse by the bridle and followed me down the mountain in cautious zigzags, while I kept as nearly as I could in the track of our leader. At the buttress the guide tightened my forward and after saddle-girths until my horse groaned and grunted an inarticulate protest, and I climbed again into the saddle. It seemed to me safer, on the whole, to ride down than to try to walk down leading my horse, since in the latter case he was constantly sliding upon me, or dislodging loose stones which threatened to knock my legs from under me and launch me into space like a projectile from a catapult. The first hundred feet of the descent were very bad.   It was

THE DESCENT INTO THE GORGE OF THE KATÚN.

almost impossible to keep in the saddle on account of the steepness of the incline, and once I just escaped being pitched over my horse's head at the end of one of his short slides. We finally reached a very steep but grassy slope, like the side of a titanic embankment, down which we zigzagged, with much discomfort but without any danger, to the bottom of the Katún valley. As we rode towards the great peaks, and finally, leaving our horses, climbed up on the principal glacier, I saw how greatly we had underestimated distances, heights, and magnitudes, from the elevated

THE KATÚN RIVER.

position which we had previously occupied. The Katún River, which, from above, had looked like a narrow, dirty white ribbon that a child could step across, proved to be a torrent thirty or forty feet wide, with a current almost deep and strong enough to sweep away a horse and rider. The main glacier, which I had taken to be about three hundred feet wide, proved to have a width of more than half a mile; and its central moraine, which had looked to me like a strip of black sand piled up to the height of six or seven feet like a long furnace dump, proved to be an enormous mass of

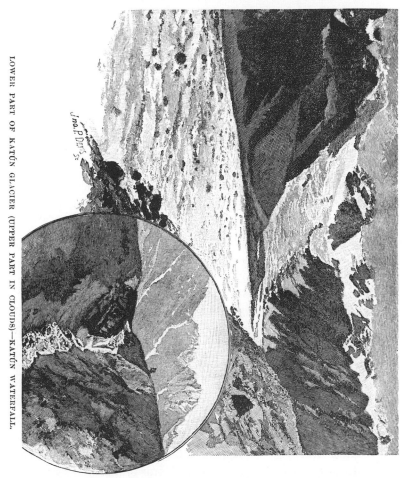

LOWER PART OF KATÚN GLACIER (UPPER PART IN CLOUDS)—KATÚN WATERFALL.

gigantic rocks, three or four miles long, and from 300 to 400 feet wide, piled up on the glacier in places to the height of 75 feet. Mr. Frost estimated the width of this glacier at two-thirds of a mile, and the extreme height of the moraine at 100 feet.

I took the photographic apparatus, and in the course of an hour and an half succeeded in climbing up the central moraine about two miles towards the foot of the great ice fall; but by that time I was tired out and dripping with perspiration. I passed many wide crevasses into which were running streams of water from the surface of the glacier; and judging from the duration of the sound made by stones that I dropped into some of them, they must have had a depth of a hundred feet, perhaps much more. This was only one of eleven glaciers that I counted from the summit of the high ridge which divides the water-shed of the Írtish from that of the Ob. Seven glaciers descend from the two main peaks alone.

We spent all the remainder of the day in sketching, taking photographs, and climbing about the glacier and the valley, and late in the afternoon returned to our camp in the valley of the White Berél. That night—the 2d of August—was even colder than the preceding one. Ice formed to the thickness of more than a quarter of an inch in our tea-kettle, and my blankets and pillow, when I got up in the morning, were covered with thick white frost.

Monday we made another excursion to the summit of the ridge that overlooks the valley of the Katún, and succeeded in getting a good photograph of the two big peaks, against a background of cloudless sky. Our little instrument, of course, could not take in a quarter of the mighty landscape, and what it did take in it reduced to so small a scale that all of the grandeur and majesty of the mountains was lost; but it was a satisfaction to feel that we could carry away something that would suggest and recall to us in later years the sublimity of that wonderful alpine picture.

Monday noon we broke camp and started for the Rak-mánofski hot springs; and on the 5th of August, after an absence of ten days, we returned to the Altái Station.

CHAPTER X

TWO COLONIES OF POLITICAL EXILES

FEW pages in my Siberian note-books are more suggestive of pleasant sensations and experiences than the
pages that record the incidents of our life in the mountains
of the Altái. As I now turn over the flower-stained leaves
dated "Altái Station, August 5, 1885," every feature of that
picturesque Cossack village comes back to me so vividly
that, if for a moment I close my eyes, I seem to hear again
the musical plash and tinkle of the clear, cold streams that
tumble through its streets; to see again the magnificent
amphitheater of flower-tinted slopes and snowy peaks that
encircles it; and to breathe once more the fresh, perfumed
air of the green alpine meadow upon which it stands. If
the object of our Siberian journey had been merely enjoy-
ment, I think we should have remained at the Altái Station
all summer; since neither in Siberia nor in any other country could we have hoped to find a more delightful place for
a summer vacation. The pure mountain air was as fragrant and exhilarating as if it had been compounded of
perfume and ozone; the beauty and luxuriance of the flora
were a never-failing source of pleasure to the eye;[1] the
clear, cold mountain streams were full of fish; elk, argali,
wild goats, bears, foxes, and wolves were to be found by
an enterprising hunter in the wooded ravines and the high
mountain valleys south of the station; troops of Kírghis

---

[1] I brought back with me from the Altái an herbarium consisting of nearly a
thousand species of flowering plants.

horsemen were ready to escort us to the Mongolian boundary post, to the beautiful alpine lake of Márka Kul, or to the wild, unexplored fastnesses of the Chinese Altái; and Captain Maiéfski, the hospitable commandant of the post, tempted us to prolong our stay, by promising to organize for us all sorts of delightful excursions and expeditions. The season of good weather and good roads, however,

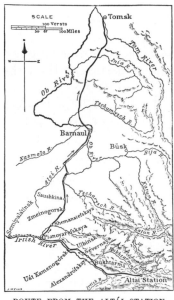

ROUTE FROM THE ALTÁI STATION
TO TOMSK.

was rapidly passing; and if we hoped to reach the mines of Kará before winter should set in, we had not a day to spare. It was already the first week in August, and a distance of 2500 miles lay between us and the head-waters of the Amúr.

Our next objective point was the city of Tomsk, distant from the Altái Station about 750 miles. In order to reach it we should be obliged to return over a part of the road that we had already traversed, and to descend the Írtish as far as the station of Piánoyarófskaya. At that point the road to Tomsk leaves the Semipalátinsk road, and runs northward through the great Altái mining district and the city of Barnaül. There were two colonies of political exiles on our route—one of them at the Cossack station of Ulbínsk, 160 miles from the Altái Station, and the other in the town of Ust Kámenogórsk. In each of these places, therefore, we purposed to make a short stay.

On the morning of Thursday, August 6th, we packed our baggage in the *tárantás*, ordered horses from the post station, took breakfast for the last time with Captain Maiéfski and his wife, whose kindness and warm-hearted hospitality had made their house seem to us like a home, and after drinking to the health of all our Altái friends, and bidding everybody good-by three or four times, we rode reluctantly out of the beautiful alpine village and began our descent to the plains of the Írtish.

It is not necessary to describe our journey down the valley of the Búkhtarmá and across the gray, sterile steppes of the upper Írtish. It was simply a reversal of the experience through which we had passed in approaching the Altái Station three weeks before. Then we were climbing from the desert into the alps, while now we were descending from the alps to the desert.

At six o'clock Friday afternoon we reached the settlement of Búkhtarmá, where the Írtish pierces a great outlying spur of the Altái chain, and where the road to Ust Kámenogórsk leaves the river and makes a long détour into the mountains. No horses were obtainable at the post station; the weather looked threatening; the road to Alexandrófskaya was said to be in bad condition owing to recent rains; and we had great difficulty in finding a peasant with "free" horses who was willing to take our heavy *tárantás* up the steep, miry mountain road on what promised to be a dark and stormy night. With the coöperation of the station master, however, we found at last a man who was ready, for a suitable consideration, to make the attempt, and about an hour before dark we left Búkhtarmá for Alexandrófskaya with four "free" horses. We soon had occasion to regret that we had not taken the advice of our driver to stop at Búkhtarmá for the night and cross the mountains by daylight. The road was worse than any neglected wood-road in the mountains of West Virginia; and before we had made half the distance to Alexandrófskaya, night came on, with a violent storm accompanied by lightning, thunder, and heavy rain. Again and again we lost the road in the darkness; two or three times we became almost hopelessly mired in bogs and sloughs; and finally our *tárantás* capsized, or partly capsized, into a deep ditch or gully worn out in the mountain-side by falling water. The driver shouted, cursed, and lashed his dispirited horses, while Mr. Frost and I explored the gully with lighted wisps of hay, and lifted, tugged, and pulled at the heavy vehicle until we were tired out, drenched with rain, and covered from head to foot with mud; but all our efforts were fruitless. The *tárantás* could not be extricated. From this predicament we were finally rescued by the drivers of three or four *telégas*, who left Búkhtarmá with the mail shortly after our departure and who overtook us just at the time when their services were most needed. With their aid we righted the capsized vehicle, set it again on the road, and proceeded. The lightly loaded *telégas* soon left us behind, and knowing that we could expect no more help from that source, and that another capsize would probably end our travel for the night, I walked ahead of our horses in the miry road for half or three-quarters of an hour, holding up a white hand-kerchief at arm's-length for the guidance of our driver, and shouting directions and warnings to him whenever it seemed necessary. Tired, at last, of wading through mud in Cimmerian darkness, and ascertaining the location of holes, sloughs, and rocks by tumbling into or over them, I climbed back into the *tárantás* and wrapped myself up in a wet blanket, with the determination to trust to luck. In less than fifteen minutes our vehicle was again on its side in another deep gully. After making a groping investigation by the sense of touch, we decided that the situation this time was hopeless. There was nothing to be done but to send the driver on horseback in search of help, and to get through the night as best we could where we were. It was then about eleven o'clock. The wind had abated, but the rain was still falling, and the intense darkness was relieved only by an occasional flash of lightning. Cold, tired, and hungry, we crawled into our capsized vehicle, which still afforded us some little shelter from the rain, and sat there in sleepless discomfort until morning. Just before daylight our driver returned with a Cossack from Alexandrófskaya,

COMING UP THE ALEXANDRÓFSKAYA-SÉIVERNAYA RAVINE.

bringing lanterns, ropes, crowbars, and fresh horses, and with these helps and appliances we succeeded in righting the *tárantás* and dragging it back to the road.

We reached Alexandrófskaya in the gray light of early
dawn, and after drinking tea and sleeping two hours on the
floor of the post station, we resumed our journey with eight
horses and three drivers. The road from Alexandrófskaya
to Séivernaya runs for five or six miles up the steep, wild
ravine that is shown in the illustration on page 231.
It then crosses a series of high, bare ridges running generally at right angles to the course of the Írtish, and finally
descends, through another deep, precipitous ravine, into
the valley of Ulbínsk, which it follows to Ust Kámenogórsk. The mountains which compose this spur, or outlying branch, of the Altái system are not high, but, as will
be seen from the illustration on page 235, they are picturesque and effective in outlining and grouping, and are
separated one from another by extremely beautiful valleys
and ravines.

Owing to the bad condition of the roads and the mountainous nature of the country, we were more than ten hours
in making the nineteen miles between Séivernaya and Ulbínsk, although we had eight horses on the first stretch
and five on the second. The slowness of our progress gave
us an opportunity to walk now and then, and to make collections of flowers, and we kept the *tárantás* decorated all
day with goldenrod, wild hollyhocks, long blue spikes of
monk's-hood, and leafy branches of *zhímolost* or Tatár
honeysuckle, filled with showy scarlet or yellow berries.

Late Saturday afternoon, as the sun was sinking behind
the western hills, we rode at a brisk trot down the long,
beautiful ravine that leads into the valley of the Ulbá, and
before dark we were sitting comfortably in the neat waiting-room of the Ulbínsk post station, refreshing ourselves
with bread and milk and raspberries.

Among the political exiles living in Ulbínsk at that time
were Alexander L. Blok, a young law student from the city
of Sarátof on the Vólga; Apollo Karélin, the son of a well-
known photographer in Nízhni Nóvgorod; Séiverin Gross,

a young lawyer from the province of Kóvno, and Mr. Vítort, a technologist from Ríga.

Mr. Karélin had been accompanied to Siberia by his wife, but the others were, I believe, unmarried. I had

THE ULBÍNSK RAVINE.

learned the names, and something of the histories, of these exiles from the politicals in Semipalátinsk, and there were several reasons why I particularly wished to see them and to make their acquaintance. I had an idea that perhaps the politicals in Semipalátinsk were above the average level of administrative exiles in intelligence and education

—that they were unusually favorable specimens of their class,—and it seemed to me not improbable that in the wilder and remoter parts of Western Siberia I should find types that would correspond more nearly to the conception of nihilists that I had formed in America.

Before we had been in the village an hour, two of the exiles—Messrs. Blok and Gross—called upon us and introduced themselves. Mr. Blok won my heart from the very first. He was a man twenty-six or twenty-eight years of age, of medium height and athletic figure, with light-brown hair, blue eyes, and a beardless but strong and resolute face, which seemed to me to express intelligence, earnestness, and power in every line. It was, in the very best sense of the word, a *good* face, and I could no more help liking and trusting it than I could help breathing. Marcus Aurelius somewhere says, with coarse vigor of expression, that "a man who is honest and good ought to be exactly like a man who smells strong, so that the bystander, as soon as he comes near, must smell, whether he choose or not." Mr. Blok's honesty and goodness seemed to me to be precisely of this kind, and I found myself regarding him with friendly sympathy, and almost with affection, long before I could assign any reason for so doing. Mr. Gross was a rather handsome man, perhaps thirty years of age, with brown hair, full beard and mustache, gray eyes, and clearly cut, regular features. He talked in an eager, animated way, with an affectionate, caressing modulation of the voice, and had a habit of unconsciously opening his eyes a little more widely than usual as an expression of interest or emotion. Both of the young men were university graduates; both spoke French and German, and Mr. Gross read English; both were particularly interested in questions of political economy, and either of them might have been taken for a young professor, or a post-graduate student, in the Johns Hopkins University. I had not talked with them an hour before I became satisfied that in intelligence and culture

they were fully abreast of the Semipalátinsk exiles, and
that I should have to look for the wild, fanatical nihilists
of my imagination in some part of Siberia more remote
than Ulbínsk.

We talked in the post station until about nine o'clock,
and then, at Mr. Blok's suggestion, made a round of calls

THE VALLEY OF ULBÍNSK.

upon the other political exiles in the village. They were
all living in wretchedly furnished log houses rented from
the Ulbínsk Cossacks, and were surrounded by unmistakable evidences of hardship, privation, and straiténed circumstances ; but they seemed to be trying to make the best of
their situation, and I cannot remember to have heard anywhere that night a bitter complaint or a single reference to

personal experience that seemed to be made for the purpose of exciting our sympathy. If they suffered, they bore their suffering with dignity and self-control. All of them seemed to be physically well except Mrs. Karélin, who looked thin, pale, and careworn, and Mr. Vítort, who had been three times in exile and ten years in prison or in Siberia, and who, I thought, would not live much longer to trouble the Government that had wrecked his life. Although only forty-five years of age, he seemed greatly broken, walked feebly with a cane, and suffered constantly from rheumatism contracted in damp prison cells. He was one of the best-informed exiles that I met in Western Siberia, and was the first to tell me of the death of General Grant. We had a long talk about the United States, in the course of which he asked many questions concerning our civil war, the constitutional amendments adopted after the war, the balance of parties in Congress, and the civil service reform policy of President Cleveland, which showed that he had more than a superficial acquaintance with our political history. In the houses of all the exiles in Ulbínsk, no matter how wretchedly they might be furnished, I found a writing-desk or table, books, and such magazines as the *Revue des Deux Mondes*, and the *Rússki Véistnik*, or *Russian Messenger*. In the house of Mr. Blok there was a small but well-selected library, in which I noticed, in addition to Russian books, a copy of Longfellow's poems, in English; Maine's "Ancient Law," and "Village Communities"; Bain's "Logic"; Mill's "Political Economy"; Lecky's "History of Rationalism" (an expurgated Russian edition); Spencer's "Essays: Moral, Political, and Esthetic," and his "Principles of Sociology"; Taine's "History of English Literature"; Laboulaye's "History of the United States," and a large number of French and German works on jurisprudence and political economy. I need hardly call attention, I think, to the fact that men who read and carry to Siberia with them such books as these are not wild fanatics, nor "ignorant shoemakers and mechanics," as they were once contemptuously described to me by a Russian officer, but are serious, cultivated, thinking men. If such men are in exile in a lonely Siberian village on the frontier of Mongolia, instead of being at home in the service of the state— so much the worse for the state!

We spent with the political exiles in Ulbínsk the greater part of one night and a day. I became very deeply interested in them, and should have liked to stay there and talk with them for a week; but our excursion to the Katúnski Alps had occupied more time than we had allotted to it, and it was important that we should, if possible, reach the convict mines of Eastern Siberia before the coming on of winter. Sunday afternoon at four o'clock we set out for Ust Kámenogórsk. Messrs. Blok and Karélin accompanied us on horseback as far as the ferry across the Ulbá, and then, after bidding us a hearty and almost affectionate good-by, and asking us not to forget them when we should return to "a freer and happier country," they remounted their horses and sat motionless in their saddles, watching us while we were being ferried over the river. When we were ready to start on the other side, a quarter of a mile distant, they waved their handkerchiefs, and then, taking off their hats, bowed low towards us in mute farewell as we dashed away into the forest. If these pages should ever be read in one of the lonely cabins of the political exiles in Ulbínsk, the readers may feel assured that "in a freer and happier country" we have not forgotten them, but think of them often, with the sincerest esteem and the most affectionate sympathy.

We reached Ust Kámenogórsk before dark Sunday afternoon and took up our quarters in the post station. The town, which contains about 5000 inhabitants, is a collection of 600 or 800 houses, built generally of logs, and is situated in the midst of a treeless plain on the right bank of the Írtish, just where the latter is joined by its tributary the

Ulbá. It contains one or two Tatár mosques, two or three Russian churches with colored domes of tin, and an *ostrog*,

THE TOWN OF UST KÁMENOGÓRSK.

or fortress, consisting of a high quadrangular earthen wall or embankment, surrounded by a dry moat, and inclosing a white-walled prison, a church, and a few Government buildings. The mosques, the white-turbaned mullas, the hooded Kírghis horsemen in the streets, the morning and evening cry of the muezzins, and the files of Bactrian camels, which now and then come pacing slowly and solemnly in from the steppe, give to the town the same Oriental appearance that is so noticeable in Semipalátinsk, and that suggests the idea that one is in northern Africa or in Central Asia, rather than in Siberia.

While we were drinking tea in the post station we were surprised by the appearance of Mr. Gross, who had come from Ulbínsk to Ust Kámenogórsk that morning, and had been impatiently awaiting our arrival. He had hardly taken his seat when the wife of the station-master announced that a Russian officer had come to call on us, and before I had time to ask Mr. Gross whether his relations with the Russian authorities were pleasant or unpleasant, the officer, dressed in full uniform, had entered the room. I was embarrassed for an instant by the awkwardness of the situation. I knew nothing of the officer except his name, and it was possible, of course, that upon finding a political exile there he might behave towards the latter in so offensive a manner as to make some decisive action on my part inevitable. I could not permit a gentleman who had called upon us to be offensively treated at our table, even if he was officially regarded as a "criminal" and a "nihilist." Fortunately my apprehensions proved to be groundless. Mr. Shaitánof, the Cossack officer who had come to see us, was a gentleman, as well as a man of tact and good breeding, and whatever he may have thought of the presence of a political exile in our quarters so soon after our arrival, he manifested neither surprise nor annoyance. He bowed courteously when I introduced Mr. Gross to him, and in five minutes they were engaged in an animated discussion of bee-keeping, silk-worm culture, and tobacco-growing. Mr. Shaitánof said that he had been making some experiments near Ust Kámenogórsk with mulberry trees and Virginian and Cuban tobacco, and had been so successful that he hoped to introduce silk-worm culture there the next year, and to substitute for the coarse native tobacco some of the finer sorts from the West Indies and the United States.

After half an hour of pleasant conversation Mr. Shaitánof bade us good-night, and Mr. Gross, Mr. Frost, and I went to call on the political exiles. In anticipation of our coming, ten or fifteen of them had assembled in one of the large upper rooms of a two-story log building near the center of the town, which served as a residence for one of them and a place of rendezvous for the others. It is, of course, impracticable, as well as unnecessary, to describe and characterize all of the political exiles in the Siberian towns and villages through which we passed. The most that I aim to do is to give the reader a general idea of their appearance and behavior, and of the impression that they made upon me. The exiles in Ust Kámenogórsk did not differ essentially from those in Ulbínsk, except that, taken as a body, they furnished a greater variety of types and represented a larger number of social classes. In Ulbínsk there were only professional men and students. In Ust Kámenogórsk there was at one end of the social scale a peasant shoemaker and at the other a Caucasian princess, while between these extremes were physicians, chemists, authors, publicists, university students, and landed proprietors. Most of them were of noble birth or belonged to the privileged classes, and some of them were men and women of high cultivation and refinement. Among those with whom I became best acquainted were Mr. Kanoválof, who read English well but spoke it imperfectly;[1] Mr. Milinchúk, a dark-haired, dark-bearded Georgian from Tiflís; and Mr. Adam Bialovéski, a writer and publicist from the province of Mohílef. The last-named gentleman, who was a graduate of the university of Kíev, impressed me as a

[1] Mr. Kanoválof committed suicide in Ust Kámenogórsk about six months after we left there.

man of singular ability, fairness, and breadth of view. He
was thoroughly acquainted with Russian history and jurisprudence, as well as with the history and literature of the
west European nations; and, notwithstanding the fact that
he had been in prison or in exile most of the time since his
graduation from the university, he regarded life and its
problems with undiminished cheerfulness and courage. I
had a long talk with him about the Russian situation, and
was very favorably impressed by his cool, dispassionate
review of the revolutionary movement and the measures
taken by the Government for its suppression. His statements were entirely free from exaggeration and prejudice,
and his opinions seemed to me to be almost judicially fair
and impartial. To brand such a man as a nihilist was absurd, and to exile him to Siberia as a dangerous member
of society was simply preposterous. In any other civilized
country on the face of the globe except Russia he would
be regarded as the most moderate of liberals.

CHAPTER XI

THE colony of political exiles in Ust Kámenogórsk was the last one that we saw in the steppe territories, and it seems to me desirable, before proceeding with the narrative of our Siberian journey, to describe more fully and carefully the particular form of punishment that these offenders were undergoing — a form of punishment that is known in Russia as "exile by administrative process."

Exile by administrative process means the banishment of an obnoxious person from one part of the empire to another without the observance of any of the legal formalities that, in most civilized countries, precede the deprivation of rights and the restriction of personal liberty. The obnoxious person may not be guilty of any crime, and may not have rendered himself amenable in any way to the laws of the state, but if, in the opinion of the local authorities, his presence in a particular place is "prejudicial to public order," or "incompatible with public tranquillity," he may be arrested without a warrant, may be held from two weeks to two years in prison, and may then be removed by force to any other place within the limits of the empire and there be put under police surveillance for a period of from one year to ten years. He may or may not be informed of the reasons for this summary proceeding, but in either case he is perfectly helpless. He cannot examine the witnesses upon whose testimony his presence is declared to be "prejudicial to public order." He cannot

242

summon friends to prove his loyalty and good character, without great risk of bringing upon them the same calamity that has befallen him. He has no right to demand a trial, or even a hearing. He cannot sue out a writ of habeas corpus. He cannot appeal to his fellow-citizens through the press. His communications with the world are so suddenly severed that sometimes even his own relatives do not know what has happened to him. He is literally and absolutely without any means whatever of self-defense. To show the nature of the evidence upon which certain classes of Russians are banished to Siberia, and to illustrate the working of the system generally, I will give a few cases of administrative exile from the large number recorded in my note-books.

Some of the readers of this chapter will perhaps remember a young naval officer named Constantine Staniukóvich, who was attached to the staff of the Grand Duke Alexis at the time of the latter's visit to the United States. From the fact that I saw in Mr. Staniukóvich's house in Tomsk the visiting cards of people well known in New York and San Francisco, I infer that he went a good deal into society here and that he may still be recalled to mind by persons who met him. He was the son of a Russian admiral, was an officer of great promise, and had before him the prospect of a brilliant career in the Russian naval service. He was, however, a man of broad and liberal views, with a natural taste for literary pursuits, and after his return from America he resigned his position in the navy and became an author. He wrote a number of novels and plays which were fairly successful, but which, in the language of the censor, " manifested a pernicious tendency," and in 1882 or 1883 he purchased a well-known Russian magazine in St. Petersburg called the *Diélo* and became its editor and proprietor. He spent a considerable part of the summer of 1884 abroad, and in the latter part of that year left his wife and children at Baden-Baden and started for St. Petersburg.

At the Russian frontier station of Vérzhbolof he was suddenly arrested, was taken thence to St. Petersburg under guard, and was there thrown into the fortress of Petropávlovsk. His wife, knowing nothing of this misfortune, continued to write to him at St. Petersburg without getting any answers to her letters, until finally she became alarmed, and telegraphed to the editorial department of the *Diélo*, asking what had happened to her husband and why he did not write to her. The managing editor of the magazine replied that Mr. Staniukóvich was not there, and that they had supposed him to be still in Baden-Baden. Upon the receipt of this telegram, Mrs. Staniukóvich, thoroughly frightened, proceeded at once with her children to St. Petersburg. Nothing whatever could be learned there with regard to her husband's whereabouts. He had not been seen at the editorial rooms of the *Diélo*, and none of his friends had heard anything of or from him in two weeks. He had suddenly and mysteriously disappeared. At last, after days of torturing anxiety, Mrs. Staniukóvich was advised to make inquiries of General Órzhefski, the chief of gendarmes. She did so, and found that her husband was a prisoner in one of the casemates of the Petropávlovsk fortress. The police, as it afterward appeared, had for some time been intercepting and reading his letters, and had ascertained that he was in correspondence with a well-known Russian revolutionist who was then living in Switzerland. The correspondence was perfectly innocent in its character, and related solely to the business of the magazine; but the fact that an editor, and a man of known liberal views, was in communication with a political refugee was regarded as sufficient evidence that his presence in St. Petersburg would be "prejudicial to public order," and his arrest followed. In May, 1885, he was exiled for three years by administrative process to the city of Tomsk in Western Siberia. The publication of the magazine was of course suspended in consequence of the imprisonment and ultimate banishment of its owner, and Mr. Staniukóvich was financially ruined. If the Russian Government deals in this arbitrary way with men of rank, wealth, and high social position in the capital of the empire, it can be imagined what treatment is accorded to authors, physicians, students, and small landed proprietors whose presence is regarded as "prejudicial to public order" in the provinces.

In the year 1880 the well-known and gifted Russian novelist Vladímir Korolénko, two of whose books have recently been translated into English and published in Boston,[1] was exiled to Eastern Siberia as a result of what the Government itself finally admitted to be an official mistake. Through the influence of Prince Imeretínski, Mr. Korolénko succeeded in getting this mistake corrected before he reached his ultimate destination and was released in the West Siberian city of Tomsk. Hardly had he returned, however, to European Russia, when he was called upon to take the oath of allegiance to Alexander III., and to swear that he would betray every one of his friends or acquaintances whom he knew to be engaged in revolutionary or anti-Government work. No honorable and self-respecting man could take such an oath as that, and of course Mr. Korolénko declined to do so. He was thereupon exiled by administrative process to the East Siberian territory of Yakútsk, where, in a wretched native *ulús*, he lived for about three years.[2]

Mr. Boródin, another Russian author and a well-known contributor to the Russian magazine *Annals of the Fatherland*, was banished to the territory of Yakútsk on account of the alleged "dangerous" and "pernicious" character of a certain manuscript found in his house by the police during

---

[1] "The Vagrant," a series of sketches of Siberian life and experience, and "The Blind Musician."

[2] A statement of the circumstances of Mr. Korolénko's first exile to Siberia was published over the signature of the well-known author S. A. Priklónski in the newspaper *Zémstvo* for 1881, No. 10, p. 19. Korolénko has been four times banished to various parts of the empire without trial or hearing.

a search. This manuscript was a spare copy of an article upon the economic condition of the province of Viátka, which Mr. Boródin had written and sent to the above-named magazine, but which, up to that time, had not been published. The author went to Eastern Siberia in a convict's gray overcoat with a yellow ace of diamonds on his back, and three or four months after his arrival in Yakútsk he had the pleasure of reading in the *Annals of the Fatherland* the very same article for which he had been exiled. The Minister of the Interior had sent him to Siberia merely for having in his possession what the police called a "dangerous" and "pernicious" manuscript, and then the St. Petersburg committee of censorship had certified that another copy of that same manuscript was perfectly harmless, and had allowed it to be published, without the change of a line, in one of the most popular and widely circulated magazines in the empire.[1]

A gentleman named Achkín, in Moscow, was exiled to Siberia by administrative process in 1885 merely because, to adopt the language of the order that was issued for his arrest, he was "suspected of an intention to put himself into an illegal situation." The high crime which Mr. Achkín was "suspected of an intention" to commit was the taking of a fictitious name in the place of his own. Upon what ground he was "suspected of an intention" to do this terrible thing he never knew.

Another exile of my acquaintance, Mr. Y——, was banished merely because he was a friend of Mr. Z——, who was awaiting trial on the charge of political conspiracy. When Mr. Z——'s case came to a judicial investigation he was found to be innocent and was acquitted; but in the mean-

[1] *Zémstvo*, 1881, No. 10, p. 19. It is not often, of course, that facts of this kind, which are so damaging to the Government, get into the Russian newspaper press. The account of Mr. Boródin's experience and of the exile of Mr. Korolénko was published at the time when the liberal ministry of Loris-Mélikof was in power, just at the close of the reign of the late Tsar, when the strictness of the censorship was greatly relaxed.

time Mr. Y——, merely for being a friend of this innocent man, had gone to Siberia by administrative process.

In another case a young student, called Vladímir Sidórski (I use a fictitious name), was arrested by mistake instead of another and a different Sidórski named Victor, whose presence in Moscow was regarded by somebody as "prejudicial to public order." Vladímir protested that he was not Victor, that he did not know Victor, and that his arrest in the place of Victor was the result of a stupid blunder; but his protestations were of no avail. The police were too much occupied in unearthing what they called "conspiracies" and looking after "untrustworthy" people to devote any time to a troublesome verification of an insignificant student's identity. There must have been something wrong about him, they argued, or he would not have been arrested, and the safest thing to do with him was to send him to Siberia, whoever he might be—and to Siberia he was sent. When the convoy officer called the roll of the out-going exile party, Vladímir Sidórski failed to answer to Victor Sidórski's name, and the officer, with a curse, cried " Victor Sidórski! Why don't you answer to your name?"

"It is not my name," replied Vladímir, " and I won't answer to it. It 's another Sidórski who ought to be going to Siberia."

" What is your name, then?"

Vladímir told him. The officer coolly erased the name " Victor" in the roll of the party, inserted the name " Vladímir," and remarked cynically, " It does n't make a —— bit of difference!"

In the years 1877, 1878, and 1879, no attempt was made, apparently, by the Government to ascertain whether an arrested person was deserving of exile or not, nor even to ascertain whether the man or woman exiled was the identical person for whom the order of banishment had been issued. The whole system was a chaos of injustice, accident, and caprice. Up to November, 1878, as appears from an official circular to provincial governors, the local authorities did not even take the trouble to make a report of political arrests to the Minister of the Interior.[1] If a man was taken into custody as a political offender, that, in many cases, was the end of it so far as an investigation was concerned. The fact that he had been arrested by mistake, or in the place of some other person, did not necessarily insure his release. The local authorities reversed the humane rule of Catharine II. and acted, in political cases, upon the principle that it is better to punish ten innocent persons than to allow one criminal to escape.

The above-cited case of the student Sidórski is by no means exceptional. In the open letter to the Tsar for which Madame Tsébrikova has recently been exiled to the province of Vólogda, the reader will find a brief statement of a similar case in which two brothers were banished by mistake in place of two other brothers of like name but of different family. The banished young men were the sole support of their widowed mother and a fifteen-year-old sister. When, at last, the blunder was discovered and the innocent brothers were permitted to return to their home, they found that their mother had died of grief and privation, and that, after her death, their child-sister had been sold by a boarding-house keeper into a house of prostitution. "What must have been the feeling of those young men towards the Government," Madame Tsébrikova asks, "when they came back and were informed of their mother's death and their sister's shame?" In the light of such facts terrorism ceases to be an unnatural or an inexplicable phenomenon. Wrong a man in that way, deny him all redress, exile him again if he complains, gag him if he cries out, strike him in the face if he struggles, and at last he will stab and throw bombs. It is useless to say that the Russian Government does not exasperate men and women in this way.

[1] Circular letter from the Department of Executive Police No. 159, November 4, 1878, in "Prison Circulars," p. 655. Ministry of the Interior, St. Petersburg, 1880.

The case of Madame Tsébrikova herself is a recent case in point. For merely writing out the above story of injustice and other stories like it, and sending them to Alexander III. with an earnest and respectful letter imploring him to right such wrongs, Madame Tsébrikova has been exiled by administrative process to a remote village in the province of Vólogda. The only results of her letter were a decree of banishment and a contemptuous inquiry from the Tsar, " What business is it of hers ? "

The two things that are most exasperating to a liberal and warm-hearted young Russian are, first, official lawlessness [*próizvól*] in the sphere of personal rights, and second, the suffering brought by such lawlessness upon near relatives and dear friends. In exile by administrative process these two exasperating agencies operate conjointly. The suffering of a loved wife, or the loss of an affectionate child, is hard enough to bear when it comes in the ordinary course of nature and seems to be inevitable ; but when it comes as the direct result of unnecessary causes, such as injustice, tyranny, and official caprice, it has more than the bitterness of death, and it arouses fiercer passions than those that carry men into the storm of battle. As an illustration of this I will relate briefly the story of a young Russian surgeon who is known to a number of persons in the United States.

In the year 1879 there was living in the town of Ivángorod, in the province of Chernígof, a skilful and accomplished young surgeon named Dr. Biéli. Although he was a man of liberal views, he was not an agitator nor a revolutionist, and had taken no active part in political affairs. Some time in the late winter or early spring of 1879 there came to him, with letters of introduction, two young women who had been studying in one of the medical schools for women in St. Petersburg, and had been expelled and ordered to return to their homes in central Russia on account of their alleged political " untrustworthiness " [*neblagonadiózhnost*]. They were very anxious to complete their education and to fit themselves for useful work among the peasants; and they begged Dr. Biéli to aid them in their studies, to hear their recitations, and to allow them to make use of his library and the facilities of his office. As they were both in an "illegal" position,—that is, were living in a place where, without permission from the authorities, they had no right to be,—it was Dr. Biéli's duty as a loyal subject to hand them over to the police, regardless of the fact that they had come to him with letters of introduction and a petition for help. He happened, however, to be a man of courage, independence, and generous instincts; and, instead of betraying them, he listened with sympathy to their story, promised them his aid, introduced them to his wife, and began to give them lessons. The year 1879 in Russia was a year of intense revolutionary activity. Attempts were constantly being made by the terrorists to assassinate high Government officials; and the police, in all parts of the empire, were more than usually suspicious and alert. The visits of the young girls to Dr. Biéli's house and office soon attracted the attention of the local authorities in Ivángorod, and they took steps to ascertain who they were and where they had come from. An investigation showed that one of them was living on a forged passport, while the other had none, and that both had been expelled from St. Petersburg for political "untrustworthiness." Their unauthorized appearance in Ivángorod, when they should have been at their homes, and their half-secret visits—generally at night—to the house of Dr. Biéli were regarded as evidence of a political conspiracy, and on the 10th of May, 1879, both they and the young surgeon were arrested and exiled by administrative process to Siberia. Dr. Biéli eventually was sent to the arctic village of Verkhoyánsk, latitude 67.30°, in the province of Yakútsk, where he was seen in 1882 by Engineer Melville, Lieutenant Danenhower, Mr. W. H. Gilder, and all the survivors of the arctic exploring steamer *Jeannette*. At the time of Dr. Biéli's banishment, his wife, a beautiful young woman, twenty-four or twenty-five years of age, was expecting confinement, and was therefore unable to go to Siberia with him. As soon as possible, however, after the birth of her child, and before she had fully recovered her strength, she left her nursing baby with relatives and started on a journey of more than 6000 miles to join her husband in a village situated north of the arctic circle and near the Asiatic pole of cold. She had not the necessary means to make such a journey by rail, steamer, and post, as Lieutenant Schuetze made it in 1885–86, and was therefore forced to ask permission of the Minister of the Interior to travel with a party of exiles.[1] As far as the city of Tomsk in Western Siberia both political and common-criminal exiles are transported in convict trains or barges. Beyond that point the common criminals walk, and the politicals are carried in *telégas*, at the rate of about sixty miles a week, stopping in an *étape* every third day for rest. At this rate of progress Mrs. Biéli would have reached her husband's place of exile only after sixteen months of incessant hardship, privation, and suffering. But she did not reach it. For many weeks her hope, courage, and love sustained her, and enabled her to endure without complaint the jolting, the suffocating dust, the scorching heat, and the cold autumnal rains on the road, the bad food, the plank sleeping-benches, the vermin, and the pestilential air of the *étapes;* but human endurance has its limits. Three or four months of this unrelieved misery, with constant anxiety about her husband and the baby that, for her husband's sake, she had abandoned in Russia, broke down her health and her spirit. She sank into deep despondency and eventually began to show signs of mental aberration. After passing Krasnoyársk her con-

---

[1] By Russian law a wife may go to her exiled husband at the expense of the Government, provided she travels with an exile party, lives on the exile ration, sleeps in the roadside *étapes,* and submits generally to prison discipline.

dition became such that any sudden shock was likely completely to overthrow her reason—and the shock soon came. There are two villages in Eastern Siberia whose names are almost alike—Verkholénsk and Verkhoyánsk. The former is situated on the river Léna, only 180 miles from Irkútsk, while the latter is on the head-waters of the Yána, and is distant from Irkútsk nearly 2700 miles. As the party with which she was traveling approached the capital of Eastern Siberia, her hope, strength, and courage seemed to revive. Her husband she thought was only a few hundred miles away, and in a few more weeks she would be in his arms. She talked of him constantly, counted the *verst*-posts which measured her slow progress towards him, and literally lived upon the expectation of speedy reunion with him. A few stations west of Irkútsk she accidentally became aware, for the first time, that her husband was not in Verkholénsk, but in Verkhoyánsk; that she was still separated from him by nearly 3000 miles of mountain, steppe, and forest; and that in order to reach his place of banishment that year she would have to travel many weeks on dog or reindeer sledges, in terrible cold, through the arctic solitudes of northeastern Asia. The sudden shock of this discovery was almost immediately fatal. She became violently insane, and died insane a few months later in the Irkútsk prison hospital, without ever seeing again the husband for whose sake she had endured such mental and physical agonies.

I have been compelled to restrict myself to the barest outline of this terrible tragedy; but if the reader could hear the story, as I heard it, from the lips of exiles who traveled with Mrs. Biéli, and who saw the flickering spark of her reason go out, in an East Siberian *étape*, he would not wonder that exile by administrative process makes terrorists, but rather that it does not make a nation of terrorists.[2]

---

[2] My authorities for the facts of this case are: first, a well-known member of a Russian provincial assembly, a man of the highest character, who was

A recent writer in the German periodical *Unsere Zeit* of Leipzig, who signs himself "A Russian Resident of Eastern Siberia," and who is, apparently, a sincere and earnest man, attempts to lay the whole responsibility for exile by administrative process upon the Russian revolutionists. He admits the truth of all I have said on the subject, and acknowledges that "no man knows at what moment he may be seized and cast into prison or doomed to exile without even a hearing"; but he declares that "all this has been brought upon us by a band so vile — so horribly vile — that their crimes are without parallel. . . . . But for the nihilists of Kará there would have never been any administrative exile." [1]   The "Russian Resident of Eastern Siberia," however, is as much mistaken in the explanation that he gives of the origin of administrative exile, as in the character

personally cognizant of the circumstances attending Dr. Biéli's arrest and banishment; second, exiles who went to Siberia in the same party with Dr. Biéli; and third, exiles — one of them a lady — who were in the same party with Dr. Biéli's wife.

[1] The passages of the "Russian Resident's" article to which I desire to call the reader's attention are as follows: "And now came the most terrible calamity of all — the delegation by the Tsar to the administrative authorities of the power of exile, which, until then, had been the imperial prerogative. It was a measure resorted to in a time of terrible necessity, when the nihilists, in the indulgence of their bloody phantasy, were recklessly wielding the assassin's dagger, and not hesitating even to hurl railway trains to destruction by dynamite. The power of exile was committed to the administration as a means of precaution. The governors-general were intrusted with power to banish all suspected persons. It appeared to be the only possible means to counteract the nefarious doings of these dark conspirators. It was an unfortunate decision and a

serious error. It did not save the Tsar and has done nothing for the suppression of nihilism; but the incalculable evil and misery to which the wretched system has reduced us is indescribable. What Kennan writes on this head is true, every word of it. The word *neblagonadiózhni* [untrustworthy] has become a curse-word in the Russian language and will be recalled with a shudder by latest generations. This is the unspeakable misery that the terrorists have plunged us into with their murders. From the day this power was delegated, no man knows at what moment he may be seized and cast into prison or doomed to exile without even a hearing. All this has been brought upon us by a band so vile — so horribly vile — that their crimes are without parallel; young people from eighteen to twenty-three, without ideals, without moral restraint, without regard for family, fatherland, or station, spreading blood and ruin at the prompting of their presumptuous fancies. . . . . . The same author who knew so well how to stir our sympathies for undeserved sorrow wields his pen with equal facility in denunciation of the just fate that he attributes to the Russian revolutionists. Exile by administrative process is not a new thing in Russia,[1] nor was it first resorted to by the Russian Government as an extraordinary and exceptional measure of self-defense in the struggle with the revolutionists. It is older than nihilism, it is older than the modern revolutionary movement, it is older than the imperial house of Románof. It has been practised for centuries as a short and easy method of dealing with people who happen to be obnoxious or in

of a band of profligates. . . . . . Are Kennan and Frost, perhaps, of opinion that the murders of Lincoln and Garfield are to be reckoned as benefactions to the race? Did it never occur to Kennan that for all the nameless miseries which he depicts in the first part of his book" [the first of my magazine articles republished in Germany in book form] "we are indebted to the heroes of the second part—that but for the nihilists of Kará there never would have been any administrative exile?" [*Unsere Zeit*, Leipzig, August, 1890. Translation in the *Literary Digest* of the same month and year.]

I shall recur in a later chapter to the controverted question of the moral character of the Russian revolutionists, but, in the meantime, it may not be out of place to ask the "Russian Resident of Eastern Siberia" whether it never occurred to him that an unprejudiced investigator who, he admits, is perfectly right in his description of Siberian prisons, right "beyond question" in his account of common-criminal exile, and right "to a word" in his statements concerning administrative banishment, may, possibly, be right also in his estimate of the character of men with whom he lived for a whole year upon terms of the closest intimacy? Did it never occur to the "Russian Resident" that a man who tells the exact truth in ninety-nine consecutive instances is likely to tell the exact truth also in the one hundredth, unless there be, in that particular case, some good and previously

non-existent reason for deception or error?

[1] Administrative punishments generally, as distinguished from judicial punishments, have been inflicted in Russia from the very dawn of history. At the beginning of the eighteenth century the right to inflict punishment by administrative process was vested in more than twenty different classes of Russian officials, including governors, vice-governors, *voevóds*, commandants, chiefs of detective police, ecclesiastical authorities, chiefs of provincial bureaus, excise officers, landed proprietors, chief foresters, post-station masters, officers of the mints, and managers of Government salt works. Most of these officials were empowered not only to exile at their own discretion, but to confiscate property, to inflict torture, to brand, and to flog with the *knut*. For references to the laws that conferred such powers upon Russian officials see "Personal Detention as a Police Measure to Insure Public Safety," by I. Tarásof, Professor of Criminal Law and Jurisprudence in the Demídof Juridical Lyceum, part 2, p. 9. Yaroslavl, 1886. Exile by administrative process is also specifically authorized in the "Statutes Relating to the Anticipative Prevention and Frustration of Crime," articles 1, 300, 316, and 334–339; in the "Exile Statutes," article 11, and in article 667, part 1, Vol. II, of the "Collection of Russian Laws." All of these legal enactments originated long prior to the existence in Russia of a revolutionary party.

the way, but who cannot conveniently be tried or convicted in a court of justice. If the "Russian Resident of Eastern Siberia" will read attentively the works of Tarásof, Sergéyefski, Maxímof, and Anúchin, he will find that administrative exile has been not only a recognized, but a well established, method of dealing with certain classes of offenders ever since the seventeenth century. In the reign of the Emperor Nicholas, for example, nihilism had not been so much as heard of,— the very word was unknown,— and yet men and women were being exiled to Siberia by administrative process, not in hundreds merely, but in thousands, and not only by order of the Tsar, but by order of the administrative authorities, by order of the ecclesiastical authorities, by order of the village communes, and even by order of private landowners. Most of them, it is true, were not political offenders; but they were none the less entitled to a trial, and they were all victims of the system that the "Russian Resident" says was brought into existence half a century later, "in a time of terrible necessity, as the only possible means to counteract the nefarious doings of those dark conspirators," the nihilists.

The careful and exhaustive researches of Anúchin in the archives of the chief exile bureau [*Prikáz o Sílnikh*] at Tobólsk, show that between 1827 and 1846 there was not a year in which the number of persons sent to Siberia by administrative process fell below three thousand, and that it reached a maximum, for a single year, of more than six thousand.[1] The aggregate number for the twenty-year period is

[1] The precise figures are as follows:

1827	6,326	1837	3,976
1828	5,613	1838	4,077
1829	3,509	1839	4,552
1830	3,377	1840	4,683
1831	4,050	1841	4,125
1832	3,395	1842	3,737
1833	3,371	1843	4,067
1834	3,134	1844	3,741
1835	3,618	1845	3,184
1836	4,469	1846	2,905

Total 79,909

See "An Investigation of the Percentages of Siberian Exiles," by E. N. Anúchin, chap. ii, p. 22. Memoirs of the Imperial Russian Geographical Society, Statistical Section, Vol. III, St. Petersburg, 1873.

As an evidence of the trustworthiness of Mr. Anúchin's statistics, it is only proper to mention the fact that, for the great work above cited, the author was awarded the Constantine medal of the Imperial Russian Geographical Society

79,909. It can hardly be contended, I think, that the nihilists or the terrorists are responsible for a system that had sent eighty thousand persons to Siberia without judicial trial, long before such a thing as a nihilist or a terrorist was known, and before most of the modern Russian revolutionists were born. The "Russian Resident of Eastern Siberia" has simply put the cart before the horse. It was administrative exile, administrative caprice, and the absence of orderly and legal methods in political cases generally, that caused terrorism, and not terrorism that necessitated official lawlessness. The wolf always contends, with a show of virtuous indignation, that while he was peacefully drinking as usual, the lamb muddied the brook, and thus compelled him to "take exceptional measures for the reëstablishment of public tranquillity"; but his statement is very properly discredited when it appears that he was above the lamb on the brook, and that, for years, he had been taking "exceptional measures" of the same kind with other lambs that had not been near the brook. To defend or to justify the crimes of the terrorists is not the object of my work; but when the history of the nineteenth century in Russia shall have been written by some one having access to the secret archives of the Ministry of the Interior and the Third Section of the Tsar's Chancellery, it will appear, I think, to the satisfaction of all men, that most of the so-called terroristic crimes in Russia were committed, not, as the "Russian Resident" asserts, by "bloodthirsty tigers in human form at the prompting of

for 1869. The book was intended to comprise two volumes, but the second volume, containing statistics of the exile system since 1846, has never appeared, owing to "circumstances over which the author has no control." The censor has even mutilated the first volume by striking out Anúchin's condemnation of exile by administrative process—the very subject now under consideration. The author's expres- sions of disapproval are contained in the copy sent to the Smithsonian Institution at Washington, but they are not to be found in my copy, nor in any other of later date than the first edition. The fact is not without interest as a significant proof that the Russian Government itself is ashamed of this atrociously unjust form of exile, although not yet willing to abandon it.

presumptuous fancies," but by ordinary men and women exasperated to the pitch of desperation by administrative suppression of free speech and free thought, administrative arrest without warrant, administrative imprisonment for years upon suspicion, administrative banishment to the arctic regions without trial, and, to crown all, administrative denial of every legal remedy and every peaceful means of redress.

It is true that in 1879, as a result of the criminal activity of the terrorists, martial law was declared throughout European Russia, unlimited discretionary power was given to governors-general, and exile by administrative process, as a quick and convenient method of dealing with political suspects, was expressly authorized by the Tsar; but the imperial authorization was nothing more than a formal sanction of a preëxisting measure, and an intimation that it might, thenceforth, be given a wider scope. To say that this form of exile was previously unknown, and that it was forced upon the Government by the crimes of the terrorists, is to set chronology at naught and to ignore all the historical facts of the case. The first attempt on the part of the terrorists to assassinate a Government official was the attempt of Véra Zasúlich to kill General Trepof, the St. Petersburg chief of police, on the 5th of February, 1878. Administrative exile for political reasons had then been common for almost a decade. If I mistake not, Véra Zasúlich herself had been one of its victims seven or eight years before. I think she was one of twenty or thirty persons who were tried before a special session of the Governing Senate in 1871 upon the charge of complicity in the Necháief conspiracy, who were judicially declared to be not guilty, but who were immediately rearrested, nevertheless, and exiled by administrative process, in defiance of all law and in contemptuous disregard of the judgment of the highest court in the empire. A government that acts in this way sows dragons' teeth and has no right to complain of the harvest. The so-called "propagandists" of 1870-74 did not resort to violence in any form, and did not even make a practice of resisting arrest, until after the Government had begun to exile them to Siberia for life with ten or twelve years of penal servitude, for offenses that were being punished at the very same time in Austria with only a few days—or at most a few weeks—of personal detention.[1] It was not terrorism that necessitated administrative exile in Russia; it was merciless severity and banishment without due process of law that provoked terrorism.

In the latter part of the reign of Alexander II., and particularly between the years 1870 and 1880, administrative exile was resorted to, in political cases, upon a scale never before known, and with a recklessness and cynical indifference to personal rights that were almost unparalleled. In Odessa, General Todleben, by virtue of the unlimited discretionary power given him in the Imperial *ukáz* of April 17, 1879, proceeded to banish, without inquiry or discrimination, the whole "politically untrustworthy" class—that is, to exile every person whose loyalty to the existing Government was even doubtful.[2] The mere fact that a man had been registered as a suspect in the books of the secret police, or had been accused, even anonymously, of political disaffection, was a sufficient reason for his deportation to the remotest part of the empire. Parents who had never had a disloyal thought were exiled because their children had become revolutionists; school-boys who happened to be acquainted with political offenders were exiled because they had not betrayed the latter to the police;

1 See the reference by W. R. S. Ralston to the trial of Austrian socialists at Lemberg in March, 1877. ["Russian Revolutionary Literature," by W. R. S. Ralston, *Nineteenth Century*, May, 1877, p. 413.] See also official report of the trial of Austrian socialists in Cracow, where the severest sentence imposed was one month of imprisonment.[Newspaper *Golos*, St. Petersburg, 1880, Nos. 122, 123, 125, 126, 127, and 128.]

2 See the article upon Count Lóris-Mélikof in the Russian historical review *Rússkaya Stariná* for the month of January, 1889, p. 62.

teachers were exiled for circulating copies of the Russian magazine *Annals of the Fatherland;* members of provincial assemblies were exiled because they insisted upon their right to petition the crown for the redress of grievances; and university students who had been tried for political crime and duly acquitted by the courts were immediately rearrested and exiled by administrative process, in violation of the most elementary principles of justice.

In December, 1879, a young revolutionist — a Jew — named Maidánski, was hanged in Odéssa by sentence of a court-martial for having taken part in a conspiracy to assassinate a Government spy named Gorinóvich. His old father and mother, who lived in Elizabethgrad, came to Odéssa to have a last interview with him before he should be put to death; but the authorities, instead of allowing the aged parents to see their condemned son, promptly arrested them both and sent them to Eastern Siberia by administrative process. They were nothing but poor illiterate peasants, and there was not the least evidence to show that they had encouraged their son's criminal activity, or even that they had been aware of it; but the opinion of the Government seemed to be that they deserved punishment for having brought such a son into the world. It may be thought, in the light of more recent events, that they were treated in this merciless way because they were Jews; but the Government, at that time, was dealing in precisely the same manner with orthodox Russians belonging to the educated and privileged classes.

In the late summer or early fall of 1879 two educated young women from Nikoláief — the sisters Livandófskaya — were exiled for political reasons to different parts of Eastern Siberia. One of them, named Véra, was banished by administrative process to Mínusínsk in the province of Yeniséisk, while the other was sentenced by a court-martial to forced colonization in the little town of Kírensk on the river Léna.[1] If the Government had been satisfied with the deportation of these two young women only, there would have been nothing unusual or particularly noteworthy in the case; but it went much further than this. The family of the two exiled girls consisted of a father aged about seventy, a mother aged fifty-five or sixty, and two younger sisters fifteen and sixteen years of age respectively.

After the banishment of Véra and the other elder sister to Eastern Siberia, all the remaining members of the family were exiled by administrative process for a term of three years to a village near the sub-arctic coast of the White Sea in the province of Archángel. As long as their term of banishment lasted they received a small monthly allowance from the Government for their maintenance, and so managed to exist; but when, in 1882, they were informed that they were at liberty to return to Nikoláief, and that their allowance would no longer be paid to them, they were left without any means of support in the place where they were, and had no money with which to get back to their home. They wrote a piteous letter to Véra in Mínusínsk, describing their sufferings and their almost helpless situation, and Véra, upon receipt of it, determined to make her escape, return to European Russia, and there, under an assumed name, earn money enough, if possible, to bring her aged parents and her two younger sisters back to their home in Nikoláief. Her attempt to escape was successful, she reached European Russia in safety, and began, in the city of Kiev, her search for employment. Failing to get anything to do, she used up, little by little, the small sum of money that she had brought with her from Siberia, and at last, to escape starvation, she was forced, in despair, to give herself up to the police. She lay for some months in

[1] Véra was first banished in 1878 to the village of Velíki Ústia in the European province of Vólogda. When, about a year later, her sister, with twenty-seven other political offenders, was tried by court-martial in Odéssa and sentenced to forced colonization in Kírensk, Véra was rearrested and exiled to Mínusínsk.

prison, while the authorities were investigating her story, and was then sent back to Mínusínsk. In the meantime her aged father and mother had succeeded in obtaining from friends money enough to get as far south as Moscow, and when the unfortunate daughter passed through that city on her way to Eastern Siberia, her parents and sisters, whom she had hoped to help, came to see her in prison and were permitted to have a brief interview with her. Véra subsequently married, in Mínusínsk, the talented young author, publicist, and political exile, Iván Petróvich Belokónski, and lived there with him until the termination of her period of banishment. She then returned to European Russia in order that she might help take care of her aged father, who had gone insane, and her feeble and almost heart-broken mother. At the time when we left Siberia, she, herself, was living with her parents in the city of Kiev, her exiled husband was more than three thousand miles away in Mínusínsk, and her exiled sister was more than four thousand miles away on the head-waters of the river Léna.

To one who lives in a country where personal rights are secured by all sorts of legal and constitutional guarantees, it may seem, perhaps, that nothing could be more unjust and tyrannical than the banishment of an infirm father, an aged mother, and two helpless children, merely because certain other members of the family had become disloyal; but in the history of administrative exile in Russia there are things even more extraordinary and unreasonable than this.

Towards the close of the Russo-Turkish war of 1877-1878, when the conspicuous gallantry of General Skóbelef had attracted to him the attention of the world, and had made him the idol of enthusiastic young men throughout Russia, a large number of students in the university of Kiev undertook to give formal expression to their feeling of admiration for the great popular hero by getting up an address to him. There happened, at that time, to be more or less political excitement among a certain class of the Kiev university students, and the meetings that were held for the purpose of drafting and discussing the proposed address to Skóbelef were thought by the Government to have in view another and a more dangerous end.　They were soon prohibited, therefore, by the authorities, and several of the students who had taken a prominent part in them were arrested on suspicion, held for a time in prison, and then sent by administrative process to the northern province of Vólogda.　Among the students thus exiled was Iván N——, the son of a wealthy landed proprietor in Khersón.　When the young man had spent three or four months in the northern village to which he had been banished, his father, by means of a liberal expenditure of money, succeeded in getting him transferred to the province of Khersón, where the climate is milder than in Vólogda, and where the young exile was nearer his home.　He was still kept, however, under police surveillance, and was regarded by the authorities as "politically untrustworthy."　In April, 1879, General Todlében was appointed governor-general of Odéssa, with unlimited discretionary power, and as soon as he reached his post he proceeded to extirpate "sedition" in the provinces under his jurisdiction by banishing to Siberia, without trial or hearing, every man, woman, or child who was registered as a suspect in the books of the secret police, or who happened at that time to be under police surveillance. Among such persons was the unfortunate Kiev student Iván N——.　His transfer from the province of Vólogda to the province of Khersón had brought him within the limits of the territory subject to the authority of Governor-general Todlében, and had thus rendered his situation worse instead of better.　It was of no use for him to plead that the Government, in consenting to his transfer from a northern to a southern province, had intended to show him mercy, and that to send him to Siberia would be to punish him a second time, and with redoubled severity, for an action that was wholly innocent in the first place, and that ought not to have been punished at all. The chinóvniks in the office of the governor-general had no time to investigate or to make discriminations. The orders were to banish to Siberia all persons then under police surveillance ; and if they should once begin to inquire, and investigate, and grant hearings, they would never get anybody banished at all. If he felt aggrieved he could send a petition to the Minister of the Interior from Siberia. All the young man's efforts to get his case reconsidered on its merits were fruitless, and in the summer of 1879 he was sent to Eastern Siberia by administrative process. In the prison of Krasnoyársk, where the exile party to which he belonged was detained for a few days, a misunderstanding of some sort arose between the prison officials and the politicals, in the course of which the latter became insubordinate and turbulent. The inspector of exile transportation came to the prison in a state of semi-intoxication to quiet the disturbance, and while he was haranguing and threatening the politicals, one of them exclaimed ironically, " Vazhno ! " which may be rendered in English, " How important we are ! " The inspector was beside himself with fury, and, not being able to find out who had uttered the offensive exclamation, he caused all the prisoners in that *kámera* to be sent to the sub-arctic territory of Yakútsk. The young student from Kiev was not a political and had taken no active part in the disorder, but he happened to be in the cell from which the ironical cry, " Vazhno ! " came, and that circumstance alone was sufficient to send him to the arctic regions. In the next five years of enforced solitude he had ample time to reflect upon the danger of falling under suspicion in a country where the will of a *chinóvnik* is the law of the land, and where patriotic admiration for a great general may be punished as severely as an assault with intent to kill. The Persian poet Saadi, who evidently saw practised at Bagdad in the twelfth century the same governmental

methods that prevail in Russia now, tells a story in the
"Gulistan" of a terror-stricken fox who was seen limping and
running away, and who, upon being asked what he was
afraid of, replied, " I hear they are going to press a camel
into the service."

" Well, what of it ?"said the interrogator; "what relation-
ship is there between that animal and you ? "

" Be silent ! " rejoined the fox.   " If the malignant, out
of evil design, should say, ' This is a camel,' who would
be so solicitous for my relief as to order an inquiry
into my case? and 'before the antidote can be brought
from Irak he who has been bitten by the serpent may
be dead.'"

In the year 1879 there was living in the Russian city of
Pultáva a poor apothecary named Schiller, who desired for
some reason to change the location of his place of business.
As druggists in Russia are not allowed to migrate from one
town to another without the permission of the Government,
Schiller wrote to the Minister of the Interior, stating his
desire to move and the reasons for it, and asking that he
be authorized to close his shop in Pultáva and open another
in Kharkóf.   Week after week passed without bringing
any answer to his request.   At last, the Minister of the Interior happened to stop in Pultáva for a day or two on one
of his journeys from St. Petersburg to the Crimea, and
Schiller, regarding this as a providential opportunity, attempted to get an interview with him for the purpose of
presenting his petition in person.   Of course the guard at
the door of the house occupied by the Minister refused to
admit a poor apothecary with a paper, and Schiller, indignant at what he thought was an injustice, wrapped his
petition around a stone, to give it weight, and threw it into
the window of the Minister's room.   He was at once arrested
and imprisoned, and a few months later, upon the charge
of having behaved in a disorderly manner and shown gross
disrespect to the higher authorities, he was banished by

administrative process, as a political offender, to the village of Varnavin in the province of Kostromá. This was not regarded by the authorities as a particularly severe punishment; but Schiller, finding enforced residence in an unfamiliar village to be irksome and tedious, and having no further confidence in petitions, changed his location between sunset and dawn without asking leave of anybody — in other words, ran away. About this time the Tsar issued a *poveléinie,* or command, directing that all administrative exiles found absent from their places of banishment without leave should be sent to the East-Siberian province of Yakútsk.[1] When, therefore, a few months later, Schiller was rearrested in a part of the empire where he had no right to be, he was sent by *étape* to Irkútsk, and the governor-general of Eastern Siberia was requested to put him under police surveillance in some part of the territory named in the Imperial command. Governor-general Anúchin, who had then recently come to Irkútsk, and who had not had time, apparently, to familiarize himself with the vast region intrusted to his care,[2] directed that Schiller be sent to the district town of Zashíversk, which was supposed to be situated on the river Indigírka, a few miles south of the arctic circle. A century or a century and a half ago, this

[1] This Imperial command was issued on the 2d of April, 1880, and was intended to discourage attempts on the part of political exiles to escape. In the hands of local police officials it was soon made an instrument for the punishment of politicals who incurred their hostility. The first time, for example, that an obnoxious exile went two hundred yards beyond the limits of the village — perhaps only into a neighboring forest to gather flowers or berries — he was arrested upon the charge of attempting to escape and immediately banished to the province of Yakútsk — the wildest part of northeastern Asia. It made little difference whether the charge rested upon any basis of fact or not. In the latter part of the year 1880, a political named Peter Mikháilovich Volokhóf — an acquaintance of the Russian novelist Korolénko — was banished to the province of Yakútsk for an alleged attempt to escape from Archángel. As a matter of fact he had never even been in Archángel, much less attempted to escape from there.

[2] Eastern Siberia has an area considerably greater than that of the United States and Alaska taken together, and most of the vast territory of Yakútsk is as wild and unsettled as the northern part of British North America.

town of Zashíversk was a place of considerable local importance ; but, for some reason, it lost its preëminence as a fur-trading center, fell gradually into decay, and finally ceased to exist. Its location was still marked with two concentric circles on all the maps,[1] its name continued to appear annually in the records of the governor-general's office, and I have no doubt that a coterie of *chinóvniks* in Irkútsk were dividing and pocketing every year the money appropriated for repairs to its public buildings; but, as a matter of fact, it had not contained a building nor an inhabitant for more than half a century, and forest trees were growing on the mound that marked the site of its *ostróg*.[2] Poor Schiller, after having been carried three or four thousand miles up and down the rivers Léna and Indigírka in a vain search for a non-existent arctic town, was finally brought back to Yakútsk; and a report was made to the governor-general that Zashíversk, apparently, had ceased to exist. The governor-general thereupon ordered that the prisoner be taken to Srédni Kolímsk, another " town " of forty-five houses, situated on the river Kolymá north of the arctic circle, 3700 miles from Irkútsk and 7500 miles from the capital of the empire. When, after more than a year of *étape* life, the unfortunate druggist from Pultáva reached the last outpost of Russian power in northeastern Asia and was set at liberty, he made his way to the little log church, entered the belfry, and proceeded to jangle the church bells in a sort of wild, erratic chime. When the

[1] It is shown as a district town on an official map of the Russian general staff published as late as 1883.

[2] The site of Zashíversk is about 3200 miles by the usually traveled route from Irkútsk and about 7000 miles from St. Petersburg. Exiles have been sent there more than once. A political named Pik very nearly starved to death there in the reign of Catherine II., from which I infer that the town was virtually extinct before the beginning of the present century. Seventy-five or eighty years later, however, Governor-general Fredericks is said to have sent there a drunken and incorrigible exile named Tsigankof, who had been banished to Siberia for impertinence to a gendarme officer in a St. Petersburg restaurant. [See newspaper *Volzhski Vestnik*, Kazán, September 23, 1885, and newspaper *Vostochnoe Obozrénie*, St. Petersburg, April 24, 1886, p. 9.]

people of the town ran to the belfry in alarm and inquired what was the matter, Schiller replied with dignity that he wished the whole population to know that by the grace of God, Herman Augustóvich Schiller, after long and perilous wanderings, had reached in safety the town of Srédni Kolímsk. Whether the mind of the exile had given way under the prolonged strain of hardship and suffering, or whether, as some assert, he had become intoxicated and rang the church bells merely as a drunken freak, I do not know; but the local police reported to the governor-general that the "political" exile Schiller was disorderly and turbulent, and that he had caused a public scandal before he had been in Srédni Kolímsk twenty-four hours. Upon this report the governor-general indorsed an order to remove the offender to some place at least twelve versts distant from the town. His idea probably was to have Schiller sent to some small suburban village in the general neighborhood of Srédni Kolímsk, but far enough away so that he could not easily get into the town to make a disturbance. Unfortunately there was no suburban village within a hundred versts in any direction, and the local authorities, not knowing what else to do, carried the wretched druggist about twelve versts out into the primeval wilderness, erected a log cabin for him, and left him there — assuring him cheerfully, as they bade him good-by, that "káknibúd" [somehow or other] he would get along. With a little help occasionally from wandering Chúkchi and Tongusí he did get along, catching fish, gathering berries, and snaring ptarmigan for his subsistence, and living, for several years, the life of a continental Crusoe. What eventually became of him I do not know.

Of course cases of this kind are exceptional. The Russian Government does not make a practice of sending to the arctic regions druggists who wish to change their places of business, neither does it regularly banish to the territory of Yakútsk students who express admiration for Skóbelef.

Nevertheless, under a system of administration that allows an irresponsible official to punish at his own discretion, such results are not only possible but probable.

In the year 1874, a young student named Egór Lázaref was arrested in one of the south-eastern provinces of European Russia upon the charge of carrying on a secret revolutionary propaganda. He was taken to St. Petersburg and kept in solitary confinement in the House of Preliminary Detention and in the fortress of Petropávlovsk for about four years. He was then tried with one hundred and ninety-two other political suspects before the Governing Senate, found to be not guilty, and acquitted.[1] As there still existed, however, a possibility that he might be guilty on some future occasion, he was punished in advance by being sent as a soldier to a regiment then engaged in active service in the Trans-Cáucasus.[2] One would suppose that to be arrested without cause, to be held four years in solitary confinement, to be declared innocent by the highest court in the empire, and then to be punished with compulsory military service in Asia Minor for an offense prophetically foreseen, but not yet committed, would make a revolutionist, if not a terrorist, out of the most peaceable citizen; but Mr. Lázaref, as soon as he had been released from the army, quietly completed his education in the university, studied law, and began the practice of his profession in the city of Sarátof on the Vólga. He had no more trouble with the Government until the summer of 1884, when a police

[1] Official certified copy of the sentence in the case of "the 193," p. 8.

[2] This was a favorite method of Nicholas for the punishment of literary men and students whose opinions were too liberal for his taste. He compelled the gifted Russian poet Shevchénko to serve ten years as a common soldier, and kept him most of that time in the hottest and most desolate part of Central Asia — the district of Mángishlák. The talented novelist Dostoyéfski was also forced to serve as a common soldier after the expiration of his term of hard labor in the Omsk convict prison. I cannot now recall any case in which Nicholas insulted his own courts by punishing administratively persons whom they had just declared to be innocent, but such cases were common in the reign of Alexander II. Most of the prisoners acquitted by the Senate in the trial of "the 193" were immediately rearrested and banished by administrative process, or sent as common soldiers into the ranks.

officer suddenly appeared to him one morning and said that the governor of the province would like to see him. Mr. Lázaref, who was on pleasant personal terms with the governor, went at once to the latter's office, where he was coolly informed that he was to be exiled by administrative process to Eastern Siberia for three years. Mr. Lázaref stood aghast.

"May I ask your high excellency for what reason?" he finally inquired.

"I do not know," replied the governor. "I have received orders to that effect from the Ministry of the Interior, and that is all I know about it."

Through the influence of friends in St. Petersburg, Mr. Lázaref obtained a respite of two weeks in which to settle up his affairs, and he was then sent as a prisoner to Moscow. He reached that city after the last party of political exiles had been despatched for the season, and had to live in the Moscow forwarding prison until the next spring. While there he wrote a respectful letter to the Department of Imperial Police, asking, as a favor, that he might be informed for what reason he was to be exiled to Eastern Siberia. The reply that he received was comprised in two lines, and was as follows: "You are to be put under police surveillance in Eastern Siberia because you have not abandoned your previous criminal activity." In other words, he was to be banished to the Trans-Baikál because he had not "abandoned" the "previous criminal activity" of which a court of justice had found him not guilty! In the Moscow forwarding prison, soon after Mr. Lázaref's arrival, a number of the political prisoners were comparing experiences one day, and asking one another for what offenses they had been condemned to banishment. One said that forbidden books had been found in his house; another said that he had been accused of carrying on a revolutionary propaganda; and a third admitted that he had been a member of a secret society. Finally Mr. Lázaref's turn came, and upon being asked why he was on his way to Siberia, he replied simply, " I don't know."

" Don't know!" exclaimed one of his comrades. " Did n't your father have a black-and-white cow?"

"Very likely," said Mr. Lázaref. " He had a lot of cows."

" Well!" rejoined his comrade triumphantly, "what more would you have? That 's enough to exile twenty men — and yet he says he does n't know!"

On the 10th of May, 1885, Mr. Lázaref left Moscow with an exile party for Siberia, and on the 10th of October, 1885, after twenty-two weeks of travel "by *étape*," reached the town of Chíta, in the Trans-Baikál, where I had the pleasure of making his acquaintance.

The grotesque injustice, the heedless cruelty, and the preposterous "mistakes" and " misunderstandings" that make the history of administrative exile in Russia seem to an American like the recital of a wild nightmare are due to the complete absence, in the Russian form of government, of checks upon the executive power, and the almost equally complete absence of official responsibility for unjust or illegal action. The Minister of the Interior, in dealing with politicals, is almost wholly unrestrained by law; and as it is utterly impossible for him personally to examine all of the immense number of political cases that come to him for final decision, he is virtually forced to delegate a part of his irresponsible power to chiefs of police, chiefs of gendarmes, governors of provinces, and subordinates in his own ministry. They in turn are compelled, for similar reasons, to intrust a part of their authority and discretion to officers of still lower grade; and the latter, who often are stupid, ignorant, or unscrupulous men, are the persons who really make the investigations, the searches, and the examinations upon which the life or liberty of an accused citizen may depend. Theoretically, the Minister of the Interior, aided by a council composed of three of his own subordinates and two officers from the Ministry of Justice, reviews and reëxamines the cases of all political offenders who are dealt with by administrative process;[1] but practically he does nothing of the kind, and it is impossible that he should do anything of the kind for the very simple reason that he has not the time.

In the years 1886 and 1887 there came before the Department of Justice 1883 political cases, involving no less than 2972 persons.[2] A very large proportion of these cases were dealt with by administrative process, and if the Minister of the Interior had given to each one of them a half, or one-quarter, of the study which was absolutely essential to a clear comprehension of it, he would have had no time to attend to anything else. As a matter of fact he did not give the cases such study, but, as a rule, simply signed the papers that came up to him from below. Of course he would not have signed the order for the exile of Mr. Korolénko to the province of Yakútsk if he had known that the whole charge against the young novelist was based on a mistake; nor would he have signed the order for the exile of Mr. Boródin if he had been aware that the magazine article for which the author was banished had been approved by the St. Petersburg Committee of Censorship. He accepted the statements passed up to him by a long line of subordinate officials, and signed his name merely as a formality and as a matter of course. How easy it is in Russia to get a high official's signature to any sort of a document may be illustrated by an anecdote that I have every reason to believe is absolutely true. A *stóla-nachálnik*, or head of a bureau, in the provincial administration of Tobólsk, while boasting one day about his power to shape and direct governmental action, made a wager with another *chinóvnik* that he could get the governor of the province — the late Governor Lisogórski — to sign a manuscript copy of the

[1] See "Rules Relating to Measures for the Preservation of National Order and Public Tranquillity." Appendix D.

[2] Report of the Minister of Justice for 1886-7.

Lord's Prayer. He wrote the prayer out in the form of an
official document on a sheet of stamped paper, numbered
it, attached the proper seal to it, and handed it to the governor with a pile of other papers which required signature.
He won his wager. The governor duly signed the Lord's
Prayer, and it was probably as harmless an official document as ever came out of his office.

How much of this sort of careless and reckless signing there
was in the cases of political offenders dealt with by administrative process may be inferred from the fact that, when
the liberal minister Loris-Melikof came into power in 1880,
he found it necessary to appoint a revisory commission,
under the presidency of General Cherévin, to investigate
the cases of persons who had been exiled and put under
police supervision by administrative process, and to correct,
so far as possible, the "mistakes," "misunderstandings,"
and "irregularities" against which the sufferers in all parts
of the empire began to protest as soon as the appointment
of a new Minister of the Interior gave them some reason to
hope that their complaints would be heeded. There were
said to be at that time 2800 political offenders in Siberia
and in various remote parts of European Russia who had
been exiled and put under police surveillance by administrative process. Up to the 23d of January, 1881, General
Cherévin's commission had examined the cases of 650 such
persons, and had recommended that 328, or more than half
of them, be immediately released and returned to their
homes.[1]

Of course the only remedy for such a state of things as
this is to take the investigation of political offenses out of
the hands of an irresponsible police, put it into the courts,
where it belongs, and allow the accused to be defended there
by counsel of their own selection. This remedy, however,
the Government persistently refuses to adopt. The Moscow

[1] An official announcement by the Government, quoted in the newspaper
Sibir for Jan. 31, 1881, p. 1.

Assembly of Nobles, at the suggestion of Mr. U. F. Samárin, one of its members, sent a respectful but urgent memorial to the Crown, recommending that every political exile who had been dealt with by administrative process should be given the right to demand a judicial investigation of his case. The memorial went unheeded, and the Government, I believe, did not even make a reply to it.[1]

Before the year 1882 the rights, privileges, and obligations of political offenders exiled to Siberia by administrative process were set forth only in secret circular-letters, sent from time to time by the Minister of the Interior to the governors of the different Siberian provinces. Owing to changes in the ministry, changes in circumstances, and changes of ministerial policy, these circular-letters of instruction ultimately became so contradictory, or so inconsistent one with another, and led to so many "misunderstandings," "irregularities," and collisions between the exiles and the local authorities in the Siberian towns and villages, that on the 12th of March, 1882, the Minister of the Interior drew up, and the Tsar approved, a set of rules for the better regulation of police surveillance and administrative exile. An official copy of this paper, which I brought back with me from Siberia, lies before me as I write. It is entitled: "Rules Relating to Police Surveillance" [Polozhénie o Politséiskom Nadzóre].[2] The first thing that strikes the reader in a perusal of this document is the fact that it declares exile and police surveillance to be, not *punishments* for crimes already committed, but measures of precaution to prevent the commission of crimes that evil-minded men may contemplate. The first section reads as follows: "Police surveillance [which includes administrative exile] is a means of preventing crimes against the existing imperial order [the present form of government]; and it is applicable to all persons who are prejudicial to public tranquillity."

1 Newspaper *Zemstvo*, 1881, No. 10, p. 21.

2 For a translation of these "Rules" see appendix D.

The power to decide when a man is " prejudicial to public tranquillity," and when exile and surveillance shall be resorted to as a means of " preventing crime," is vested in the governors-general, the governors, and the police; and in the exercise of that power they pay quite as much attention to the opinions that a man holds as to the acts that he commits. They can hardly do otherwise. If they should wait in all cases for the commission of criminal acts, they would not be "*preventing* crime," but merely watching and waiting for it, while the object of administrative exile is to *prevent* crime by anticipation. Clearly, then, the only thing to be done is to nip crime in the bud by putting under restraint, or sending to Siberia, every man whose political opinions are such as to raise a presumption that he *will* commit a crime "against the existing imperial order" if he sees a favorable opportunity for so doing. Administrative exile, therefore, is directed against ideas and opinions from which criminal acts may come, rather than against the criminal acts themselves. It is designed to anticipate and prevent the acts by suppressing or discouraging the opinions; and, such being the case, the document which lies before me should be called, not " Rules Relating to Police Surveillance," but " Rules for the Better Regulation of Private Opinion."[1] In the spirit of this latter title, the "Rules" are interpreted by most of the Russian police.

The pretense that administrative exile is not a punishment, but only a precaution, is a mere juggle with words. The Government says, " We do not exile a man and put him under police surveillance as a punishment for holding certain opinions, but only as a means of preventing him from giving such opinions outward expression in criminal

[1] This is the view of the " Rules" taken by the most competent Russian authorities. In the *Annals of the Fatherland* for May, 1882, will be found a very full discussion of administrative exile, with quotations from the principal newspapers of the empire to show the view generally taken of the " Rules," and some interesting and pertinent remarks by Professor Kistiakófski upon " punishment on suspicion."

acts." If the banishment of a man to the province of Yakútsk for five years is not a " punishment," then the word " punishment" must have in Russian jurisprudence a very peculiar and restricted signification. In the case of women and young girls a sentence of banishment to Eastern Siberia is almost equivalent to a sentence of death, on account of the terrible hardships of the journey and the bad sanitary condition of the *étapes* — and yet the Government says that exile by administrative process is not a punishment!

In 1884 a pretty and intelligent young girl named Sophia Nikítina, who was attending school in Kiev, was banished by administrative process to one of the remote provinces of Eastern Siberia. In the winter of 1884–85, when she had accomplished about 3000 miles of her terrible journey, she was taken sick, on the road between Tomsk and Áchinsk, with typhus fever, contracted in one of the pestilential *étapes*. Physicians are not sent with exile parties in Siberia, and politicals who happen to be taken sick on the road are carried forward, regardless of their condition and regardless of the weather, until the party comes to a lazaret, or prison hospital. There are only four such lazarets between Tomsk and Irkútsk, a distance of about a thousand miles, and consequently sick prisoners are sometimes carried in sleighs or telegas, at a snail's pace, for a week or two — if they do not die — before they finally obtain rest, a bed, and a physician. How many days of cold and misery Miss Nikítina endured on the road that winter after she was taken sick, and before she reached Áchinsk and received medical treatment, I do not know ; but in the Áchinsk lazaret her brief life ended. It must have been a satisfaction to her, as she lay dying in a foul prison hospital, 3000 miles from her home, to think that she was not undergoing "punishment" for anything that she had done, but was merely being subjected to necessary restraint by a parental Government, in order that she might not sometime be tempted to do something that would have a tendency to raise a presumption that her presence in Kiev was about to become more or less "prejudicial to public tranquillity."

I have not space for a quarter of the evidence that I collected in Siberia to show that administrative exile is not only cruelly unjust, but, in hundreds of cases, is a punishment of barbarous severity. If it attained the objects that it is supposed to attain, there might, from the point of view of a despotic Government, be some excuse if not justification for it; but it does not attain such objects. Regarded even from the side of expediency, it is uselessly and needlessly cruel. In a recent official report to the Minister of the Interior, Major-General Nicolái Baránof, the governor of the province of Archangel, in discussing the subject of administrative exile says:

From the experience of previous years, and from my own personal observation, I have come to the conclusion that administrative exile for political reasons is much more likely to spoil the character of a man than to reform it. The transition from a life of comfort to a life of poverty, from a social life to a life in which there is no society whatever, and from a life of activity to a life of compulsory inaction, produces such ruinous consequences, that, not infrequently, especially of late, we find the political exiles going insane, attempting to commit suicide, and even committing suicide. All this is the direct result of the abnormal conditions under which exile compels an intellectually cultivated person to live. There has not yet been a single case where a man, suspected with good reason of political untrustworthiness and exiled by administrative process, has returned from such banishment reconciled to the Government, convinced of his error, and changed into a useful member of society and a faithful servant of the Throne. On the other hand, it often happens that a man who has been exiled in consequence of a misunderstanding, or an administrative mistake, becomes politically untrustworthy for the first time in the place to which he has been banished — partly by reason of his association there with real enemies of the Government, and partly as a result of personal exasperation. Furthermore, if a man is infected with anti-Government ideas, all the circumstances of exile tend only to increase the infection, to sharpen his faculties, and to change him from a theoretical to a practical — that is, an extremely dangerous — man.   If, on the contrary, he has not been guilty of taking part in a revolutionary movement, exile, by force of the same circumstances, develops in his mind the idea of revolution, or, in other words, produces a result directly opposite to that which it was intended to produce.   No matter how exile by administrative process may be regulated and restricted, it will always suggest to the mind of the exiled person the idea of uncontrolled official license, and this alone is sufficient to prevent any reformation whatever.[1]

Truer words than these were never written by a high Russian official, and so far as the practical expediency of exile by administrative process is concerned, I should be content to rest the case against it upon this frank report of the governor of Archangel.   The subject, however, may be regarded from a point of view other than that of expediency — namely, from the point of view of morals, justice, and humanity.   That side of the question I shall reserve for further discussion in later chapters.

[1] *Juridical Messenger* (the journalistic organ of the Moscow Juridical Society, or Bar Association), October, 1883, p. 332.

CHAPTER XII

THE rapidity with which the season of good weather and good roads was passing, and the length and arduous nature of the journey that still lay before us, compelled us to make our stay in the city of Ust Kámenogórsk very brief. The work that we accomplished there, however, had an important bearing upon the prosecution of our researches in the field of political exile, and rendered our success in that field almost certain. I had always anticipated great difficulty in ascertaining where political exiles were to be found, and how they could be approached without the asking of too many dangerous questions. We could not expect in every town to stumble, by good luck, upon a liberal and sympathetic official who would aid us in our search, and yet experience had shown us the absolute necessity of knowing definitely in advance where to go and whom to approach. We had already passed through half a dozen towns or villages where there were colonies of interesting political exiles, and where, if we had been aware of their existence, we should have stopped; but we had no clues whatever to them, and I feared that if, in searching for clues, we made a practice of asking questions at random, we should soon attract the attention of the police and be called upon to explain what business we had with political exiles, and why we were everywhere looking them up. At Ust Kámenogórsk this source of embarrassment was finally removed. We not only obtained there a mass of useful information and a great number of valuable hints and suggestions, but we carried away with us notes, of recommendation to people who could aid us, letters of introduction to liberal officials in the towns through which we were yet to pass, and a manuscript list, or directory, in which were set forth the names, ages, professions, and places of banishment of nearly seven hundred political exiles in all parts of Siberia. After we had obtained these letters of introduction and this "underground" directory, the Government could have prevented us from investigating the exile system only by removing us forcibly from the country. We no longer had to grope our way by asking hazardous questions at random. We could take every step with a certainty of not making a mistake, and could go, in every village, directly to the persons whom we wished to see.

On Monday, August 10th, we dined for the last time with the politicals in Ust Kámenogórsk, sang to them once more, by special request, "John Brown's Body" and "The Starspangled Banner," and at six o'clock in the evening set out by post for Barnaül and Tomsk. The road, as far as the post-station of Piánoyarófskaya, was the same that we had followed in going from Semipalátinsk to the Altái Station. The country that it intersected seemed to us more parched and barren than ever, but here and there, in the moister places, we passed large flocks of fat-tailed sheep, guarded and watched by Kírghis horsemen, whose hooded heads and black faces, with the immense goggles of horsehair netting that they wore to protect their eyes from the glare of the sun, gave them an almost demoniacal appearance. Occasionally, in the outskirts of the villages, we saw fields of cultivated sunflowers, or of half-ripe watermelons and cantaloups; but as a rule the steppe was uncultivated and could not be cultivated without artificial irrigation. The weather was still very warm, and in almost every village we noticed naked children playing in the streets.

A POST-STATION ON THE BARNAÜL ROAD.

At Piánoyarófskaya we left the Semipalátinsk road and the valley of the Írtish, and, turning to the northward, crossed the low divide which separates the water-shed of the Írtish from that of the Ob, and entered the province of Tomsk. A large quantity of rain had fallen, and had been followed by a comfortable temperature; but the muddy roads hindered us, and the post-stations, where we got very little to eat, were filthy and swarming with bedbugs. In the stations of Shemanáiefskaya and Saüshkina, after vainly attempting to sleep, I sat up and wrote throughout the whole of two nights, killing fifteen or twenty bedbugs each night on my writing-table. The lack of proper food, the constant jolting, and the impossibility of getting any sleep, soon reduced us to an extremely jaded and exhausted condition, and when we reached the town of Barnaül, Friday afternoon, August 14, after an almost sleepless journey of ninety-six hours, I was hardly able to sit up.

Barnaül is a large town of 17,000 inhabitants, and is the center of the rich and important mining district of the Altái. It contains an unusual number of pretentious dwelling-houses and residences with columns and imposing façades, but most of them have fallen into decay. They were erected many years ago, at a time when a mining officer of the Crown in Barnaül received 2000 or 3000 rubles a year as salary, and stole 100,000 rubles a year by means of "cooked" accounts, and when, according to tradition, he paid twice the amount of his own salary to a French governess for his children, and as much more to a French culinary chef, and sent his soiled linen to Paris by mail to be washed and starched.

The mines of the Altái are, for the most part, the private property of the Tsar. In the nine years from 1870 to 1879 they produced 6984 pounds of gold, 206,964 pounds of silver, 9,639,620 pounds of copper, and 13,221,396 pounds of lead. A large part of the gold and silver ore is smelted in Barnaül.

MARKET-PLACE IN BARNAÜL.

Mr. Frost, with an amount of enterprise which was in
the highest degree creditable to him, explored the city with
sketch-book and camera, and took photographs of the bazar,

of peasant women carrying stones on hand-barrows near the mining "works," and of a curious building, not far from our hotel, which seemed to have been intended for a Russo-Ionic temple, but which afterward had apparently been transformed into a jail, in order to bring it more nearly into harmony with the needs of the place. I should have accompanied him upon some of these excursions, but I was nearly sick from sleeplessness. The dirty hotel in Barnaül was alive with bedbugs, and I was compelled to sleep every night on a table, or rather stand, about four feet long by three wide, set out in the middle of the room. Owing to the fact that I generally rolled off or capsized the table as soon as I lost consciousness, my sleep was neither prolonged nor refreshing, and before we left Barnaül I was reduced to a state bordering on frenzy. Almost the only pleasant recollection that I have of the city is the memory of receiving there eighteen letters from home — the first I had had since our departure from Tiumén.

Tuesday afternoon, August 18th, we left Barnaül for Tomsk. The part of Western Siberia that lies between these two cities is a fertile rolling country, diversified by birch groves and wide stretches of cultivated land, and suggestive a little of the southern part of New England. Mr. Frost, whose home is in Massachusetts, said he could easily imagine that he was "up Berkshire way." The scenery, although never wild, is everywhere pleasing and picturesque; the meadows, even in August, are carpeted with flowers, and the greenness and freshness of the vegetation, to a traveler who comes from the desert-like steppes of the upper Irtish, are a source of surprise and gratification. Near the first station we passed the small lake of Koliván, which is celebrated in all that part of Siberia for the picturesque beauty of its scenery, and Mr. Frost made a sketch of some fantastic rocks by the roadside. It is a favorite place of resort in summer for the wealthy citizens of Barnaül and Tomsk. It had been our intention to spend a day or two

in exploring this picturesque sheet of water, but we finally
decided that we could not spare the time.   We crossed the
river Ob on a curious *paróm*, or ferry-boat, consisting of a
large platform supported upon two open hulks and pro-

OLD PRISON OR GUARD-HOUSE IN BARNAÚL.

pelled by a paddle-wheel at one end, the crank of which
was turned by two ragged-bearded old *muzhíks*.   Most of
the Siberian rivers are crossed by means of what are known
as "pendulum ferries," in which the boat is anchored by a
long cable made fast in the middle of the stream, and is

swung from shore to shore pendulum-wise by the force of the current. The Ob ferry-boat, of which Mr. Frost made a sketch, was the first one we had seen propelled by a paddle-wheel.

So far as I can remember, there was little on the route between Barnaül and Tomsk to attract a traveler's attention. I was terribly jaded and exhausted from lack of sleep, and spent a large part of the time in a state which was little more than one of semi-consciousness.

At four o'clock on the afternoon of Thursday, August 20th, we rode at last into the city of Tomsk. We had made, with horses, in the 51 days which had elapsed since our departure from Tiumén, a journey of more than 1500 miles, in the course of which we had inspected two large prisons, made the acquaintance of three colonies of political exiles, and visited the wildest part of the Russian Altái. We drove at once to the European Hotel, which is the building shown at the extreme right of the illustration on page 300, secured a fairly comfortable room, and as soon as possible after dinner removed our clothing and stretched our weary bodies out in civilized beds for the first time in nearly two months.

Tomsk, which is the capital of the province of the same name, is a city of 31,000 inhabitants, and is situated partly on a bluff, and partly on low land adjoining the river Tom, a short distance above its junction with the Ob. In point of size and importance it is the second city in Siberia, and in enterprise, intelligence, and prosperity it seemed to me to be the first. It contains about 8000 dwelling-houses and other buildings, 250 of which are brick; 33 churches, including a Roman Catholic church, a Mohammedan mosque, and 3 Jewish synagogues; 26 schools, attended by about 2500 scholars; a very good public library; 2 tri-weekly newspapers, which, however, the Minister of the Interior keeps closed a large part of the time on account of their "pernicious tendency"; and a splendid new university building.[1]   The streets of the city are not paved and are very imperfectly lighted, but at the time of our visit they seemed to be reasonably clean and well cared for, and the town, as a whole, impressed me much more favorably than many towns of its class in European Russia.

The province of which Tomsk is the capital has an area of 330,000 square miles, and is therefore about seven times as large as the State of Pennsylvania. It contains 8 towns, each of which has on an average 14,000 inhabitants, and 2719 villages, each of which has on an average 366 inhabitants, so that its total population is about 1,100,000. Of this number 90,000 are aborigines, and 30,000 communal exiles, or common criminals banished from European Russia. The southern part of the province is very fertile, is well timbered and watered, and has a fairly good climate. The 3,600,000 acres of land which it has under cultivation yield annually about 30,000,000 bushels of grain and 4,500,000 bushels of potatoes, with smaller quantities of hemp, flax, and tobacco, while the pastures around the villages support about 2,500,000 head of live stock.

From these statistics it will be seen that, in spite of bad government, restricted immigration, and the demoralizing influence of criminal exile, the province of Tomsk is not wholly barren or uncivilized. If it were in the hands of Americans, and if free immigration from European Russia

[1] The building of the Tomsk university had been completed at the time of our visit, but the Government seemed to be unable or unwilling to throw the institution open for the reception of students. It was thought and said, by a certain class of reactionists and obscurantists, that a Siberian university would be a nucleus or rallying-point for "Siberian patriots," that it would foster a spirit of independence and a desire for separation from European Russia, and that, consequently, it ought not to be opened at all. Prince Meshchérski, for example, in his newspaper *Grazhdanín*, attacked the Tomsk university repeatedly upon this ground. [*Grazhdanín*, Nos. 275 and 279, St. Petersburg, 1888.] In July, 1888, however, after three years' consideration, the Government decided to open one "faculty," or department, of the new university, and selected, as the most useful and least "dangerous," the department of medicine. Since that time it has been possible for young Siberians to get a university training in medicine, but not in any branch of human knowledge that has a tendency to "excite the mind," such as history, political economy, or law.

PEASANT WOMEN AT WORK IN BARNAÜL.

to it were allowed, it might soon become as densely popu-
lated and as prosperous as any of our northwestern States.
Its resources are almost illimitable, and all that it needs is
good government and freedom for the play of private enter-

prise. As long, however, as a despotic administration at St. Petersburg can gag its newspapers for months at a time, keep its university closed, choose the teachers and prescribe the courses of study for its schools, prohibit the reading of the best books in its libraries, bind its population hand and foot by a rigid passport system, govern it through corrupt and wretchedly paid *chinóvniks*, and pour into it every year a flood of common criminals from European Russia, just so long will it remain what it now is—a naturally enterprising and promising colony strangled by oppressive and unnecessary guardianship. The Government, just at the present time, proposes to develop the resources of the province by building through it a railroad. It might much better loosen the grasp in which it holds the people by the throat, permit them to exercise some judgment with regard to the management of their own affairs, allow them freely to discuss their needs and plans in their own newspapers, abolish restrictions upon personal liberty of movement, stop the sending there of criminal exiles, and then let the province develop itself. It does not need "development" half as much as it needs to be let alone.

Our first step in Tomsk was to call upon the political exiles, and upon several army officers to whom we had letters of introduction, and ascertain from them the facts that were necessary for our guidance. We were received by everybody with the utmost courtesy and kindness, and Colonel Yágodkin, the chief military officer of the district, not only welcomed us to his house with cordial hospitality, but took a friendly interest in all of our prison investigations. Only a day or two after our arrival he called at our hotel to inform us that a convict barge from Tiumén had arrived that morning at the steamer-landing two or three miles from the city, and to say that if we would like to see the reception of a convict party, he would go to the landing with us and introduce us to the chief officer of the local exile bureau. I thanked him for his thoughtfulness, and in ten minutes Mr. Frost, Colonel Yágodkin, and I were driving furiously over a muddy road toward the *prístan*, or landing-place. Although we made all possible haste, the prisoners had disembarked before we reached our destination. We found them assembled in two dense gray throngs at the ends of a long wooden shed, which was surrounded and turned into a sort of cattle-pen by a high plank wall. Here they were identified, counted, and turned over by the con-

KOLIVÁN LAKE.

voy officer to the warden of the Tomsk forwarding prison. The shed was divided transversely through the middle by a low wooden barricade, at one end of which was a fenced inclosure, about ten feet square, for the accommodation of the officers who had to take part in the reception of the party. About half the exiles had been formally "received" and were standing at the eastern end of the shed, while the other half were grouped in a dense throng at the western end, waiting for their names to be called. The women, who stood huddled together in a group by themselves, were mostly in peasant costumes, with bright-colored kerchiefs over their heads, and their faces, I thought, showed great anxiety and apprehension. The men all wore long gray overcoats over coarse linen shirts and trousers; most of them were in chains, and the bare heads of the convicts and the penal colonists had been half shaved longitudinally in such a way that one side of the scalp was smooth and blue while the other side was hidden by long, neglected hair. Soldiers stood here and there around the shed, leaning upon their bayoneted rifles, and inside the little inclosure were the convoy officer of the party, the warden and the surgeon of the Tomsk forwarding prison, the chief of the local bureau of exile administration, and two or three other officers, all in full uniform. Colonel Yágodkin introduced us as American travelers who desired to see the reception of an exile party, and we were invited to stand inside the inclosure.

The officer who was conducting the examination of the convicts drew a folded paper from a large bundle in his hand, opened and glanced at it, and then shouted, "Nikolái Koltsóf!" A thin, pale man, with heavy, wearied eyes and a hopeless expression of face, who was standing in the front rank of the exile party, picked up the gray linen bag that lay beside him on the floor, and with a slow clink, clink, clink of chains walked to the inclosure. The examining officer compared his face carefully with a photograph attached to the *statéini spísak* or "identification paper," in order to make sure that the pale man had not "exchanged names" with some other exile, while a Cossack orderly examined him from head to foot and rummaged through his bag to see that he had neither lost nor surreptitiously sold the articles of clothing that he had received in Moscow or Tiumén, and that his *statéini spísak* called for.

"Is everything there?" inquired the officer.

"Everything," replied the Cossack.

"Stupái!" [Pass on!] said the lieutenant; and the pale-faced man shouldered his bag and joined the ranks of the "received" at the eastern end of the shed.

"The photographs are a new thing," whispered Colonel Yágodkin to me; "and only a part of the exiles have them. They are intended to break up the practice of exchanging names and identities."

"But why should they wish to exchange names?" I inquired.

"If a man is sentenced to hard labor at the mines," he replied, "and has a little money, he always tries to buy secretly the name and identity of some poor devil of a colonist who longs desperately for a drink of *vódka*, or who wants money with which to gamble. Of course the convoy officer has no means of preventing this sort of transaction, because he cannot possibly remember the names and faces of the four or five hundred men in his party. If the convict succeeds in finding a colonist who is willing to sell his name, he takes the colonist's place and is assigned a residence in some village, while the colonist takes the convict's place and goes to the mines. Hundreds of hard-labor convicts escape in this way."[1]

"Hassán Abdállimof!" called the examining officer. No one moved.

"Hassán Abdállimof!" shouted the Cossack orderly, more loudly.

"Go on, Stumpy; that's you!" said half a dozen exiles in an undertone as they pushed out of the throng a short, thickly set, bow-legged Tatár, upon whose flat, swarthy face there was an expression of uncertainty and bewilderment.

"He does n't know Russian, your High Nobility," said one of the exiles respectfully, "and he is glupováti" [dull-witted].

[1] I shall explain this practice of exchanging names more fully in a later chapter.

"Bring him here," said the officer to the Cossack orderly.

When Hassán had been examined, he did not shoulder his bag and go to his place as he should have done, but began to bow and gesticulate, and to make supplications in

GROTESQUE ROCKS NEAR KOLIVÁN LAKE.

the Tatár language, becoming more and more excited as he talked.

"What does he say?" inquired the officer. "Find some soldier who knows Tatár." An interpreter was soon found and Hassán repeated his story.

"He says, your High Nobility," translated the interpreter, "that when he was arrested they took eight *rúbles* from him and told him the money would be given back to him in Siberia. He wants to know if he cannot have some of it now to buy tea."

"Nyettoo chai!" [No tea!] said the Tatár mournfully, with a gesture of utter desolation.

"To the devil with him!" cried the officer furiously. "What does the blank blank mean by delaying the reception of the party with such a trifle? This is no place to talk about tea! He'll receive his money when he gets to his destination. Away with him!" And the poor Tatár was hustled into the eastern end of the shed.

"Iván Dontremember — the red-headed," shouted the examining officer.

"That's a *brodyág*" (a vagrant or tramp), whispered Colonel Yágodkin to me as a sun-burned, red-headed *muzhík* in chains and leg-fetters, and with a tea-kettle hanging from his belt, approached the inclosure. "He has been arrested while wandering around in Western Siberia, and as there is something in his past history that he does n't want brought to light, he refuses to disclose his identity, and answers all questions with 'I don't remember.' The tramps all call themselves 'Iván Dontremember,' and they're generally a bad lot. The penalty for belonging to the 'Dontremember' family is five years at the mines." The examining officer had no photograph of "Iván Dontremember, the red-headed," and the latter's identity was established by ascertaining the number of teeth that he had lost, and by examining a scar over his right ear.

One by one the exiles passed in this way before the examining officer until all had been identified, counted, and turned over, and then the warden of the Tomsk forwarding prison gave a receipt to the convoy officer of the barge for 551 prisoners, including 71 children under 15 years of age, who were accompanying their fathers or mothers into exile.

At the end of the verification and reception some of the officers returned to the city; but Colonel Yágodkin, Mr. Frost, and I remained to see the surgical examination of the sick and disabled, and to inspect the convict barge. Doctor Órzheshkó, the surgeon of the Tomsk prison, then took the place that had been occupied by the examining officer, laid a stethoscope and two or three other instruments upon a small table beside him, and began a rapid examination of a long line of incapacitated men, some of whom were really sick and some of whom were merely shamming. The object of the examination was to ascertain how many of the prisoners were unable to walk, in order that the requisite number of *telégas* might be provided for their transportation to the city. The first man who presented himself was thin, pale, and haggard, and in reply to a question from the surgeon said, with a sepulchral cough, that his breast hurt him and that he could not breathe easily. Dr. Órzheshkó felt his pulse, put a stethoscope to his lungs, listened for a moment to the respiratory murmur, and then said briefly, " Pass on; you can walk." The next man had a badly swollen ankle, upon which his leg-fetter pressed heavily, evidently causing him great pain. He looked imploringly at the doctor while the latter examined the swollen limb, as if he would beseech him to have mercy; but he said not a word, and when his case was approved and a wagon was ordered for him, he crossed himself devoutly three times, and his lips moved noiselessly, as if he were saying softly under his breath, "I thank thee, O God!"

There were forty or fifty men in the line of prisoners awaiting examination, and the surgeon disposed of them at the rate of about one a minute. Some had fever, some were suffering from rheumatism, some were manifestly in an advanced stage of prison consumption, and all seemed to me sick, wretched, or weak enough to deserve wagons; but the experienced senses of the surgeon quickly detected the malingerers and the men who were only slightly indisposed, and quietly bade them "Pass on!" At the end of the examination Dr. Órzheshkó reported to the prison

FERRY ON THE RIVER OB NEAR BARNAÜL

warden that there were twenty-five persons in the party who were not able to walk to the city, and who, therefore, would have to be carried. The necessary wagons were ordered, the sick and the women with infants were placed

in them, and at the order "Stroisa!" [Form ranks!] the
convicts, with a confused clinking of chains, took positions outside the shed in a somewhat ragged column; the
soldiers, with shouldered rifles, went to their stations in
front, beside, and behind the party; and Mr. Pépeláief, the
chief of the local exile bureau, stepping upon a chair, cried,
"Nu rebatta" [Well, boys], "have you anything to say or
any complaints to make?"

"No; nothing, your Nobility," replied seventy-five or a
hundred voices.

"Well, then, S'Bógem" [Go with God].

The soldiers threw open the wooden gate of the yard or
pen; the under-officer shouted "Ready — March!" and
with a renewed jingling of multitudinous chains, the gray
column moved slowly out into the muddy road.

As soon as an opportunity presented itself, Colonel Yágodkin introduced us to Mr. Pépeláief, the chief officer of
the local exile bureau, who supervised the reception and
the forwarding of exile parties, the equipment of the convicts with clothing, and the examination and verification of
their papers.   Mr. Pépeláief, a rather tall, thin man, with a
hard, cold face, greeted us politely, but did not seem pleased
to see us there, and was not disposed to permit an inspection of the convict barge.

"What do they want to go on board the barge for?" he
inquired rather curtly of Colonel Yágodkin. "There is
nothing to see there, and besides it is inconvenient; the
women are now cleaning it."

Colonel Yágodkin, however, knew that I was particularly
anxious to see in what condition the floating prison was
when the convicts left it, and, a few moments later, he introduced us to the convoy officer, and again suggested
a visit to the barge. This time he was successful. The
convoy officer evidently did not see any reason why Colonel Yágodkin should not go on board the barge with his
friends if he wished to do so, and he at once cheerfully

offered to accompany us. The barge was, apparently, the same one that I had inspected in Tiumén two months before. Then it was scrupulously clean, and the air in its cabins was fresh and pure; but now it suggested a recently vacated wild-beast cage in a menagerie. It was no more dirty, perhaps, than might have been expected; but its atmosphere was heavy with a strong animal odor; its floors were covered with dried mud, into which had been trodden refuse scraps of food; its *nári*, or sleeping-benches, were black and greasy, and strewn with bits of dirty paper; and in the gray light of a cloudy day its dark *kámeras*, with their small grated port-holes, muddy floors, and polluted ammoniacal atmosphere, chilled and depressed me with suggestions of human misery.

The Rev. Henry Lansdell, in a magazine article published two or three years ago,[1] says, "I have seen some strong statements, alleging the extreme unhealthiness of these barges, . . . and I do not suppose that they are as healthy as a first-class sanatorium."

If Mr. Lansdell made a careful examination of a convict barge immediately after the departure from it of a convict party, the idea of a "sanatorium" certainly could not have been suggested to him by anything that he saw, touched, or smelled. It suggested to me nothing so much as a recently vacated den in a zoölogical garden. It was, as I have said, no more dirty and foul than might have been expected after ten days of such tenancy; but it could have been connected in one's mind with a "sanatorium" only by a violent wrench of the imagination. As a proof, however, that a convict barge in point of healthfulness does not fall far short of "a first-class sanatorium," Mr. Lansdell quotes a statement made to him by "an officer who had charge of the prisoners between Tiumén and Tomsk," to the effect that "during the season of 1882, 8 barges car-

[1] "Russian Convicts in the Salt Mines of Iletsk"; *Harper's Magazine*, May, 1888, pp. 894–910.

ried 6000 prisoners a voyage of nearly 2000 miles, and yet only two [and one of them a child] died on the passage, while only 20 were delivered invalided at Tomsk."

Inasmuch as I once took the same view of the exile system that Mr. Lansdell now takes, and have been forced to confess myself in error, it may be proper for me to say, without reflecting in any way upon Mr. Lansdell's conscientiousness and sincerity, that the statement which he quotes has not the slightest foundation in fact, and was probably made to him by the convoy officer with a deliberate intention to deceive. According to the official report of the inspector of exile transportation for 1882,— the year to which Mr. Lansdell's information relates,— the number of prisoners carried on convict barges was not 6000, but 10,245. Of this number 279 were taken sick on the barges, 22 died, and 80 were left dangerously sick at river ports, or were delivered in that condition at Tomsk.[1] These, it must be remembered, were the cases of sickness and the deaths that occurred in a voyage which averages only ten days in duration. If, in a population of 10,245 souls, 279 persons were taken sick and 22 died every 10 days, we should have an annual sick-rate of nearly 99 per cent., and an annual death-rate of nearly 8 per cent. It would not, I think, be a very popular " sanatorium " in which 99 per cent. of all the persons who entered it comparatively well became seriously sick in the course of the year, and eight per cent. of the whole number died. But sickness on the convict barges has been far more prevalent than this — and within recent years. In 1879, 724 prisoners were taken sick between Tiumén and Tomsk, and 51 died; and in 1871, 1140 were taken sick out of a whole number of 9416 carried, and 111 died. Such a rate of mortality as that shown by the death of 111 persons out of 9416 in 10 days would entirely depopulate

[1] Annual Report of the Inspector of Exile Transportation for Western Siberia, p. 12 of the manuscript.

in a single year, not only "a first-class sanatorium," but a village of 4000 inhabitants.

In a foot-note below will be found a tabulated statement of the cases of sickness and death which occurred on the convict barges between Tiumén and Tomsk in the fifteen years beginning with 1870 and ending with 1884. I copied the figures myself from the manuscripts of the official reports, and so far as transcription is concerned, I will guarantee their accuracy.[1]

It will be seen that during this period there has been, on the whole, a steady improvement in the hygienic condition of the barges, and a corresponding decrease in the sick- and death-rates. The mortality now is chiefly among children,

[1] SICKNESS AND MORTALITY ON CONVICT BARGES BETWEEN TIUMÉN AND TOMSK — TEN DAYS.

YEAR.	NUMBER CARRIED.		TAKEN SICK.			DIED.			DELIVERED SICK.		
	Adults.	*Children.*	*Adults.*		*Children.*	*Adults.*		*Children.*	*Adults.*		*Children.*
1870	7444	1492	No information.			...	85	...	No information.		
1871	8202	1214	...	1140	...	...	111	...	...	301	...
1872	7246	1098	...	486	...	...	30	...	...	70	...
1873	7923	1090	...	673	...	...	23	...	...	190	...
1874	8068	1269	...	574	...	...	21	...	...	196	...
1875	7771	1301	...	579	...	...	16	...	...	115	...
1876	8878	1455	492	....	121	2	....	19	119	....	24
1877	9065	1499	300	....	133	2	....	35	143	....	44
1878	8749	1688	193	....	151	2	....	27	216	....	38
1879	8977	1342	570	....	154	4	....	47	182	....	39
1880	8844	1425	391	....	138	2	....	23	85	....	21
1881	9011	1452	197	....	22	4	....	23	71	....	23
1882	8832	1413	202	...	77	4	....	18	62	....	18
1883	9506	1543	150	....	107	4	....	38	66	....	37
1884	9004	1688	103	....	113	1	....	28	67	....	55
	127520	20969	2598	3452	1016	25	286	258	1011	872	299
Grand Totals.	148489		7066			569			2182		

It must be borne in mind that these figures show only a small part of the sickness and mortality in convict parties from points of departure to points of destination. Before reaching Tiumén the convicts travel by barge from Nízhni Nóvgorod to Perm, a distance of nearly 1000 miles, and after leaving Tomsk many of them walk nearly 2000 miles into Eastern Siberia. In a subsequent paper I shall give statistics of sickness and mortality for the whole journey from Moscow to Irkútsk.

who, of course, are less able than adults to endure the
hardships, the privations, and exposures of barge life. I
am glad to be able to say that, in my judgment, the inspector of exile transportation and the local Siberian author-

A PART OF THE MARKET SQUARE IN TOMSK.

ities are now doing all that lies in their power to do for
the comfort and health of exiles on the voyage between
Tiumén and Tomsk. The barges are thoroughly cleaned
and fumigated after every trip, and the prisoners are as
well fed and cared for as they can be with the limited sum

of money that the Government appropriates for the purpose. The suffering and disease which still exist are attributable mainly to overcrowding, and overcrowding the Siberian officials cannot prevent. Ten or twelve thousand exiles are turned over to them every summer, and they must send them eastward as best they can while the season of navigation lasts. They have only three barges, and eighteen round trips are all that can be made during the time that the river remains open. They are therefore compelled to send from 600 to 800 exiles in a single barge at every trip, and this inevitably results in a great deal of sickness and suffering.

CHAPTER XIII

THE TOMSK FORWARDING PRISON

AMONG the questions most frequently asked me since my return from Russia are, "How did you manage to gain admittance to Siberian prisons and *étapes*, to make the acquaintance everywhere of banished political offenders, and to get access to so many official documents and reports? Did not the local authorities know what you were doing, and, if so, why did they not put a stop to your investigations, or at least throw more obstacles in your way?"

I cannot give perfectly satisfactory answers to these questions, because I do not know what instructions were given to the local authorities concerning us, nor what view was taken of our movements by the Siberian police. I can, however, indicate the policy that we pursued, and the measures that we adopted to avert suspicion when it became necessary to do so, and can suggest some of the reasons for the generally non-aggressive attitude taken towards us by the Siberian officials.

In the first place, it seems to me probable that when I called upon the high authorities in St. Petersburg and asked permission to go to Siberia to inspect prisons and study the exile system, the officials reasoned somewhat in this way: "It is neither practicable nor politic to exclude foreigners from Siberia altogether. Americans and West Europeans will not be satisfied until they have investigated this exile question; and if we deny them opportunities for such investigation, they will say that we are afraid to have the condition of our prisons known. Mr. Kennan is a friendly observer; he has defended us and the exile system in an address before the American Geographical Society; he has publicly taken our side as against the nihilists; and his main object in going to Siberia seems to be to get facts with which to fortify his position as our champion. Under such circumstances he is not likely to take a very pessimistic view of things, and if somebody must go to Siberia and look through our prisons, he is the very man to do it.[1] Mr. Lansdell gave, on the whole, a favorable account of the working of our penal institutions, and there is every reason to suppose that Mr. Kennan, who is already friendly to us, will follow his example. The reports of these two gentlemen will satisfy the curiosity of the western world, and thus prevent further research; while, at the same time, they will furnish us with a means of silencing foreign critics and accusers. If an English clergyman and an American journalist declare, after personal investigation on the ground, that there is nothing particularly terrible about the exile system, the world will probably accept the judgment. We will, therefore, allow Messrs. Kennan and Frost to go to Siberia, and will give them letters of recommendation; but we will make them apply to the local authorities, in all cases, for permission to inspect prisons, and then, if necessary or expedient, we can direct secretly that such permission be denied. There is, of course, some danger that

---

[1] Mr. Vlangálli, the Assistant Minister of Foreign Affairs, had already seen a copy of my address before the American Geographical Society upon "Siberia and the Exile System"; and the conclusions which I here attribute to him might have been drawn, fairly enough, from the frank and honest statements that I made to him. I did not promise that I would defend the Russian Government, but I did assure him that I had no intention of writing a sensational narrative; that in my opinion the exile system had been painted in too dark colors; and that a fair statement of the real facts would, I thought, interest the whole civilized world, and, at the same time, be of service to the Government. In this, as I have before said, there was not the least insincerity or diplomacy. My statements were strictly and exactly in accordance with my opinions.

they will meet political exiles, but they seem already to be strongly prejudiced against such offenders, and we will prejudice them still further by giving them a letter of introduction to Mr. Katkóff, and by instructing the latter to see that they are furnished in advance with proper information. If their relations with political criminals in Siberia become, nevertheless, too close and intimate, we can at any time direct that they be warned, or, if necessary, that they be put under surveillance."

My belief that this was the reasoning of the high officials in St. Petersburg is based mainly, of course, upon conjecture; but it is supported collaterally by the whole of our Siberian experience. It was everywhere apparent that the question of admitting us to prisons or excluding us therefrom had been left to the discretion of the Siberian authorities; and that the latter, in their dealings with us, were guided mainly by circumstances and by personal views and impressions. It was in the highest degree important, therefore, that we should so conduct ourselves as to gain the confidence and good-will of these officers, and that we should prosecute our researches in the field of political exile in such a manner as not to excite comment or give occasion for report. Nine-tenths of the towns and villages through which we passed were in communication with St. Petersburg by telegraph. If the police should discover that we were systematically visiting the political exiles and taking letters of introduction from one colony to another, they might send a telegram any day to the Minister of the Interior, saying, "Kennan and Frost are establishing intimate relations everywhere with administrative exiles and state criminals. Was it the intention of the Government that this should be permitted?" I did not know what answer would be made to such a telegram; but there certainly was a strong probability that it would at least result in an official "warning," or in a stricter supervision of our movements, and thus render the accomplishment of our purposes extremely difficult. Our letters of recommendation might protect us from unauthorized interference at the hands of the local authorities; but they could not save us from an arrest or a search ordered by telegraph from St. Petersburg. That telegraph line, therefore, for nearly a year hung over our heads like an electric sword of Damocles, threatening every moment to fall and cut short our career of investigation.

Up to the time of our arrival at Ust Kámenogórsk we had had no trouble with the police, and our intercourse with the political exiles had been virtually unrestricted. As we began, however, to accumulate letters and documents that would be compromising to the writers and givers if discovered, we deemed it prudent to mask our political investigations, as far as practicable, under a semblance of interest in other things, and, at the same time, to cultivate the most friendly possible relations with the local authorities. It seemed to me that to avoid the police, as if we were afraid of them or had something to conceal from them, would be a fatal error. Safety lay rather in a policy of extreme boldness, and I determined to call at the earliest moment upon the *isprávnik*, or chief of police, in every village, and overwhelm him with information concerning our plans, purposes, and previous history, before he had time to form any conjectures or suspicions with regard to us, and, if possible, before he had even heard of our arrival. After we began to make the acquaintance of the political exiles we had no difficulty in getting from them all necessary information with regard to the history, temperament, and personal characteristics of an official upon whom we purposed to call, and we therefore had every possible advantage of the latter in any contest of wits. He knew nothing about us, and had to feel his way to an acquaintance with us experimentally; while we knew all about him, and could, by virtue of our knowledge, adapt ourselves to his idiosyncrasies, humor his tastes, avoid dangerous topics, lead up to subjects upon which we were sure to be in enthusiastic agreement, and

thus convince him that we were not only good fellows, but
men of rare sagacity and judgment — as of course we were!
We made it a rule to call in evening dress upon every official, as a means of showing him our respectful appreciation
of his rank and position; we drank *vódka* and bitter cordial
with him — if necessary, up to the limit of double vision;
we made ourselves agreeable to his wife, and Mr. Frost
drew portraits of his children; and, in nine cases out of
ten, we thus succeeded in making ourselves "solid with the
administration" before we had been in a town or village
forty-eight hours.

The next steps in our plan of campaign were, first, to
forestall suspicion in the minds of the subordinate police,
by showing ourselves publicly as often as possible in the
company of their superiors; and, secondly, to supply the
people of the village with a plausible explanation of our
presence there by making visits to schools, by ostentatiously
taking notes in sight of the scholars, and by getting the
teachers to prepare for us statistics of popular education.
This part of the work generally fell to me, while Mr. Frost
attracted public attention by sketching in the streets, by collecting flowers and butterflies, or by lecturing to station-mas-
ters and peasants upon geography, cosmography, and the
phenomena of the heavens. This last-mentioned occupation afforded him great amusement, and proved at the same
time to be extremely useful as a means of giving a safe
direction to popular speculations concerning us. Jointly
I think we produced upon the public mind the impression that we had come to Siberia with what is known in
Russia as an *uchónni tsel* [a scientific aim], and that we
were chiefly interested in popular education, art, botany,
geography, and archæology. After we had thus forestalled
suspicion by calling promptly upon the police, and by furnishing the common people with a ready-made theory to
explain our presence and our movements, we could go
where we liked without exciting much remark, and we

devoted four or five hours every night to the political exiles. Now and then some peasant would perhaps see us
going to an exile's house; but as many of the politicals
were known to be scientific men, and as we were travelling
with a "scientific aim," no particular significance was attached to the circumstance. Everybody knew that we spent
a large part of our time in visiting schools, collecting flowers, sketching, taking photographs, and hobnobbing with
the local authorities; and the idea that we were particularly
interested in the political exiles rarely occurred, I think, to
any one. As we went eastward into a part of Siberia where
the politicals are more closely watched, we varied our policy
somewhat to accord with circumstances; but the rules that
we everywhere observed were to act with confidence and
boldness, to make ourselves socially agreeable to the local
authorities, to attract as much attention as possible to the
side of our life that would bear close inspection, and to
keep the other side in the shade. We could not, of course,
conceal wholly from the police our relations with the political
exiles; but the extent and real significance of such relations
were never, I think, suspected. At any rate, the telegraphic
sword of Damocles did not fall upon us, and until we reached
the Trans-Baikál we did not even receive a "warning."

Our work in all parts of Siberia was greatly facilitated
by the attitude of honest and intelligent officials towards
the system that we were investigating. Almost without
exception they were either hostile to it altogether, or op-
posed to it in its present form; and they often seemed glad
of an opportunity to point out to a foreign observer the
evils of exile as a method of punishment, and the frauds,
abuses, and cruelties to which, in practice, it gives rise.
This was something that I had neither foreseen nor counted
upon; and more than once I was surprised and startled by
the boldness and frankness of such officials, after they had
become satisfied that they could safely talk to me without
reserve.

"I get my living by the exile system," said a high officer of the prison department to me one day, "and I have no fault to find with my position or my pay; but I would gladly resign both to-morrow if I could see the system abolished. It is disastrous to Siberia, it is ruinous to the criminal, and it causes an immense amount of misery; but what can be done? If we say anything to our superiors in St. Petersburg, they strike us in the face; and they strike hard — it hurts! I have learned to do the best I can and to hold my tongue."

"I have reported upon the abuses and miseries in my department," said another officer, "until I am tired; and I have accomplished little or nothing. Perhaps if you describe them, something will be done. The prison here is unfit for human habitation, — it is n't fit for a dog, — and I have been trying for years to get a new one; but my efforts have resulted in nothing but an interminable correspondence."

Statements similar to these were made to me by at least a score of officers who held positions of trust in the civil or military service of the state, and many of them furnished me with abundant proof of their assertions in the shape of statistics and documentary evidence.

In Tomsk the condition of the prisons and the evils of the exile system were so well known to everybody, and had been so often commented upon in the local newspapers, that the higher officials did not think it worth while apparently to try to conceal anything from us. The governor of the province, Mr. Krasófski, happened at that time to be absent from the city, but his place was being filled by State Councilor Nathaniel Petukhóf, the presiding officer of the provincial administration, who was described to us as a man of intelligence, education, and some liberality. As soon as I conveniently could, I called upon Mr. Petukhóf, and was received by him with great cordiality. He had read, as I soon learned, my book upon northeastern Siberia; and since it had made a favorable impression upon him, he was predisposed to treat me with consideration and with more than ordinary courtesy. I, in turn, had heard favorable reports with regard to his character; and under such circumstances we naturally drifted into a frank and pleasant talk about Siberia and Siberian affairs. At the end of half an hour's conversation he asked me if there was any way in which he could be of assistance to me. I replied that I should like very much to have permission to visit the exile forwarding prison. I fancied that his face showed, for an instant, a trace of embarrassment; but as I proceeded to describe my visits to prisons in two other provinces, he seemed to come to a decision, and, without asking me any questions as to my motives, said, " Yes, I will give you permission; and, if you like, I will go with you." Then, after a moment's hesitation, he determined, apparently, to be frank with me, and added gravely, " I think you will find it the worst prison in Siberia." I expressed a hope that such would not be the case, and said that it could hardly be worse than the forwarding prison in Tiumén. He shrugged his shoulders slightly, as if to say, " You don't know yet what a Siberian prison may be," and asked me what could be expected when buildings were crowded with more than twice the number of persons for which they were intended. "The Tomsk forwarding prison," he continued, " was designed to hold 1400 prisoners.[1] It now contains more than 3000, and the convict barges, as they arrive from Tiumén, increase the number by from 500 to 800 every week, while we are able to forward eastward only 400 a week. The situation is, therefore, becoming worse and worse as the summer advances. The prison *kámeras* are terribly over-

---

[1] According to the report of the inspector of exile transportation for 1885, this prison would accommodate 1900 prisoners, with an allowance of eight-tenths of a cubic fathom of air space per capita. (Page 27 of the manuscript report.) Mr. Petukhóf, in his estimate, did not perhaps allow for such close packing as this. In private houses in Russia the amount of air space regarded as essential for one grown person is a little more than five cubic fathoms (*Rússkaya Misl*, May 1891, p. 61).

crowded; it is impossible to keep them clean; the vitiation of the air in them causes a great amount of disease, and the prison hospital is already full to overflowing with the dangerously sick."

"But," I said, "why do you not forward exiles eastward more rapidly and thus relieve the congestion in this prison? Why can you not increase the size of your marching parties, or send forward two parties a week instead of one?"

"It is impracticable," replied the acting governor. "The exile administration of Eastern Siberia says that it cannot receive and distribute prisoners faster than it does now. Its *étapes* are too small to accommodate larger parties, and the convoying force of soldiers is not adequate to take care of two parties a week. We tried one year the plan that you suggest, but it did not work well."

"Does the Government at St. Petersburg know," I inquired, "of this state of affairs?"

"Certainly," he replied. "It has been reported upon every year, and, besides writing, I have sent four urgent telegrams this summer asking if something cannot be done to relieve this prison."

"And has nothing been done?"

"Nothing whatever. The number of prisoners here will continue to increase steadily up to the close of river navigation, when the convict barges will stop running, and then we shall gradually clear out the prison during the winter months. In the mean time typhus fever will prevail there constantly, and great numbers of sick will lie uncared for in their cells because there is no room for them in the hospitals. If you visit the prison, my advice to you is to breakfast heartily before starting, and to keep out of the hospital wards."

I thanked him for his caution, said that I was not afraid of contagion, and asked when it would be convenient for him to go with me to the prison. A day was agreed upon, and I took my leave.

On Wednesday, August 26,—the day appointed,—Mr. Petukhóf sent word to me that unforeseen circumstances would prevent him from going to the prison with us, but that we need not postpone our visit on his account. An inspecting party therefore was made up of Colonel Yágodkin, Mr. Pépeláief (the chief of the local exile bureau), and the convoy officer of the barge, Mr. Frost, and myself. It was one of the cold, gray, gloomy days that often come to Western Siberia in the late summer, when the sky is a canopy of motionless leaden clouds, and the wind blows sharply down across the *túndras* from the arctic ocean. The air was raw, with a suggestion of dampness, and an overcoat was not uncomfortable as we rode out to the eastern end of the city.

The first glimpse that we caught of the Tomsk forwarding prison showed us that it differed widely in type from all the Siberian prisons we had previously seen. Instead of the huge white, three-story, stuccoed building, with narrow arched windows and red tin roof, that we had expected to find, we saw before us something that looked like the permanent fortified camp of a regiment of soldiers, or like a small prairie village on the frontier, surrounded by a high stockade of sharpened logs to protect it from hostile Indians. With the exception of the zigzag-barred sentry-boxes at the corners, and the soldiers, who with shouldered rifles paced slowly back and forth along its sides, there was hardly a suggestion of a prison about it. It was simply a stockaded inclosure about three acres in extent, situated on an open prairie beyond the city limits, with a pyramidal church-tower and the board roofs of fifteen or twenty log buildings showing above the serrated edge of the palisade. If we had had any doubts, however, with regard to the nature of the place, the familiar jingling of chains, which came to our ears as we stopped in front of the wooden gate, would have set such doubts at rest.

In response to a summons sent by Mr. Pépeláief through the officer of the day, the warden of the prison, a short,

stout, chubby-faced young officer, named Ivanénko, soon
made his appearance, and we were admitted to the prison
yard. Within the spacious inclosure stood twelve or fifteen
one-story log buildings, grouped without much apparent
regularity about a square log church. At the doors of most
of these buildings stood armed sentries, and in the unpaved
streets or open spaces between them were walking or sitting on the bare ground hundreds of convicts and penal
colonists, who, in chains and leg-fetters, were taking their
daily outing. The log buildings with their grated windows,
the high stockade which surrounded them, the armed sentries here and there, and the throngs of convicts who in
long, gray, semi-military overcoats roamed aimlessly about
the yard, would doubtless have reminded many a Union soldier of the famous prison pen at Andersonville. The prison
buildings proper were long, one-story, barrack-like houses
of squared logs, with board roofs, heavily grated windows,
and massive wooden doors secured by iron padlocks. Each
separate building constituted a *kazárm*, or prison ward, and
each ward was divided into two large *kámeras*, or cells, by a
short hall running transversely through the middle. There
were eight of these *kazárms*, or log prisons, and each of them
was designed to accommodate 190 men, with an allowance
of eight-tenths of a cubic fathom of air space per capita.[1]
They were all substantially alike, and seemed to me to be
about 75 feet long by 40 feet wide, with a height of 12 feet
between floors and ceilings. The first *kámera* that we examined was perhaps 40 feet square, and contained about
150 prisoners. It was fairly well lighted, but its atmosphere was polluted to the last degree by over-respiration,
and its temperature, raised by the natural heat of the pris-

[1] The report of the inspector of exile
transportation for 1884 says that the
Tomsk prison contains ten of these *kazárms*. The warden told me that there
were only eight. Accounts also differ
as to the normal capacity of the prison.
Acting-Governor Petukhóf said that it
was originally intended to hold 1400
prisoners, while the inspector of exile
transportation reported in 1884 that
its normal capacity was 1900. It contained, at the time of our visit, about
3500.

A "FAMILY KÁMERA" IN THE TOMSK FORWARDING PRISON.

oners' bodies, was fifteen or twenty degrees above that of the air outside. Two double rows of sleeping-benches ran across the *kámera*, but there evidently was not room enough on them for half the inmates of the cell, and the remainder were forced to sleep under them, or on the floor in the gangways between them, without pillows, blankets, or bedclothing of any kind. The floor had been washed in anticipation of our visit, but the warden said that in rainy weather it wàs always covered with mud and filth brought in from the yard by the feet of the prisoners, and that in this mud and filth scores of men had to lie down at night to sleep. Many of the convicts, thinking that we were officers or inspectors from St. Petersburg, violated the first rule of prison discipline, despite the presence of the warden, by complaining to us of the heat, foulness, and oppressiveness of the prison air, and the terrible overcrowding, which made it difficult to move about the *kámera* in the daytime, and almost impossible to get any rest at night. I pitied the poor wretches, but could only tell them that we were not officials, and had no power to do anything for them.

For nearly an hour we went from *kazárm* to *kazárm* and from cell to cell, finding everywhere the same overcrowding, the same inconceivably foul air, the same sickening odors, and the same throngs of gray-coated convicts. At last Mr. Pépeláief, who seemed disposed to hurry us through the prison, said that there was nothing more to see except the kitchen and the hospital, and that he presumed we would not care to inspect the hospital wards, inasmuch as they contained seventy or eighty patients sick with malignant typhus fever. The young convoy officer of the barge, who seconded all of Colonel Yágodkin's efforts to make us thoroughly acquainted with the prison, asked the warden if he was not going to show us the "family *kámeras*" and the "*balagáns.*"

"Certainly," said the warden; "I will show them anything that they wish to see."

I had not before heard of the *balagáns*, and Mr. Pépeláief, who had to some extent taken upon himself the guidance of the party, seemed as anxious to prevent us from seeing them as he had been to prevent us from seeing the convict barge.

The *balagáns* we found to be long, low sheds, hastily built of rough pine boards, and inclosed with sides of thin, white cotton-sheeting. They were three in number, and were occupied exclusively by family parties, women, and children. The first one to which we came was surrounded by a foul ditch half full of filth, into which water or urine was dripping here and there from the floor under the cotton-sheeting wall. The *balagán* had no windows, and all the light that it received came through the thin cloth which formed the sides.

A scene of more pitiable human misery than that which was presented to us as we entered the low, wretched shed can hardly be imagined. It was literally packed with hundreds of weary-eyed men, haggard women, and wailing children, sitting or lying in all conceivable attitudes upon two long lines of rough plank sleeping-benches, which ran through it from end to end, leaving gangways about four feet in width in the middle and at the sides. I could see the sky through cracks in the roof; the floor of unmatched boards had given way here and there, and the inmates had used the holes as places into which to throw refuse and pour slops and excrement; the air was insufferably fetid on account of the presence of a great number of infants and the impossibility of giving them proper physical care; wet underclothing, which had been washed in camp-kettles, was hanging from all the cross-beams; the gangways were obstructed by piles of gray bags, bundles, bedding, and domestic utensils; and in this chaos of disorder and misery hundreds of human beings, packed together so closely that they could not move without touching one another, were trying to exist, and to perform the necessary duties of everyday life. It was enough to make one sick at heart to see, subjected to such treatment and undergoing such suffering, hundreds of women and children who had committed no crime, but had merely shown their love and devotion by going into Siberian exile with the husbands, the fathers, or the brothers who were dear to them.

As we walked through the narrow gangways from one end of the shed to the other, we were besieged by unhappy men and women who desired to make complaints or petitions.

"Your High Nobility," said a heavy-eyed, anxious-looking man to the warden, "it is impossible to sleep here nights on account of the cold, the crowding, and the crying of babies. Can't something be done?"

"No, brother," replied the warden kindly; "I can't do anything. You will go on the road pretty soon, and then it will be easier."

"Dai Bogh!" [God grant it!] said the heavy-eyed man as he turned with a mournful look to his wife and a little girl who sat near him on the sleeping-bench.

"Bátiushka!" [My little father! My benefactor!] cried a pale-faced woman with an infant at her naked breast; "won't you, for God's sake, let me sleep in the bath-house with my baby? It's so cold here nights; I can't keep him warm."

"No, mátushka" [my little mother], said the warden; "I can't let you sleep in the bath-house. It is better for you here."

Several other women made in succession the same request, and were refused in the same way; and I finally asked the warden, who seemed to be a kind-hearted and sympathetic man, why he could not let a dozen or two of these unfortunate women, who had young babies, go to the bath-house to sleep. "It is cold here now," I said, "and it must be much worse at night. These thin walls of cotton-sheeting don't keep out at all the raw night air."

"It is impossible," replied the warden. "The atmosphere of the bath-house is too hot, close, and damp. I tried letting some of the nursing women sleep there, but one or two of their babies died every night, and I had to stop it."

I appreciated the hopelessness of the situation, and had nothing more to say. As we emerged from the *balagán*, we came upon Mr. Pépeláief engaged in earnest conversation with one of the exiles, a good-looking, blond-bearded man about thirty-five years of age, upon whose face there was an expression of agitation and excitement, mingled with a sort of defiant despair.

"I have had only one shirt in months," the exile said in a trembling voice, "and it is dirty, ragged, and full of vermin."

"Well!" said Mr. Pépeláief with contemptuous indifference, "you 'll get another when you go on the road."

"But when will I go on the road?" replied the exile with increasing excitement. "It may be three months hence."

"Very likely," said Mr. Pópeláief coldly, but with rising temper, as he saw us listening to the colloquy.

"Then do you expect a man to wear one shirt until it drops off from him?" inquired the exile with desperate indignation.

"Silence!" roared Mr. Pépeláief, losing all control of himself. "How dare you talk to me in that way? I 'll take the skin off from you! You 'll get another shirt when you go on the road, and not before. Away!"

The exile's face flushed, and the lump in his throat rose and fell as he struggled to choke down his emotion. At last he succeeded, and, turning away silently, entered the *balagán*.

"How long will the women and children have to stay in these sheds?" I asked the warden.

"Until the 2d of October," he replied.

"And where will you put them then?"

He shrugged his shoulders, but said nothing.[1]

From the *balagáns* we went to a "family *kámera*" in one of the log *kazárms*. Here there was the same scene of disorder and wretchedness that we had witnessed in the *balagáns*, with the exception that the walls were of logs, and the air, although foul, was warm. Men, women, and children were sitting on the *nári*, lying under them, standing in throngs in the gangways, and occupying in one way or another every available square foot of space in the *kámera*. I had seen enough of this sort of misery, and asked the warden to take us to the hospital, a two-story log building situated near the church. We were met at the door by Dr. Órzheshkó, the prison surgeon, who was a large, heavily built man, with a strong, good face, and who was by birth a Pole.

The hospital did not differ materially from that in the prison at Tiumén, except that it occupied a building by itself, and seemed to be in better order. It was intended originally to hold 50 beds; but on account of the overcrowding of the prison it had been found necessary to increase the number of beds to 150, and still nearly 50 sick patients were unprovided for and had to lie on benches or on the floor. The number of sick in the hospital at the time of our visit was 193, including 71 cases of typhus fever. The wards, although unduly crowded, were clean and neat, the bed-clothing was plentiful and fresh, and the atmosphere did not seem to me so terribly heavy and polluted as that of the hospital in Tiumén. The blackboards at the heads of the narrow cots showed that the prevalent diseases among the prisoners were typhus fever, scurvy, dysentery, rheumatism, anæmia, and bronchitis. Many of

[1] I learned upon my return trip that late in October 200 women and children were transferred to an empty house, hired for the purpose in the city of Tomsk, and that 1000 or 1500 other exiles were taken from the forwarding prison to the city prison and to the prison of the convict companies [arestántski róti]. These measures were rendered imperative by the alarming prevalence of disease — particularly typhus fever — in the forwarding prison as a result of the terrible overcrowding.

the nurses, I noticed, were women from 25 to 35 years of age, who had strong, intelligent faces, belonged apparently to one of the upper classes, and were probably medical students.

Early in the afternoon, after having made as careful an examination of the whole prison as circumstances would permit, we thanked the warden, Mr. Ivanénko, for his courteous attention, and for his evident disposition to deal with us frankly and honestly, and drove back to our hotel. It was long that night before I could get to sleep, and when I finally succeeded it was only to dream of crowded *balagáns*, of dead babies in bath-houses, and of the ghastly faces that I had seen in the hospital of the Tomsk forwarding prison.

Inasmuch as we did not see this prison at its worst, and inasmuch as I wish to give the reader a vivid realization, if possible, of the awful amount of human agony that the exile system causes, it seems to me absolutely necessary to say something, in closing, with regard to the condition of the Tomsk forwarding prison two months after we made to it the visit that I have tried to describe.

On my return to Tomsk from Eastern Siberia, in February, I had a long interview with Dr. Órzheshkó, the prison surgeon. He described to me the condition of the prison, as it gradually became more and more crowded in the late fall after our departure, and said to me: "You can hardly imagine the state of affairs that existed here in November. We had 2400 cases of sickness in the course of the year, and 450 patients in the hospital at one time, with beds for only 150. Three hundred men and women dangerously sick lay on the floor in rows, most of them without pillows or bed-clothing; and in order to find even floor space for them, we had to put them so close together that I could not walk between them, and a patient could not cough or vomit without coughing or vomiting into his own face or into the face of the man lying beside him. The atmosphere in the wards became so terribly polluted that I fainted repeatedly upon coming into the hospital in the morning, and my assistants had to revive me by dashing water into my face. In order to change and purify the air, we were forced to keep the windows open; and, as winter had set in, this so chilled the rooms that we could not maintain, on the floor where the sick lay, a temperature higher than five or six degrees Réaumur above the freezing point. More than 25 per cent. of the whole prison population were constantly sick, and more than 10 per cent. of the sick died."[1]

"How long," I inquired, "has this awful state of things existed?"

"I have been here fifteen years," replied Dr. Órzheshkó, "and it has been so, more or less, ever since I came."

"And is the Government at St. Petersburg aware of it?"

"It has been reported upon every year. I have recommended that the hospital of the Tomsk forwarding prison be burned to the ground. It is so saturated with contagious disease that it is unfit for use. We have been called upon by the prison department to forward plans for a new hospital, and we have forwarded them. They have been returned for modification, and we have modified them; but nothing has been done."[2]

It is unnecessary to comment upon this frank statement of the Tomsk surgeon. Civilization and humanity can

---

[1] The report of the inspector of exile transportation shows how rapidly the sick-rate increased with the progressive overcrowding. The figures are as follows:

1885, Month.	Average daily number of sick.	Per cent. of whole prison population.	1885, Month.	Average daily number of sick.	Per cent. of whole prison population.
June	108	5.8	September	242	9.6
July	170	6.9	October	356	15.4
August	189	7.1	November	406	25.2

The sick-rate increased steadily throughout the winter until March, when it reached high-water mark — 40.7 per cent., or nearly one-half the whole prison population. [Report of Inspector of Exile Transportation for 1885, p. 30 of the manuscript.]

[2] In 1887 fifteen thousand dollars were appropriated for the erection of new hospital barracks in this prison. [Rep. of the Chief Pris. Adm. for 1887. Ministry of the Interior, St. Petersburg, 1889.]

safely rest upon it, without argument, their case against the Tomsk forwarding prison.[1]

[1] See Appendix E for statements of other observers with regard to the condition of this prison. An English traveler — Mr. H. de Windt — inspected it last year and says that he "entirely failed to recognize it" from my "ghastly descriptions." I have appended his letters and my replies together with some other material relating to the subject, so that the reader may be able to form an independent judgment, not only with regard to the condition of this particular prison, but with regard to the trustworthiness of certain writers in England who describe Siberian prisons as equal to any in Europe, and who assert that an exile in Siberia "may be more comfortable than in many, and as comfortable as in most, of the prisons of the world."

CHAPTER XIV

THE LIFE OF POLITICAL EXILES

IN the city of Tomsk, where we spent more time than in any other West-Siberian town, we had an opportunity to become well acquainted with a large colony of political exiles, and greatly to extend our knowledge of political exile life. We met there, for the first time, men and women who had taken part in the so-called "propaganda" of 1872–75, who had been banished by sentence of a court, and who might fairly be called revolutionists. They did not differ essentially from the administrative exiles in Semipalátinsk, Ulbínsk and Ust Kámenogórsk, except that they had been longer in exile and had had a much wider range of experience. Solomon Chudnófski, for example, a bright and talented publicist, about thirty-five years of age, told me that he was arrested the first time at the age of nineteen, while in the university; and that he had been under police surveillance, in prison, or in exile nearly all his life. He was held four years and three months in solitary confinement before trial, and spent twenty months of that time in a casemate of the Petropávlovsk fortress. For protesting against illegal treatment in that great state-prison, and for insisting pertinaciously upon his right to have pen, ink, and paper, in order that he might address a complaint to the Minister of the Interior, he was tied hand and foot, and was finally put into a strait-jacket. He thereupon refused to take food, and starved himself until the prison surgeon reported that his condition was becoming critical. The warden, Colonel Bogaródski, then yielded, and furnished him with writing materials, but no reply was ever made to the complaint that he drew up. He was finally tried with "the 193," in 1878, upon the charge of importing pernicious books, was found guilty, and was sentenced to five years of penal servitude, with deprivation of all civil rights. In view, however, of the length of time that he had already been held in solitary confinement while awaiting trial— four years and three months—the court recommended to the Tsar that his sentence be commuted to exile in Western Siberia for life.[1]

Most men would have been completely broken down by nearly five years of solitary confinement and seven years of exile; but Mr. Chudnófski's energy and courage were invincible. In spite of the most disheartening obstacles he completed his education, and made a name and career for himself even in Siberia. He is the author of the excellent and carefully prepared history of the development of educational institutions in Siberia, published in the "Official Year Book" of the province of Tomsk for 1885; he has made two scientific expeditions to the Altái under the auspices of the West-Siberian Branch of the Imperial Geographical Society; he has been an indefatigable contributor to the Russian periodical press; and his book upon the Siberian province of Yeniséisk took the prize offered by the Krasnoyársk city council for the best work upon that subject.[2] Mr. Chudnófski impressed me as a man who, if he had been born in America, might have had a career of usefulness and distinction, and might have been an honor to the state.

[1] Sentence in the trial of "the 193," pp. 5, 11, and 16. An official copy of the document is in my possession.

[2] "The Province of Yeniséisk, a Statistical and Politico-Economical Study," by S. Chudnófski, 195 pages. Press of the *Siberian Gazette*, Tomsk, 1885.

The value of Mr. Chudnófski's book was greatly impaired by censorial mutilation, and the last two chapters could not be printed at all; but even in its expurgated form it is acknowledged to be one of the most important works of the kind that Siberia has yet produced.

He happened to be born in Russia, and was therefore pre-destined to imprisonment and exile.

Among the most interesting of the newly arrived political exiles in Tomsk was Mr. Constantine Staniukóvich, the editor and proprietor of the Russian magazine *Diélo*,

PRINCE KROPÓTKIN.

whose history I gave briefly in Chapter XI ["Exile by Administrative Process," p. 243]. He was a close and accurate observer of Russian social life, a talented novelist, a writer of successful dramas, and a man of great force, energy, and ability. His wife, who had accompanied him to Siberia, spoke English fluently with the least perceptible accent, and seemed to me to be a woman of more than ordinary culture and refinement. They had one grown daughter, a pretty, intelligent girl seventeen or eighteen years of age, as well as two or three younger children, and the whole family made upon us an extremely pleasant impression. Some of the most delightful evenings that we had in Tomsk were spent in their cozy little parlor, where we sometimes sat until long after midnight listening to duets sung by Miss Staniukóvich and Prince Kropótkin; discussing Russian methods of government and the exile system; or comparing our impressions of London, Paris, Berlin, New York, and San Francisco. Both Mr. and Mrs. Staniukóvich had traveled in the United States, and it seemed not a little strange to find in their house in Siberia visiting-cards of such well-known American officers as Captain James B. Eads and Captain John Rodgers, a photograph of President Lincoln, and Indian bead and birch-bark work in the shape of slippers and toy canoes brought as souvenirs from Niagara Falls. We had not expected to find ourselves linked to political exiles in Siberia by such a multitude of common experiences and memories, nor to be shown in their houses such familiar things as bead-embroidered moccasins and birch-bark watch-pockets made by the Tonawanda Indians. Mr. Staniukóvich was struggling hard, by means of literary work, to support his family in exile; and his wife, who was an accomplished musician, aided him as far as possible by giving music lessons.

I am glad to be able to say that, since my return to the United States, Mr. Staniukóvich has completed his term of exile, has left the empire, and when I last heard of him was in Paris. He continues to write indefatigably for the Russian periodicals, and has recently published a volume of collected sketches entitled "Stories of the Sea."

Another political exile in whom I became deeply interested at Tomsk was Prince Alexander Kropótkin, brother of the well-known author and socialist who now resides in London. As his history clearly illustrates certain phases of political exile life I will briefly relate it.

Although banished to Siberia upon the charge of disloyalty Kropótkin was not a nihilist, nor a revolutionist, nor even an extreme radical. His views with regard to social and political questions would have been regarded in America, or even in western Europe, as very moderate, and he had never taken any part in Russian revolutionary agitation. He was, however, a man of impetuous temperament, high standard of honor, and great frankness and directness of speech; and these characteristics were perhaps enough to attract to him the suspicious attention of the Russian police.

"I am not a nihilist nor a revolutionist," he once said to me indignantly, "and I never have been. I was exiled simply because I dared to think, and to say what I thought, about the things that happened around me, and because I was the brother of a man whom the Russian Government hated."

Prince Kropótkin was arrested the first time in 1858, while a student in the St. Petersburg University, for having in his possession a copy in English of Emerson's "Self-Reliance" and refusing to say where he obtained it. The book had been lent to him by one of the faculty, Professor Tíkhonrávof, and Kropótkin might perhaps have justified himself and escaped unpleasant consequences by simply stating the fact; but this would not have been in accordance with his high standard of personal honor. He did not think it a crime to read Emerson, but he did regard it as cowardly and dishonorable to shelter himself from the consequences of any action behind the person of an instructor. He preferred to go to prison. When Professor Tíkhonrávof heard of Kropótkin's arrest he went at once to the rector of the university, and admitted that he was the owner of the incendiary volume, and the young student was thereupon released.

After his graduation from the university Kropótkin went abroad, studied science, particularly astronomy, and upon his return to Russia made a number of important translations of French and English scientific works into his native language. Finally he entered the Government service, and for a time previous to his exile held an important place in the Russian telegraph department. This place, however, he was forced to resign in consequence of a collision with the Minister of the Interior. The latter ordered Kropótkin one day to send to him all the telegrams of a certain private individual that were on file in his office. Kropótkin refused to obey this order upon the ground that such action would be personally dishonorable and degrading. Another less scrupulous officer of the department, however, forwarded the required telegrams and Kropótkin resigned. After this time he lived constantly under the secret supervision of the police. His brother Peter had already become prominent as a revolutionist and socialist; he himself was under suspicion; his record, from the point of view of the Government, was not a good one; he probably injured himself still further by frank but injudicious comments upon public affairs; and in 1876 or 1877 he was arrested and exiled to Eastern Siberia upon the vague but fatal charge of "political untrustworthiness." There were no proofs against him upon which a conviction could be had in a court of justice, and he was therefore banished by administrative process.

His place of exile was a small town called Minusínsk, situated on the Yeniséi River in Eastern Siberia, more than 3000 miles from St. Petersburg, and about 150 miles from the boundary line of Mongolia. Here, with his young wife, who had voluntarily accompanied him into exile, he lived quietly four or five years, devoting himself chiefly to reading and scientific study. There were in Minusínsk at that time no other political exiles, but Kropótkin found there, nevertheless, one congenial companion in the person of a Russian naturalist named Martiánof, with whom he wandered about the country making botanical and geological collections and discussing scientific questions. To Martiánof's enthusiasm and energy and Kropótkin's sympathy and encouragement, Minusínsk is indebted for its really excellent museum, an institution which not only is the pride of all intelligent Siberians, but is becoming known to naturalists and archæologists in Europe and the United States.

During the long series of tragic events that culminated in the assassination of Alexander II., Siberia filled up rapidly with political exiles, and the little town of Minusínsk had to take its quota. With the arrival of these new-comers began a stricter system of police supervision. As long as Kropótkin was the only political exile in the place, he was allowed a good deal of freedom, and was not harassed by humiliating police regulations; but when the number of politicals increased to twenty, the difficulty of watching them all became greater, and the authorities thought it necessary, as a means of preventing escapes, to require every exile to report himself at stated intervals to the chief of police and sign his name in a book kept for the purpose. To this regulation Kropótkin refused to submit. "I have lived here," he said to the *isprávnik*, "nearly five years and have not yet made the first attempt to escape. If you think that there is any danger of my running away now, you may send a soldier or a police officer to my house every day to watch me; but after being unjustly exiled to Siberia I don't propose to assist the Government in its supervision of me. I will not report at the police office." The *isprávnik* conferred with the governor of the province, who lived in Krasnoyársk, and by the latter's direction told Kropótkin that if he refused to obey the obnoxious regulation he would be banished to some place lying farther to the northward and eastward, where the climate would be more severe and the life less bearable. Kropótkin, however, adhered to his determination, and appealed to General Sheláshnikof, who was at that time the acting governor-general of Eastern Siberia and who had been on terms of personal friendship with Kropótkin before the latter's banishment. General Sheláshnikof replied in a cool, formal note, insisting upon obedience to the regulation, and warning Kropótkin that further contumacy would have for him disastrous consequences. While this appeal was pending, General Anúchin was appointed governor-general of Eastern Siberia, and, as a last resort, Kropótkin wrote to his aged mother in St. Petersburg to see Anúchin previous to the latter's departure for his new post and present to him a petition in her son's behalf. When the aged and heart-broken mother appeared with her petition in General Anúchin's reception-room she was treated with insulting brutality. Without reading the petition Anúchin threw it violently on the floor, asked her how she dared to come to him with such a petition from a traitor to his country, and declared that if her son "had his deserts he would be cleaning the streets in some Siberian city under guard, instead of walking about at liberty."

By this time all of the other political exiles in Minusínsk had submitted to the new regulation and were reporting at the police office, and Kropótkin was notified by the *isprávnik* that if within a stated time he did not follow their example he would be banished to Túrukhánsk, a wretched settlement of twelve or fifteen houses, situated in the province of Yeniséisk, near the coast of the arctic ocean. Kropótkin, however, still adhered to his resolution, and after a terribly trying interview with his wife, to whom he was devotedly attached, he succeeded in extorting from her a promise to return to European Russia with their young child, and let him go to Túrukhánsk alone. What this promise cost them both in misery I could imagine from the tears which suffused their eyes when they talked to me about it. At the last moment, however, while Mrs. Kropótkin was making preparations to return to European Russia, she happened to see in the *Siberian Gazette* a letter from some correspondent—a political exile, I think —in Túrukhánsk, describing the loneliness, dreariness, and unhealthfulness of the settlement, the arctic severity of the climate, the absence of all medical aid for the sick, and the many miseries of life in such a place. This completely broke down the wife's fortitude. She went to her husband, convulsed with sobs, and told him that she would send her child to European Russia, or leave it with friends in Minusínsk, but go with him to Túrukhánsk she must and should —to let him go there alone was beyond her strength. "After this," said Prince Kropótkin, "there was nothing for, me to do but put a pistol to my head, or yield, and I yielded. I went to the police office, and continued to report there as long as I remained in Minusínsk."

I have related this incident in Prince Kropótkin's Siberian life partly because it seems to have first suggested suicide to him as a means of escape from an intolerable position, and partly because it is in many ways an index to his character. He was extremely sensitive, proud, and high-spirited, and often made a fight upon some point which a cooler, more philosophic man would have taken as one of the natural incidents of his situation.

About two years ago Prince Kropótkin was transferred from Minusínsk to Tomsk, a change which brought him a few hundred miles nearer to European Russia, but which in other respects was not perhaps a desirable one. When I saw him in February he was living simply but comfortably in a rather spacious log house, ten minutes' drive from the European Hotel, and was devoting himself to literary pursuits. He had a good working library of two or three hundred volumes, among which I noticed the astronomical works of Professors Newcomb and Holden, Stallo's "Concepts of Science," of which he expressed a very high opinion, several volumes of "Smithsonian Reports," and forty or fifty other American books. His favorite study was astronomy, and in this branch of science he would probably have distinguished himself under more favorable circumstances. After his exile, however, he was not only deprived of instruments, but had great difficulty in obtaining books; his private correspondence was under control, and he was more

or less constantly disquieted and harassed by police supervision and searches of his house; so that his completed
scientific work was limited to a few articles upon astronomical subjects, written for French and German periodicals. He was a fine linguist, and wrote almost equally well
in French, German, and Russian. English he read easily
but could not speak.

On the last day before my departure from Tomsk he
came to my room, bringing a letter which I had promised
to carry for him to one of his intimate friends in western
Europe. With the keen sense of honor which was one of
his distinguishing characteristics, he brought the letter to
me open, so that I might assure myself by reading it that it
contained nothing which would compromise me in case the
Russian police should find it in my possession. I told him
that I did not care to read it, that I would run the risk of carrying anything that he would run the risk of writing—his
danger in any case would be greater than mine. He thereupon seated himself at my writing-table to address the
envelope. We happened at the moment to be talking of
his brother, Pierre Kropótkin, and his pen, taking its suggestion from his thoughts, wrote automatically upon the
envelope his brother's name instead of the name of the
person for whom the letter was intended. He discovered
the error almost instantly, and tearing up the envelope
and throwing the fragments upon the floor, he addressed
another. Late that evening, after I had gone to bed, there
came a knock at my door. I opened it cautiously, and was
confronted by Prince Kropótkin. He was embarrassed and
confused, and apologized for calling at that late hour, but
said that he could not sleep without finding and destroying
every fragment of the envelope upon which he had inad-
vertently written the name of his brother. "This may seem
to you," he said, "like absurd timidity, but it is necessary.
If the police should discover, as they probably will, that I
visited you to-day, they would not only examine the servants

as to everything which took place here, but would collect and fit together every scrap of waste paper found in your room. They would thus find out that I had addressed an envelope to my brother, and would jump at the conclusion that I had written him a letter, and had given it to you for delivery. How this would affect you I don't know, but it would be fatal to me. The least I could expect would be the addition of a year to my term of exile, or banishment to some more remote part of Siberia. I am strictly forbidden to communicate with my brother, and have not heard directly from him or been able to write to him in years." I was familiar enough with the conditions of exile life in Siberia to see the force of these statements, and we began at once a search for the fragments of the envelope. Every scrap of paper on the floor was carefully examined, but the pieces that bore the dangerous name, "Pierre A. Kropótkin," could not be found. At last my traveling companion, Mr. Frost, remembered picking up some torn scraps of paper and throwing them into the slop-basin. We then dabbled in the basin for twenty minutes until we found and burned every scrap of that envelope upon which there was the stroke of a pen, and only then could Prince Kropótkin go home and sleep. "Two years hence," he said to me as he bade me good-night, "you may publish this as an illustration of the atmosphere of suspicion and apprehension in which political exiles live. In two years I hope to be beyond the reach of the Russian police." Poor Kropótkin! In less than two years his hope was realized, but not in the way we then anticipated. I had hardly returned to my home in the United States when the *Eastern Review* of St. Petersburg, a newspaper devoted to the interests and the news of Asiatic Russia, made the following brief announcement:

"On the 25th of July, about nine o'clock in the evening, Prince A. A. Kropótkin committed suicide in Tomsk by shooting himself with a revolver. He had been in administrative exile about ten years, and his term of banishment would have expired on the 9th of next September. He had begun to make arrangements for returning to Russia, and had already sent his wife and his three children back to his relatives in the province of Khárkóf. He was devotedly attached to them, and soon after their departure he grew lonely and low-spirited, and showed that he felt very deeply his separation from them. To this reason for despondency must also be added anxiety with regard to the means of subsistence. Although, at one time, a rather wealthy landed proprietor, Prince Kropótkin, during his long period of exile in Siberia, had expended almost his whole fortune; so that on the day of his death his entire property did not amount to three hundred rubles [$150]. At the age of forty-five, therefore, he was compelled, for the first time, seriously to consider the question how he should live and support his family — a question which was the more difficult to answer for the reason that a scientific man, in Russia, cannot count upon earning a great deal in the field of literature, and Prince Kropótkin was not fitted for anything else. While under the disheartening influence of these considerations he received, moreover, several telegrams from his relatives which he misinterpreted. Whether he committed suicide as a result of sane deliberation, or whether a combination of circumstances superinduced acute mental disorder, none who were near him at the moment of his death can say." *Eastern Review*, No. 34, St. Petersburg, August 21, 1886.

Of course the editor of the *Eastern Review* was not allowed by the censor to say even one last kind word of the innocent man who had been driven to self-destruction by injustice and exile; but I will say — and say it with all my heart — that in Prince Kropótkin's death Russia lost an honest man, a cultivated scholar, a true patriot, and a most gallant gentleman.

To me perhaps the most attractive and sympathetic of the Tomsk exiles was the Russian author Felix Volkhófski, who was banished to Siberia for life in 1878, upon the charge of " belonging to a society that intends, at a more or less remote time in the future, to overthrow the existing form of government." He was about thirty-eight years of age at the time I made his acquaintance, and was a man of cultivated mind, warm heart, and high aspirations. He knew English well, was familiar with American history and literature, and had, I believe, translated into Russian many of the poems of Longfellow. He spoke to me with great admiration, I remember, of Longfellow's "Arsenal at Springfield," and recited it to me aloud. He was one of the most winning and lovable men that it has ever been my good fortune to know; but his life had been a terrible tragedy. His health had been shattered by long imprisonment in the fortress of Petropávlovsk; his hair was prematurely gray, and when his face was in repose there seemed to be an expression of profound melancholy in his dark-brown eyes. I became intimately acquainted with him and very warmly attached to him; and when I bade him good-by for the last time on my return from Eastern Siberia in 1886, he put his arms around me and kissed me, and said, "George Ivánovich, please don't forget us! In bidding you good-by, I feel as if something were going out of my life that would never again come into it."

A little more than a year after my return to the United States, Volkhófski wrote me a profoundly sad and touching letter, in which he informed me of the death of his wife by suicide. He himself had been thrown out of employment by the suspension of the liberal Tomsk newspaper, the *Siberian Gazette;* and his wife, whom I remember as a pale, delicate, sad-faced woman, twenty-five or thirty years of age, had tried to help him support their family of young children by giving private lessons and by taking in sewing. Anxiety and overwork had finally broken down her health; she had become an invalid, and in a morbid state of mind, brought on by unhappiness and disease, she reasoned herself into the belief that she was an incumbrance, rather than a help, to her husband and her children, and that they would ultimately be better off if she were dead. On the 7th of December, 1887, she put an end to her unhappy life by shooting herself through the

head with a pistol. Her husband was devotedly attached
to her; and her death, under such circumstances and in
such a way, was a terrible blow to him. In his letter to me
he referred to a copy of James Russell Lowell's poems that
I had caused to be sent to him, and said that in reading
"After the Burial" he vividly realized for the first time
that grief is of no nationality: the lines, although written
by a bereaved American, expressed the deepest thoughts
and feelings of a bereaved Russian. He sent me with his
letter a small, worn, leather match-box, which had been
given by Prince Pierre Kropótkin to his exiled brother
Alexander; which the latter had left to Volkhófski; and
which Volkhófski had in turn presented to his wife a short
time before her death. He hoped, he said, that it would
have some value to me, on account of its association with
the lives of four political offenders, all of whom I had
known. One of them was a refugee in London, another
was an exile in Tomsk, and two had escaped the jurisdiction
of the Russian Government by taking their own lives.

I tried to read Volkhófski's letter aloud to my wife; but as
I recalled the high character and lovable personality of the
writer, and imagined what this last blow of fate must have
been to such a man,— in exile, in broken health, and with
three helpless children wholly dependent upon him,— the
written lines vanished in a mist of tears, and with a choking
in my throat I put the letter and the little match-box away.

By means of secret prearranged addresses in Russia and
in the United States, I succeeded in maintaining a desul-
tory and precarious correspondence with Mr. Volkhófski
until 1889. In the spring of that year I received from him
two short letters filled with tidings of misfortune, and then—
nothing more. The two letters were, in part, as follows:

TOMSK, February 14, 1889.

My DEAR GEORGE IVÁNOVICH:

I write you a few lines first to tell you how weary I am of waiting
for a letter from you (although I know that you have not written

on account of my warning), and second to give you notice that I sent you some time since a manuscript addressed . . . so that if you have not received it you may make inquiries about it.

You have probably heard before this time of the final suppression of the *Siberian Gazette*.[1] It is hard and it is shameful! You need not hesitate any longer to write whatever you like about it for publication. You will not injure the paper because there is no hope of its resurrection. . . .

My youngest daughter is still sick and has grown so thin that it is painful to look at her. She sleeps badly and often I have to be up all night taking care of her. This, together with constant fear for her life, disorders my nerves terribly, and undermines what health I have left. I am greatly disheartened, too, by loneliness, notwithstanding my children and my friends. The affectionate tenderness of a beloved wife is a thing that some natures find it difficult to do without, no matter what else they may have. It is very hard, sometimes, my dear fellow, to live in this world!

Since it became apparent that I should no longer be able to support myself by newspaper work,[2] I have been looking for some other occupation or place; but, unfortunately, the present governor[3] is expelling political exiles from all public positions, and even debarring them, to some extent, from private employment, by showing such hostility to them that private individuals dare not give them work for fear of getting into trouble. I do not know how it will all end. I have sent four manuscripts to St. Petersburg, but none of them has been published.

My dear George Ivánovich, may you be well and happy! I am impatiently awaiting your photograph and hope that it will have your autograph on it. With most cordial remembrances to your wife, I am   Yours,   FELIX.

[1] The *Siberian Gazette*, the only liberal and progressive newspaper in Western Siberia, was suspended for eight months on the 3d of April, 1887, as the result of a secret report made by the Governor of Tobólsk to the Minister of the Interior. It survived this blow, but was finally suppressed altogether in the latter part of 1888. The only reasons assigned for this persecution of an able and honorable newspaper were first, the use by it of news and literary material furnished by political exiles, and second, the publication by it of an obituary notice of a political exile named Zabalúief, whose life and character had won the respect of everybody in Tomsk.

[2] On account of the suppression of the *Siberian Gazette*. Mr. Volkhófski had conducted the department of city news.

[3] Governor Bulubásh, formerly vice-governor of the province of Taurida. His predecessor, Governor Laks, was a comparatively liberal and enlightened man.

IRKÚTSK, EASTERN SIBERIA, May 7, 1889.

MY DEAR GOOD FRIEND:

How long it is since I last received a line from you, and how much I have needed your letters! They bring to me all the mental refreshment and all the gladness that life has for me, and at times I am sorely in need of them. Fate has dealt me another blow. My youngest daughter Katie died a month or two since of pneumonia. She had an attack of bronchitis winter before last which developed into chronic inflammation of the lungs; but in the spring of 1888 I took her into the country, where she grew better and began to run about and play. Unfortunately, however, she was exposed there to whooping-cough, took the infection, and it ended in acute pneumonia and death. She was about three years old—and such a dear lovable child! But whose child is not dear and lovable? At any rate—

No! I can't write any more about it! This is the second time within a few days that I have tried to write you of her—but I cannot—it hurts me too much! As long as I am busy and can talk or write of other things, it seems as if the wound were healed; but let my thoughts once go to her, and I feel such grief and pain that I don't know what to do with myself.

I must explain to you how I happen to be in Irkútsk. It is a very simple story. Thanks to the recommendation of some of my Irkútsk friends I was offered here a place that was suited to my tastes and abilities, and I hastened to migrate. They will always know my address here at the post-office.[1]

All of your Irkútsk friends send you their regards. I could and would write you a great deal more, but I don't want to detain this letter and will therefore postpone the rest until next time. My warmest regards to your wife. Write me!

Affectionately,   FELIX.

After the receipt of this letter I wrote Mr. Volkhófski twice, but I heard from him no more. What had happened to him I could only conjecture; but as month after month

---

[1] When political offenders sentenced merely to "domestication" [*na zhityó*] or colonization [*na poselénie*] have been ten years in exile, and have behaved during that time in a manner satisfactory to the authorities, it is customary to give them more freedom of movement. They are still kept under police surveillance, but are allowed to go anywhere within the limits of certain provinces. After I returned to the United States, Mr. Volkhófski received a "ticket of leave" of this kind.

passed without bringing any news from him, I felt more and more apprehensive that the sorrows and hardships of his life had been too great for his strength and that the next tidings of him would be the news of his death. At last, in November, 1889, when I had almost given up hope, I was astonished and delighted to receive one day a letter addressed in his familiar handwriting, but stamped with a Canadian stamp and postmarked " Vancouver."

" How did he ever get a letter mailed at Vancouver?" I said to myself, and hastily tearing open the envelope I read the first three lines. They were as follows:

" My dear George Ivánovich: At last I am *free!* I am writing this letter to you not from that land of exile, Siberia, but from free America."

If I had suddenly received a letter postmarked " Zanzibar " from a friend whom I believed to be dead and buried in Minnesota, I could hardly have been more astonished or excited. Volkhófski free and in British Columbia! It seemed utterly incredible; and in a maze of bewilderment I stopped reading the letter to look again at the postmark. It was unquestionably " Vancouver," and as I stared at it I came slowly to a realization of the fact that, in some extraordinary and incomprehensible way, Volkhófski had not only escaped, but had crossed the Pacific and was within a few days' journey of New York. His letter, which was brief and hurried, merely announced his escape from exile by way of the Amúr River, Vládivostók, and Japan, and his intention of coming to me in Washington as soon as he could be sure of finding me there. In the mean time I need not, he said, feel any anxiety about him, because he still had sixty Mexican silver dollars left, and was with a steamer acquaintance who had taken a warm and generous interest in his fortunes.

At the time when I received this letter I was lecturing six nights a week in New York and New England; but I telegraphed and wrote Volkhófski that I would meet him at the Delavan House in Albany on the morning of Sunday, December 8th. I spoke Saturday night in Utica, took the night express for Albany, and reached the Delavan House about two o'clock. Volkhófski had not yet arrived, and as it was uncertain when he would come I went to bed. Early in the morning a bell-boy knocked loudly at my door and handed me a slip of paper upon which, in Volkhófski's handwriting, were the words, "My dear fellow, I am here."

If any of the guests of the Delavan House happened to be passing through that corridor on their way to breakfast three minutes later, they must have been surprised to see, at the door of No. 90, a man with disheveled hair and nothing on but his night-shirt locked in the embrace of a traveler who had not had time to remove his Pacific-coast sombrero and heavy winter overcoat.

Volkhófski was in better health than I had expected to see him, but his face was worn and haggard, and at times there was a peculiar anxious hunted expression in his eyes which showed that he had recently been under great mental and emotional strain. We talked almost without intermission for twelve hours, and he related to me at length the story of his escape. When he wrote me the last time from Siberia in May, 1889, he was living with his little daughter Véra in Irkútsk, where he had found congenial employment, and where he was trying, by means of hard work, to lighten the sense of loneliness and bereavement that he had felt since the death of his wife and his daughter Katie. Hardly had his life begun to seem once more bearable when there came upon him a new misfortune in the shape of an order from the governor-general[1] to leave the city. He had committed no new offense, and there was no reason, so far as he was aware, for this arbitrary and imperative order; but General Ignátief seemed to be of opinion that the presence of a liberal author and journalist, and moreover a "political," in the city of

---

[1] Governor-general Ignátief, brother of the well-known diplomatist. He is now governor-general of Kiev.

Irkútsk would be "prejudicial to public tranquillity," and Volkhófski was therefore directed to "move on." Leaving his little daughter Véra with acquaintances in Irkútsk, he proceeded to Tróitskosávsk, a small town on the frontier of Mongolia, where one of his friends, a political exile named Charúshin, had for some time been living. The police there, however, had been apprised of his expulsion from Irkútsk, and assuming, of course, that he must be a very dangerous or a very troublesome man, they hastened to inform him that he could not be permitted to take up his residence in Tróitskosávsk. They did not care whither he went, but he must go somewhere beyond the limits of their jurisdiction. Indignant and disheartened, Volkhófski then resolved to abandon temporarily his little daughter Véra, whom he had left in Irkútsk, and make his escape, if possible, to the United States by way of the Pacific Ocean. He had a little money derived from the sale of a small volume of poems which he had published before leaving Tomsk[1], and if that should fail before he reached his destination, he determined to work as a stevedore, or a common laborer of some sort, until he should earn enough to go on. His objective point was the city of Washington, where he expected to find me. The nearest seaport on the Pacific where he could hope to get on board a foreign steamer was Vládivostók, about 2800 miles away. The distance to be traversed under the eyes of a suspicious and hostile police was immense; but Volkhófski was cautious, prudent, and experienced, and assuming the character of a retired army officer he set out, with "free" horses, for the head waters of the Amúr River, where he expected to take a steamer. I cannot, of course, go into the details of his difficult and perilous journey from Tróitskosávsk to Strétinsk, from Strétinsk down the Amúr by steamer to Khabarófka, and from Khabarófka up the Ússurí and across Lake Khánka to Vládivos-

---

[1] "Siberian Echoes," by Iván Brut [a pseudonym]. Mikháilof and Mákushin, Tomsk, 1889.

tók. It was a journey full of adventures and narrow escapes, and nothing but the coolness, courage, and good fortune of the fugitive carried him through in safety.   There were four foreign vessels in the port of Vládivostók at that time, and one of them, a coal steamer, was flying the flag of Great Britain. Volkhófski went on board, ascertained that the steamer was bound for Japan, and asked the captain if he would take a passenger who had neither passport nor official permission to leave the empire. The captain hesitated at first, but when Volkhófski related his story, said that he was able and willing to pay for his passage, and exhibited my photograph and letters as proofs of his trustworthiness, the captain consented to take him. A hiding-place was soon found for him, and when the Russian officials came on board to clear the vessel, he was nowhere to be seen. A few hours later the steamer was at sea, and the escaping political exile, as he stood on the upper deck and watched the slow fading of the Siberian coast in the west, drew a long deep breath of relief, and turned his face, with reviving hope, towards the land where a personal opinion concerning human affairs is not regarded as " prejudicial to public tranquillity," and where a man who tries to make the world better and happier is not punished for it with seven years of solitary confinement, eleven years of exile, and the loss of more than half his family.

After having paid his steamer fare from Vládivostók to Nagasaki, and from Nagasaki to Yokohama, Volkhófski found himself in the latter place with hardly money enough to get across the Pacific, and not half enough to reach Washington. He made inquiries concerning vessels about to sail for the western coast of America, and found that the English steamer *Batavia* was on the point of clearing for Vancouver, British Columbia. Going at once on board he asked the purser what the fare to Vancouver would be in the steerage. The officer looked at him for a moment, saw that, although a foreigner, he was unmistakably a gentleman, and then replied, bluntly but not unkindly, "You can't go in the steerage—it's jammed full of Chinese emigrants. Nobody ever goes in the steerage except Chinamen; it's no place for you." Volkhófski replied that the case was urgent — that he must get to British Columbia at once — and as he had not money enough to pay even for a second-class passage, there was nothing for him to do but go third class. The purser finally sold him a steerage ticket, but declared, nevertheless, that a white man could not possibly live for three weeks with opium-smoking Chinese coolies, and that he should put him in some other part of the vessel as soon as possible after leaving port.

Until the *Batavia* had actually sailed and was out of the harbor, Volkhófski did not dare to let the passengers, or even the officers, of the steamer know who he really was and whence he had come. The Japanese were in the habit of giving up Siberian refugees to the Russian authorities; and if it should accidentally become known that he was an escaping political exile, he might be arrested, even in Yokohama, and put on board a Russian man-of-war. He believed that he had narrowly escaped detection and capture in Nagasaki, and he did not intend to run any more risks that could be avoided. At last, however, when the *Batavia* was far at sea, and the coast of Japan had sunk beneath the rim of the western horizon, he told his story to the officers of the ship, and afterward admitted to the passengers with whom he became acquainted that he was an escaped political exile from Siberia. The interest and sympathy excited by his narrative deepened as the officers and passengers became better acquainted with him, and long before the *Batavia* reached Vancouver, he had so completely won the hearts of the whole ship's company that they took up a collection for the purpose of providing him with transportation from Vancouver to the city of Washington. To this collection every soul on board contributed, from the captain down to the steward, the cook, and the boy who cleaned the ship's lamps.[1] More than enough money was obtained to defray his expenses across the continent, and when he left the steamer he had not only the sixty Mexican silver dollars about which he wrote me, but a first-class ticket to Washington, and a cordial invitation from one of the passengers — Mr. Allan Huber of Berlin, Ontario—to stay at his house until my whereabouts could be ascertained.

When Volkhófski met me in Albany, he was terribly anxious with regard to the safety of his nine-year-old daughter Véra, whom he had left with friends in the capital of Eastern Siberia. He feared that, as soon as his escape should become known, the Government would seize the little girl, and either use her as a means of compelling him to return or put her into a state asylum, where she would virtually be lost to him forever.

"If I can only get my little girl," he said to me, "I shall feel as if I had strength and spirit enough to begin a new life; but if I lose her, I may as well give up the struggle."

"We 'll get your little girl," I replied, "if we have to resort to fraud, violence, false passports, and kidnapping"— and we *did* get her. In June, 1890, Volkhófski went to London, so as to be nearer the field of operations, and six weeks later I received from him a cablegram saying, "Hurrah! my child has arrived."

In a recent letter to a friend in Buffalo, New York, the well-known English novelist, Hesba Stretton, speaks of Volkhófski and his daughter as follows:

"Volkhófski, who escaped from Siberia rather more than a year ago, has been lecturing in England all winter. He has a charming little daughter ten years old who was born in exile. She has been staying for a fortnight with my married sister and her two daughters, and they are quite

---

[1] The steward became so much attached to Volkhófski, in the course of the voyage, that long afterward, in Montreal, he came to call upon me for the purpose of making inquiries about him.

delighted with her; she is so original and affectionate, and she has had so much tragedy in her short life, which she speaks of now and then as if horrors were a natural part of existence to her. She was brought through Siberia and Russia disguised as a boy. We hope to wean her thoughts from these terrible subjects and give her something of the ordinary joys of girlhood. But her destiny must be a sad one, for she will surely [and quite rightly] throw in her lot with the revolutionists of Russia, and unless the revolution comes soon our little Véra will spend much of her life in prison and in exile. She was showing Annie how the orthodox Russians hold their thumbs and two fingers pressed together to represent the Trinity during their worship, and then she said, 'But God does n't mind how we hold our fingers, does he?' She was moaning in her sleep one night, and when Daisy woke her she said, 'I dreamed there were spies in the room, and I pretended to be asleep till they went to sleep, and then I got up and crept to the cot where my baby brother was. I said, "Hush! don't make a noise, for there are spies in the room," and I took him up and went to the door watching the spies all the time, and I opened the door and there were some men hung up, and my father's head lay on the ground and his body was a little way off covered with a white cloth.' Think of that for the dream of a child of ten years, and think how countless are the sorrows and wrongs inflicted by the Czar of Russia and his Government! And they say he is a humane, Christian man. Alas! what horrible things are said to be Christian."

Mr. Volkhófski is now editing in London the newspaper *Free Russia*, the organ of the English society known as "The Friends of Russian Freedom."

The extension of our acquaintance in Tomsk, on one side with Government officials, and on the other with political exiles, led now and then to peculiar and embarrassing situations. A day or two before our departure for Irkútsk, while two of the politicals — Messrs. Volkhófski and Chud-nófski—were sitting in our room at the European Hotel, a servant suddenly knocked, threw open the door, and announced his Excellency Actual State Councilor Petukhóf, the governor *pro tem.* of the province. My heart, as the Russians say, went into my fingers' ends. I did not know what relations existed between the banished revolutionists and Vice-governor Petukhóf. We had called several times upon the latter without referring in any way to our acquaintance with this class of criminals; and in all our intercourse with the Tomsk officials we had treated the subject of political exile with studied indifference, in order to avert suspicion and escape troublesome inquiries. To be then surprised by the vice-governor himself while two prominent politicals were sitting in our room and writing at our table was, to say the least, embarrassing. I had just had time to ask Volkhófski and Chudnófski whether or not I should introduce them to the vice-governor, when the latter, in full uniform, entered the room. There was a curious expression of surprise in his good-humored face as he took in at a glance the situation; but the removal of his heavy overcoat and galoshes gave him an opportunity to recover himself, and as he came forward with outstretched hand to greet Mr. Frost and me there was nothing in his manner to indicate the least annoyance or embarrassment. He shook hands cordially with the two political exiles who had been condemned by a court of justice to penal servitude; began at once a conversation in which they could join, and behaved generally with so much tact and courtesy, that in five minutes we were all chatting together as unceremoniously as if we were old acquaintances who had met accidentally at a club. It was, however, a strangely constituted group: an American newspaper man; an American artist; two political exiles who had been punished with solitary confinement, leg-fetters, and the strait-jacket; and, finally, the highest provincial representative of the Government that had so dealt with these exiles—all meeting upon the common footing of personal character, and ignoring, for the time, the peculiar network of interrelations that united them. Whether or not Vice-governor Petukhóf reported to the Minister of the Interior that we had made the acquaintance of the political criminals in Tomsk, I do not know—probably not. He seemed to me to be a faithful officer of the Crown, but, at the same time, a man of culture, ability, and good sense; and while he doubtless disapproved of the revolutionary movement, he recognized the fact that among the banished revolutionists were men of education, refinement, and high personal character, who might, naturally enough, attract the attention of foreign travelers.

The number of politicals in Tomsk, at the time of our visit, was about thirty, including six or eight women. Some of them were administrative exiles, who had only just arrived from European Russia; some were *poseléntsi*, or forced colonists, who had been banished originally to "the most remote part" of Siberia, but who had finally been allowed to return in broken health to a "less remote part"; while a few were survivors of the famous "193," who had languished for years in the casemates of the Petropávlovsk fortress, and had then been sent to the plains of Western Siberia.

I was struck by the composure with which these exiles would sometimes talk of intolerable injustice and frightful sufferings. The men and women who had been sent to the province of Yakútsk for refusing to take the oath of allegiance to Alexander III., and who had suffered in that arctic wilderness all that human beings can suffer from hunger, cold, sickness, and bereavement, did not seem to be conscious that there was anything very extraordinary in their experience. Now and then some man whose wife had committed suicide in exile would flush a little and clinch his hands as he spoke of her; or some broken-hearted woman whose baby had frozen to death in her arms on the road would sob at intervals as she tried to tell me her story; but, as a rule, both men and women referred to injustice and suffering with perfect composure, as if they were nothing more than the ordinary accidents of life. Mr. Volkhófski showed me one day, I remember, a large collection of photographs of his revolutionary friends. Whenever a face struck me as being noteworthy, on account of its beauty or character, I would ask whose it was.

"That," he would say quietly, "is Miss A——, once a teacher in a peasant school; she died of prison consumption in Kiev three years ago. The man with the full beard is B——, formerly a justice of the peace in N——; he was hanged at St. Petersburg in 1879. The thin-faced girl is Miss C——, one of the so-called propagandists; she went insane in the House of Preliminary Detention while awaiting trial. The pretty young woman with the cross on the sleeve of her dress is Madame D——, a Red Cross nurse in one of the field hospitals during the late Russo-Turkish war; she was sentenced to twenty years of penal servitude and is now at the mines of Kará. The lady opposite her on the same page is Miss E——, formerly a student in the Beztúzhef medical school for women in St. Petersburg; she cut her throat with a piece of broken glass, after two years of solitary confinement in the fortress."

In this way Mr. Volkhófski went through his whole collection of photographs, suggesting or sketching hastily in a few dry, matter-of-fact words the terrible tragedies in which the originals of the portraits had been actors. He did not show the least emotional excitement, and from his manner it might have been supposed that it was the commonest thing in the world for one's friends to be hanged, sent to the mines, driven insane by solitary confinement, or tortured into cutting their throats with broken glass. His composure, however, was not insensibility, nor lack of sympathy. It was rather the natural result of long familiarity with such tragedies. One may become accustomed in time even to the sights and sounds of a field hospital, and the Russian revolutionists have become so accustomed to injustice and misery that they can speak without emotional excitement of things that made my face flush and my heart beat fast with indignation or pity.

"Twice in my life," said a well-known Russian liberal to me, "I have fully realized what it means to be a free citizen. The first time was when I returned to Russia from the United States in 187–, and noticed at the frontier the difference between the attitude taken by the gendarmes towards me and their attitude towards Englishmen who entered the empire with me. The second time was just now, when I saw the effect produced upon you by the story that Mr. B—— was relating to you. That story seemed to you — as I could plainly see from the expression of your face — something awful and almost incredible. To me it was no more surprising or extraordinary than an account of the running-over of a man in the street. As I watched the play of expression in your face — as I was forced to look at the facts, for a moment, from your point of view — I felt again, to the very bottom of my soul, the difference between a free citizen and a citizen of Russia."

In Tomsk we began to feel for the first time the nervous strain caused by the sight of irremediable human misery. Our journey through southwestern Siberia and the Altái had been off the great exile route; the politicals whose acquaintance we had made in Semipalátinsk, Ulbínsk, and Ust Kámenogórsk were fairly well treated and did not seem to be suffering; and it was not until we reached Tomsk that we were brought face to face with the tragedies of exile life. From that time, however, until we recrossed the Siberian frontier on our way back to St. Petersburg, we were subjected to a nervous and emotional strain that was sometimes harder to bear than cold, hunger, or fatigue. One cannot witness unmoved such suffering as we saw in the *balagáns* and the hospital of the Tomsk forwarding prison, nor can one listen without the deepest emotion to such stories as we heard from political exiles in Tomsk, Krasnoyársk, Irkútsk, and the Trans-Baikál. One pale, sad, delicate woman, who had been banished to Eastern Siberia, and who had there gone down into the valley of the shadow of death, undertook, one night, I remember, to relate to me her experience. I could see that it was agony for her to live over in narration the sufferings and bereavements of her tragic past, and I would gladly have spared her the self-imposed torture; but she was so determined that the world should know through me what Russians endure before they become terrorists, that she nerved herself to bear it, and between fits of half-controlled sobbing, during which I could only pace the floor, she told me the story of her life. It was the saddest story I had ever heard. After such an interview as this with a heart-broken woman —and I had many such—I could neither sleep nor sit still; and to the nervous strain of such experiences, quite as much as to hardship and privation, was attributable the final breaking down of my health and strength in the Trans-Baikál.

Before I left the city of Tomsk for Eastern Siberia, most of my long-cherished opinions with regard to nihilists and the working of the exile system had been completely overthrown. I could not, by any process of readjustment or modification, make my preconceived ideas fit the facts as I found them. In a letter written from Tomsk to the President of The Century Company on the 26th of August, 1885, I indicated the change that had taken place in my views as follows:

The exile system is much worse than I supposed. Mr. ——'s examination of prisons and study of the exile system were extremely superficial. I cannot understand how, if he really went through the Tiumén and Tomsk forwarding prisons, he could have failed to see that their condition and the condition of their wretched inmates were in many respects shocking. Nobody here has tried to conceal it from me. The acting governor of this province said to me very frankly yesterday that the condition of the Tomsk prison is *uzhásnoi* [awful], but that he cannot help it. . . . What I have previously written and said about the treatment of the political exiles seems to be substantially true and accurate,— at least so far as Western Siberia is concerned,— but my preconceived ideas as to their character have been rudely shaken. The Russian liberals and revolutionists whom I have met here are by no means half-educated enthusiasts, crazy fanatics, or men whose mental processes it is difficult to understand. On the contrary, they are simple, natural, perfectly comprehensible, and often singularly interesting and attractive. One sees at once that they are educated, reasonable, self-controlled gentlemen, not different in any essential respect from one's self. When I write up this country for *The Century*, I shall have to take back some of the things that I have said. The exile system is worse than I believed it to be, and worse than I have described it. It is n't pleasant, of course, to have to admit that one has written upon a subject without fully understanding it; but even that is better than trying, for the sake of consistency, to maintain a position after one sees that it is utterly untenable.

CHAPTER XV

THE GREAT SIBERIAN ROAD

O N Friday, August 28th, after bidding good-by to the political exiles in Tomsk and making final calls upon Colonel Yágodkin and two or three other officers who had been
particularly kind and hospitable to us, Mr. Frost and I procured a fresh *padorózhnaya*, climbed once more into our old
tárantás, and set out, with a *tróika* of good post-horses, for
Irkútsk, the capital of Eastern Siberia, which was distant
from Tomsk 1040 miles. Governor Petukhóf had promised
that he would send us an open letter directing all convoy
officers within his jurisdiction to allow us to inspect *étapes;*
but he had forgotten it, or had reconsidered his promise
after finding the political exiles in our room at the European Hotel, and we were left to gain admission to *étapes* as
best we could. Our journey of 260 miles to Áchinsk, the
first town in Eastern Siberia, was not marked by any noteworthy incident. The part of the province of Tomsk
through which we passed was generally rolling, or broken
by ranges of low hills, and in appearance it suggested at
times the thinly settled forest region of eastern Maine, and
at others the fertile farming country of western New York.
In some places we rode for hours through a dense second
growth of birches, poplars, and evergreens, which hid from
sight everything except the sky and the black muddy road,
and then, a dozen miles farther on, we would come out into
an extensive open prairie embroidered with daisies, or cross
a wide shallow valley whose bottom and sloping sides were

covered with an irregular patchwork of cultivated fields. The weather was cool and fall-like, but the mosquitos were still troublesome, and the flowers continued to be abundant. On the 6th of September I counted thirty-four different kinds of flowers in blossom beside the road, including wild roses, forget-me-nots, crane's-bill, two or three species of aster, goldenrod, wild mustard, monk's-hood, spirea, buttercups, fireweed, bluebells, vase pinks, and Kírghis caps. Many of them were blooming out of their proper season and were represented by only a few scattered specimens; but of others we might have picked millions. The most attractive and highly cultivated region that we saw was that lying between the post-stations of Itátskaya and Bogotólskaya, about fifty miles west of Áchinsk. The weather was warm and pleasant, and the picture presented by the fertile rolling country with its rich autumnal coloring, the clumps of silver birch and poplar here and there in the flowery meadows, the extensive fields of ripe yellow wheat which stretched away up the gentle sunny slopes of the hills, and the groups of men and women in scarlet or blue shirts who were harvesting the grain with clumsy sickles, or eating their noonday lunch in the shade of a frost-tinted birch by the roadside, was not unworthy of an artist's pencil, nor of comparison with any rural landscape of like character in the world.

The villages, however, in this part of Siberia were less deserving of commendation than was the scenery. They consisted generally of a double line of gray, unpainted log houses extending sometimes for two or three *versts* along the miry, chocolate-colored road, without the least sign anywhere of foliage or vegetation, except, perhaps, the leafy branch of a tree nailed up at the door of one of the numerous *kabáks*, "Rhine cellars," "drinking establishments," *pitéini doms* or *optóvi sklads*, which in every Siberian village bring revenue to the Government and demoralization to the peasants. These bush-decorated houses are of many different sorts and go by many different names; but they all sell *vódka*, and, to a great extent, they are responsible for the dirty, slovenly, and poverty-stricken appearance of the peasant villages on the great Siberian road. There are thirty rum-shops to every school throughout Western Siberia, and thirty-five rum-shops to every school throughout Eastern Siberia; and in a country where there exists such a disproportion between the facilities for education and the facilities for intoxication, one cannot reasonably expect to find clean, orderly, or prosperous villages.

The graveyards belonging to the Siberian settlements sometimes seemed to me much more remarkable and noteworthy than the settlements themselves. Near one of the villages that we passed in this part of our journey, I noticed a cemetery in which nearly half the graves were marked by jet-black, three-armed, wooden crosses, covered with narrow A-shaped roofs, and surrounded by red, green, blue, and yellow picket-fences. Some of the peculiar black crosses bore the English letters " I. H. S." on one of the arms, while others had painted on them in white the figure of Christ crucified — the legs being made extraordinarily long and thin so as to occupy the whole length of the upright shaft. Anything more remarkable than one of these ghastly white figures, on a black cross, under a gable roof, with a cheerful red, white, and blue picket-fence around it, I could hardly imagine; but it furnished a striking proof that the Russian love for crude color triumphs even over death. I do not remember to have seen bright colors used in a graveyard in any other part of the world or among any other people.

Harvesting was in progress all along the road between Tomsk and Áchinsk, and in many places the whole population, with the exception of the post-station-master and three or four drivers, had gone to the fields. In one village the only inhabitant whom we saw was a flaxen-haired child about five years of age, dressed in a dirty homespun shirt, wearing on a string about its neck a huge cow-bell, and gnawing contentedly at a big raw turnip, as it paddled along the deserted street half-way up to its knees in mud. Whether the cow-bell was one of the child's playthings, or whether the mother had made use of it as a means of finding her offspring when she should return from the harvest field, I do not know; but the combination of child, turnip, and cow-bell, in a village that did not appear to contain another living inhabitant, was novel enough to attract my attention.

In the outskirts of another settlement we were reminded once more that we were in a penal colony by the sight of a handcuffed horse grazing peacefully by the roadside. I knew that the Russian Government had once flogged and exiled to Siberia a free-thinking and insubordinate church-bell[1] because it had not self-control enough to hold its tongue when turned upside down; but I was a little startled, nevertheless, by the idea, which at once suggested itself to me, that the Government had taken to exiling and hand-cuffing "untrustworthy" horses. Upon making inquiries of the station-master, I was gratified to learn that this was not a horse that had behaved in a manner "prejudicial to public tranquillity" by refusing to neigh upon the accession to the throne of Alexander III., but was merely an animal addicted to vagrancy, whose owner had hobbled him with an old pair of Government handcuffs in order to prevent him from straying. The peasant to whom he belonged had unfortunately lost the key to the handcuffs, and for two or three months the horse had been as useless for all practical purposes as a spiked cannon.

Between the post-stations of Krasnorechínskaya and Bieloyárskaya, about twenty miles west of Áchinsk, we crossed the boundary line between the provinces of Tomsk and Yeniséisk, and entered the vast region known as Eastern Siberia. The boundary was marked by two brick columns about two feet square and seven feet high, which

[1] The celebrated bell of Uglich. It is now in Tobólsk.

bore on their eastern and western sides the coats of arms of the two coterminous provinces. The rate of postal transportation changed at this point from one and a half *kopéks* to three *kopéks* per *verst* for every horse, and our

AN OLD SIBERIAN FERRY-BOAT.

traveling expenses were thus almost doubled, without any commensurate increase in comfort or in speed. The reason assigned for this change in rate is the higher cost of forage and food in Eastern Siberia; but the Government, in dealing with its exiles, does not apparently give any weight to this consideration. If the necessaries of life are so high in Eastern Siberia as to justify the doubling of the rate for postal transportation, it would seem to follow that they are high enough to require some increase in the ration allowance of the exiles on the road; but no such increase is made. No matter whether it is in Western Siberia or in Eastern Siberia, whether black bread costs two *kopéks* a pound or seven *kopéks* a pound, the exile receives neither more nor less than ten *kopéks* a day. The result of this is that in Western Siberia he generally has enough food to sustain his strength, while in Eastern Siberia, and particularly in the Trans-Baikál, he often suffers from hunger.

We passed the town of Áchinsk on Tuesday, September 1st, and entered upon the most difficult and exhausting part of our journey. The country suddenly became wilder and more mountainous in its character; the road, for a distance of sixty or seventy miles, ran across a series of high wooded ridges, separated one from another by swampy ravines; rain fell almost incessantly; and it was all that five powerful horses could do to drag our heavy *tárantás* up the steep hills and through the abysses of tenacious semi-liquid clay in the intervening valleys. Even where the road was comparatively hard, it had been cut into deep ruts and hollows by thousands of *obózes*, or freight wagons; the attempts that had been made here and there to improve it by throwing tree-trunks helter-skelter into the sloughs and quagmires had only rendered it worse; and the swaying, banging, and plunging of the *tárantás* were something frightful. An American stage-coach would have gone to pieces on such a road before it had made a single station. In the course of the first night after leaving Áchinsk, I was thrown violently against the sides or the roof of our *tárantás* at least three or four hundred times. This incessant jolting, added to sleeplessness and fatigue, brought on a racking headache; I was in a shiver most of the night from cold and lack of nourishing food; and when we reached the station of Ibrúlskaya early Wednesday morning, after having made in twenty hours and with four changes of horses a distance of only fifty miles, I felt as if I had been beaten from head to foot with a club and left for dead. Mr. Frost was sick, and had had three severe chills in the night, and he looked so worn and haggard that I became seriously alarmed about him. He did not wish, however, to stop in the post-station of Ibrúlskaya, which was already full of travelers sleeping on benches or on the floor, and after refreshing ourselves with tea, we pushed on towards Krasnoyársk.

I cannot remember, in all Siberia, a worse road for wheeled vehicles than that between Áchinsk and Krasnoyársk. I have never, in fact, seen a worse road in my life, and it was not at all surprising that Mr. Frost was prostrated by the jolting, the consequent sleeplessness, and the lack of substantial food. We had been able to get meat at the post-stations only once in four days; we had lived almost entirely upon the bread and tea that we carried with us; and for ninety-six hours we had had only such snatches of sleep as we could get in the *tárantás* at intervals on short stretches of smooth road, or on benches in the station-houses while waiting for horses. It was some satisfaction to learn, at Ustanófskaya, that General Ignátief, the newly appointed governor-general of Eastern Siberia, who passed over the road between Áchinsk and Krasnoyársk a few days before us, was so exasperated by its condition that he ordered the immediate arrest of the contractor who had undertaken to keep it in repair, and directed that he be held in prison to await an investigation. Mr. Frost and I agreed that it was a proper case for the exercise of despotic power.

We arrived in Krasnoyársk late on the evening of Wednesday, September 2d, after a journey from Tomsk of 370 miles, which had occupied a little more than five days of incessant travel. An abundant supper and a good night's rest in a small hotel near the post-station restored our tired bodies to something like their normal condition, and Thursday afternoon we changed our travel-stained clothing and called upon Mr. Leo Petróvitch Kuznetsóf, a wealthy gold-mining proprietor to whom we had brought a letter of introduction from St. Petersburg. We little anticipated the luxurious comfort of the house and the delightful social atmosphere of the home circle to which this letter would admit us. The servant who came to the door in response

BARK-MILLS, KRASNOYÁRSK.

to our ring showed us into one of the most beautiful and tastefully furnished drawing-rooms that we had seen in Russia. It was fully fifty feet in length by thirty-five feet in width and twenty feet high; its inlaid floor of polished oak was hidden here and there by soft oriental rugs; palms, luxuriant ferns, and pots of blossoming plants occupied the lower portions of the high, richly curtained windows; the apparent size of the spacious apartment was increased by long pier-glasses interposed between the masses of greenery and flowers; a cheerful fire of birch wood was burning in an open fireplace under a massive mantel of carved marble; cabinets of polished cherry, filled with rare old china, delicate ivory carvings, bronze Buddhist idols, and all sorts of bric-à-brac, stood here and there against the walls; large oil-paintings by well-known Russian, French, and English artists occupied places of honor at the ends of the room; and at our right, as we entered, was a grand piano, flanked by a carved stand piled high with books and music.

We had hardly had time to recover from the state of astonishment into which we were thrown by the sight of so many unexpected evidences of wealth, culture, and refinement in this remote East Siberian town when a slender, dark-haired, pale-faced young man in correct afternoon dress entered the drawing-room, introduced himself as Mr. Innokénti Kuznetsóf, and welcomed us in good English to Krasnoyársk. We were soon made acquainted with the whole Kuznetsóf family, which consisted of three brothers and two sisters, all unmarried, and all living together in this luxurious house. Mr. Innokénti Kuznetsóf and his sisters spoke English fluently; they had traveled in America, and had spent more or less time in New York, Philadelphia, Washington, Saratoga, Chicago, Salt Lake City, and San Francisco. Mr. Innokénti Kuznetsóf's personal acquaintance with the United States was more extensive, indeed, than my own, inasmuch as he had twice crossed the continent; had hunted buffalo on our Western prairies; had met General Sheridan, Buffalo Bill, Captain Jack, and other frontier notables, and had even visited regions as remote as Yellowstone Park and the "Staked Plains."

How pleasant it was, after months of rough life in dirty post-stations or vermin-infested hotels, to come suddenly

into such a house as that of the Kuznetsófs; to find ourselves surrounded by flowers, books, pictures, and innumerable other evidences of cultured taste; to hear good music;
to talk with intelligent men and women who did not tell us
harrowing stories of imprisonment and exile — all this the

MONASTERY NEAR KRASNOYÁRSK.

reader can hardly imagine. We dined with the Kuznetsófs
every day that we spent in Krasnoyársk, and met at their
table some very attractive and cultivated people. Among
the latter I remember particularly Mr. Iván Sávenkof, the
director of the Krasnoyársk normal school, who had just
returned from an archæological excursion up the Yeniséi,
and who showed us some very interesting tracings and
water-color copies of the prehistoric sketches and inscriptions that abound on the "pictured rocks" along that river.
Mr. Innokénti Kuznetsóf shared Mr. Sávenkof's interest in
archæology, and both gentlemen had valuable collections
of objects dating from the stone or the bronze age that had
been taken from *kurgáns* or tumuli in various parts of the
province.

Thursday evening, after dinner, we all drove up the left
bank of the river to an old monastery about six *versts* from
the city, where the people of Krasnoyársk are accustomed
to go in summer for picnics. The road, which was a noteworthy triumph of monastic engineering, had been cut out

in the steep cliffs that border the Yeniséi, or had been carried on trestle-work along the faces of these cliffs high above the water, and at every salient angle it commanded a beautiful view of the majestic river, which, at this point, attains a width of more than a mile and glides swiftly past, between blue picturesque mountains, on its way from the wild fastnesses of Mongolia to the barren coast of the arctic ocean.

Our friends in Krasnoyársk tempted us to remain there a week or two with promises of all sorts of delightful excursions, but at that late season of the year we could not spare the time. It required not a little resolution to turn our backs on picnic parties and boating parties, on archæological excursions up the Yeniséi, on such congenial society as we found in the hospitable homes of Mr. Sávenkof and the Kuznetsófs, and to face again the old miseries of jolting, sleeplessness, cold, hunger, and fatigue

ROAD TO MONASTERY.

on the road; but it was important that we should reach the mines of the Trans-Baikál before winter set in, and we had yet 1200 miles to go.

Saturday afternoon, September 5th, we reluctantly ordered post-horses; provided ourselves with a fresh supply of bread, tea, and copper money; repacked our baggage in the old, battered, mud-splashed *tárantás*, which we were beginning to dread as a once-tortured criminal dreads the rack; and crossing the Yeniséi on a pendulum ferry-boat, resumed our journey to Irkútsk. The weather was once more pleasant and sunshiny, but the changing colors of the dying leaves showed that fall was at hand. Many of the poplars had already turned a deep brilliant red, and nearly half of the birches were solid masses of canary yellow, which, when seen against the dark background of the somber evergreens, suggested foliage in a state of incandescence. The vast fields of wheat in the valley of the Yeniséi and on the lower slopes of the hills in the neighborhood of Krasnoyársk were apparently dead ripe, and hundreds of men and women with horse-hair mosquito-protectors over their heads were reaping the grain with sickles, binding it into sheaves, and stacking the sheaves by fives in long rows.

We traveled without rest Sunday, Monday, and Tuesday, but on Wednesday morning, at the station of Kamishétskaya, about 350 miles from Irkútsk, we were forced to stop in order to have repairs made to our *tárantás*. We found the village blacksmith in a little shop near the post-station, where, with the aid of his daughter, a robust young woman eighteen or twenty years of age, he was engaged in shoeing a horse. One might infer, from the elaborate precautions taken to prevent the animal from injuring himself or anybody else while being shod, that Siberian horses were more than usually fractious, or Siberian blacksmiths more than usually careless in driving nails. The poor beast had been hoisted into the air by means of two broad belly-bands, and suspended from a stout frame so that he could not touch the ground; three of his legs had then been lashed to an equal number of posts so that he could neither kick nor struggle, and the daring blacksmith was fearlessly putting a shoe on the only hoof that the wretched and humiliated animal could move. We learned, upon inquiry, that Siberian horses are always shod in this way, and we concluded that Siberian blacksmiths must be regarded by accident insurance companies as extra-safe and very desirable risks.

While we were waiting for the repairs to our *tárantás* we were overtaken by the Moscow post. The Russian mails

A SIBERIAN BLACKSMITH.

are carried in Siberia in leathern bags or pouches as with us, and are forwarded in *telégas* under guard of an armed postilion, changing horses and vehicles at every station. There is no limit, so far as I know, to the weight or size of packages that may be sent by post,— I myself mailed a box weighing forty pounds,— and the mails are consequently very bulky and heavy, filling sometimes a dozen *telégas*. Irkútsk, the capital of Eastern Siberia, has a mail from Moscow every day and returns it three times a week; and as the imperial post takes precedence over private travelers, the latter are often forced to wait for hours at post-stations because the last horses have been taken by the Government postilion. Such was our fate at Kamishéts-kaya. The repairs to our *tárantás* were soon made, but in the mean time we had been overtaken by the post, and we were obliged to wait for horses until two o'clock in the afternoon.

From Kamishétskaya to Irkútsk we traveled night and day, stopping only now and then to inspect an *étape*, or to watch the progress of an exile party, as, with a dismal clinking of chains, it made its way slowly along the road, in a pouring rain, towards the distant mines of the Trans-Baikál.

This ride from Tomsk to Irkútsk was in some respects a harder and more exhausting journey than that from Tiumén to the mountains of the Altái. Long-continued rain had spoiled the road and rendered it in places almost impassable. The jolting of our heavy *tárantás* through deep ruts and over occasional stretches of imperfect corduroy gave us violent headaches and prevented us from getting any restful sleep; warm, nourishing food was rarely to be obtained at the post-stations; we had not yet provided ourselves with winter clothing, and suffered more or less every night from cold; and finally, we were tormented constantly by predatory insects from the roadside prisons and *étapes*. No single hardship connected with our investigation of the exile system was more trying to me than the utter impossibility of escaping from parasitic vermin. Cold, hunger, sleeplessness, and fatigue I could bear with reasonable patience and fortitude; but to be forced to live for weeks at a time in clothing infested with fleas, lice, or bedbugs from the unclean bodies of common criminal convicts not only seemed to me intolerable in itself, but gave me a hu-

THE DEPARTURE OF THE MAIL.

miliating sense of physical defilement that was almost as bad as a consciousness of moral degradation. We tried in every possible way to rid ourselves of these parasitic prison insects, but without success. The older and more neglected *étapes* along the road were swarming with vermin of all sorts, and whenever we examined one of these places we came away from it with a small but varied entomological collection in our clothing. The insects soon secured lodg-

ment in our blankets and pillows as well as in the crevices
and lining of our *tárantás*, and then it was impossible either
to exterminate or to escape them.   After throwing away successively two or three suits of underclothing, I abandoned all
hope of relief and reconciled myself to the inevitable as best
I could.   There were insects on my body or in my clothing
during the greater part of four months, and when I was
able to undress for the first time after our nine-days' journey from Krasnoyársk to Irkútsk, I found myself spotted
and blotched from head to foot as if I were suffering from
some foul eruptive disease.   It is not pleasant, of course,
to go into these details, but I wish the reader to understand
clearly and definitely what life in an *étape* is, and what Siberian exile means to a cultivated human being.[1]

I do not know that it is possible to get rid entirely of obnoxious insects in old and sometimes half-decayed buildings through which pass every year thousands of criminals
from the lowest social classes.   It is possible, however, to
keep the *étapes* decently clean and to provide the exiles,
both in the forwarding prisons and on the road, with proper
facilities for bathing and for changing and washing their
clothing.   How far these things are done now I shall try to
show in the next chapter.

As we approached the East-Siberian capital, towards the
end of the second week in September, the weather finally
cleared up, and upon the southeastern horizon, far away
in the distance, we caught sight of the blue, ethereal, snow-
crowned peaks of Tunká, situated on the frontier of Mongolia near the southern end of Lake Baikál.   They were

---

[1] A common method of gambling
among criminal convicts in Siberian
étapes is to spread down an overcoat or
a dirty linen foot-wrapper on the floor
of the *kámera*, and guess at the number of fleas that will jump upon it
within a certain length of time.   Every
convict, of course, backs his guess with
a wager.   Another method, equally
common, is to draw two small concentric circles on one of the sleeping-
platforms, put a number of lice simultaneously within the inner circle, and
then give all the money that has been
wagered on the event to the convict
whose louse first crawls across the line
of the outer circle.   Exiles on the road
are not supposed to have playing-cards,
but facilities for gambling in the manner above described are never lacking.

evidence that Irkútsk was near. When the morning of Sunday, September 13th, dawned cool and bright we found ourselves riding over a good road, along the swift but tranquil current of the river Angará, and through a country the extensive cultivation and prosperous appearance of which indicated its proximity to a market. About two o'clock in the afternoon we stopped to change horses at the last post-station, and with inspiriting anticipations of rest, sleep, clean linen, and letters from home we entered the travelers' waiting-room and read, in the official distance-table hanging against the wall, the significant words and figures:

POST-STATION OF BOKÓFSKAYA.

DISTANT

From St. Petersburg	5601 *versts.*
From Irkútsk	13 *versts.*

You may subtract thirteen from 5601, or divide 5601 by thirteen, or put the two numbers through any other mathematical process that you choose, but you will never fully appreciate the difference between them until you have traveled 5601 *versts* in the Russian Empire and have only thirteen *versts* more to go.

As soon as fresh horses could be harnessed we dashed away up the Angará towards Irkútsk, looking eagerly forward to catch the first possible glimpse of its gilded domes and its snowy cathedral walls. I had not seen the city in eighteen years, and meanwhile it had been almost entirely destroyed by fire, and had been rebuilt. I feared, therefore, that it would not present so beautiful and striking an appearance as it did when I saw it first, in the winter of 1867. About five *versts* from the city we passed the picturesque white-walled monastery of Vosnesénsk, with a throng of dirty, ragged, long-haired pilgrims gathered about its principal entrance, and beyond it we began to meet unarmed soldiers, peasants, peddlers, tramps, and nondescript vagabonds of all sorts who had been spending the Sabbath-day in the city and were straggling back on foot to their respective places of abode in the suburban villages. Nearly half of them were more or less intoxicated, and the number of open *kabáks*, or drinking-places, that we saw by the road seemed fully adequate to explain if not to excuse their condition

We crossed the swift current of the Angará by means of a "swing," or pendulum, ferry, and drove up from the landing into the streets of the city. I was somewhat disappointed in its appearance. Its gilded or colored domes, white belfries, and scattered masses of foliage, when seen from the opposite side of the river, give to it a certain half-oriental picturesqueness; but to an observer in its streets it presents itself as a large, busy, thriving, but irregularly built and unattractive Russian provincial town. After unsuccessfully seeking shelter in the new and pretentious Moscow House and in the Siberian Hotel, we finally went to the Hotel Dekó, where, as we were informed, Lieutenants Harber and Schuetze stayed when they passed through the city in 1882 on their way to the Lena Delta. An elderly and rather talkative servant who brought our luggage to our room introduced himself by saying that he always used to wait on Mr. Harber and Mr. Schuetze, and that the former loved him so that he called him "Zhan" (John). He seemed to think that "Zhan" was an American nickname expressive of the tenderest and most affectionate regard, and that he needed no other recommendation than this to an American traveler. I told him that if he would take care of us properly we also would call him "Zhan," at which he seemed very much gratified. From the frequency and the pride with which he afterwards referred to this caressing nickname, I feel confident that when he comes to die, and a tombstone is placed over his mortal remains, no possible enumeration thereon of his many virtues will give to his freed spirit half so much pleasure as the simple epitaph,

THE AMERICANS CALLED HIM "ZHAN."

CHAPTER XVI

DEPORTATION BY ÉTAPE

IN Tomsk, and during our journey from that city to Irkútsk, we had for the first time a satisfactory opportunity to study the life of Siberian exiles on the road. Marching parties of convicts three or four hundred strong leave Tomsk for Irkútsk weekly throughout the whole year, and make the journey of 1040 miles in about three months. *Étapes*, or exile station-houses, stand along the road at intervals of from twenty-five to forty miles; and at every *étape* there is a "convoy command" consisting of a commissioned officer known as the "*nachálnik* of the convoy," two or three under-officers, and about forty soldiers. As the distance from one *étape* to another is too great to be walked in a single day by prisoners in leg-fetters, buildings known as *polu-étapes*, or "half-étapes," have been constructed midway between the true *étapes* for the shelter of the convicts at night. These half-way houses are generally smaller than the regular *étapes*, as well as somewhat different from the latter in architectural plan, and they have no "convoy commands." Marching parties are expected to make about 500 versts, or 330 miles, a month, with twenty-four hours of rest every third day. If a party leaves Tomsk Monday morning, it reaches a *polu-étape* Monday night, arrives at the first regular *étape* Tuesday night, and rests in the latter all day Wednesday. Thursday morning it resumes its journey with another convoy, Thursday night it spends in the second *polu-étape*, Friday night it reaches the second regular *étape*, and Saturday it again rests and changes convoy. In this way the party proceeds slowly for months, resting one day out of every three, and changing convoys at every other station. Each prisoner receives five cents a day in money for his subsistence, and buys food for himself from peasants along the road who make a business of furnishing it. The dress of the exiles in summer consists of a shirt and a pair of trousers of coarse gray linen; square foot-wrappers of the same material in lieu of stockings; low shoes or slippers called *kati;* leather ankle-guards to prevent the leg-fetters from chafing; a visorless Glengarry cap; and a long gray overcoat. The dress of female convicts is the same, except that a petticoat takes the place of the trousers. Women and children who voluntarily accompany relatives to Siberia are permitted to wear their own clothing, and to carry severally as much baggage as can be put into a two-bushel bag. No distinction is made between common convicts and political convicts, except that the latter, if they are nobles or belong to one of the privileged classes, receive seven and a half cents a day for their subsistence instead of five, and are carried in *telégas* instead of being forced to walk.[1]

Up to the year 1883 there was no separation of the sexes in marching parties; but since that time an attempt has been made to forward unmarried male prisoners apart from "family parties," and to include in the latter all children and unmarried women. This reform has lessened somewhat the demoralization resulting from the promiscuous association of men, women, and children for months in overcrowded *étapes;* but the state of affairs is still very

[1] At one time politicals were sent to Siberia separately in post vehicles under guard of gendarmes, and were carried to their destinations almost as quickly as if they had been private travelers. That practice, however, has been abandoned on account of its inconvenience and expense, and all politicals are now forwarded with common criminal parties. The result of the change is to prolong by many months the miseries of *étape* life, and to increase enormously the chances of sickness and death.

bad, since even "family parties" contain large numbers of depraved men and boys.

Three or four days before we left Tomsk for Irkútsk, Mr. Frost and I, by invitation of Captain Gudím, the *nachálnik* of the Tomsk convoy command, drove to the forwarding prison at 7 A. M. to see the departure of a marching party. The morning was cool, but a clear sky gave promise of a warm, sunshiny day. As we drew up before the prison we saw that the party had not yet made its appearance; and, presuming that Captain Gudím was busy, we did not send for him, but sat in our *dróshky* watching the scenes at the gate. On each side of the lead-colored portal was a long wooden bench, upon which half-a-dozen soldiers, in dark green uniforms, were sitting in lazy attitudes, waiting for the party to come out, and amusing themselves meanwhile by exchanging coarse witticisms with three or four female provision-venders, squatted near them on the ground. An occasional high-pitched jingle of chains could be heard from within the inclosure, and now and then half of the double gate was thrown open to admit a couple of fettered convicts carrying water in a large wooden bucket slung between them on a shoulder-pole. Every person who entered the prison yard was hastily searched from head to foot by one of the two sentries at the gate, in order to prevent the smuggling in of prohibited articles, and especially of *vódka*.

About eight o'clock *telégas* for the transportation of the weak and infirm began to gather in the street in front of the prison; a shabby under-officer who had been lounging with the soldiers on one of the benches rose, yawned, and went discontentedly into the prison courtyard; the soldiers put on their blanket-rolls and picked up their Berdan rifles; and a louder and more continuous jingling of chains from the other side of the palisade announced that the convict party was assembling. At last the prison blacksmith came out, bringing a small portable forge, a lap anvil, a hammer or two, and an armful of chains and leg-fetters, which he threw carelessly on the ground beside him; the soldiers shouldered their guns and took positions in a semicircle so as to form a cordon; an under-officer with the muster-roll of the party in his hand and another with a leather bag of copper coins slung over his shoulder stationed themselves near the gate; and at the word "Gatóva!" [Ready!] the convicts, in single file, began to make their appearance. The officer with the muster-roll checked off the prisoners as they answered to their names; the blacksmith, with the aid of a soldier, examined their leg-fetters to see that the rivets were fast and that the bands could not be slipped over the heel; and, finally, the second under-officer gave to every man ten cents in copper coin for two days' subsistence between *étapes*. When all of the *kátorzhniki*, or hard-labor convicts, had come out of the prison yard, they arranged themselves in two parallel lines so that they could be conveniently counted, and removed their caps so that the under-officer could see that their heads had been half shaved as required by law. They were then dismissed, and the *poseléntsi*, or penal colonists, went through the same routine—the soldiers of the convoy stepping backward and extending the limits of their cordon as the number of prisoners outside the palisade gradually increased.

At length the whole party, numbering 350 or 400, was assembled in the street. Every prisoner had a gray linen bag in which were stored his scanty personal effects; many of them were provided with copper kettles which dangled from the leather belts that supported their leg-fetter chains; and one convict was carrying to the mines in his arms a small brown dog.

When the whole party had again been counted, and while the gray bags were being put into *telégas*, I availed myself of what seemed to be a favorable opportunity to talk with the prisoners. In a moment, to my great surprise, I was addressed by one of them in good English.

"Who are you?" I inquired in astonishment.

"I am a vagabond," he said quietly and seriously.

"What is your name?"

"Iván Dontremember," he replied; and then glancing around, and seeing that none of the convoy officers were near, he added in a low tone, "My real name is John Anderson, and I am from Riga."

"How do you happen to know English?" I asked.

"I am of English descent; and, besides that, I was once a sailor, and have been in English ports."

At this point the approach of Captain Gudím put a stop to our colloquy. The number of "*brodyágs*," or vagabonds, in this party was very large, and nearly all of them were runaway convicts of the "Dontremember" family, who had been recaptured in Western Siberia, or had surrendered themselves during the previous winter in order to escape starvation.

"I have no doubt," said Captain Gudím to me, "that there are *brodyágs* in this very party who have escaped and been sent back to the mines half a dozen times."

"Boys!" he shouted suddenly, "how many of you are now going to the mines for the sixth time?"

"Mnógo yest" [There are lots of them], replied several voices; and finally one gray-bearded convict in leg-fetters came forward and admitted that he had made four escapes from the mines, and that he was going into penal servitude for the fifth time. In other words, this man had traversed eight times on foot the distance of nearly 2000 miles between Tomsk and the mines of Kará.

"I know *brodyágs*," said Captain Gudím, "who have been over this road sixteen times in leg-fetters, and who have come back sixteen times across the steppes and through the woods. God only knows how they live through it!"

When one considers that crossing Eastern Siberia thirty-two times on foot is about equivalent to walking twice the circumference of the globe at the equator, one can appreciate the indomitable resolution of these men, and the strength of the influence that draws them towards home and freedom. In the year 1884, 1360 such *brodyágs* were recaptured in Western Siberia and sent back to the mines of the Trans-Baikál, and hundreds more perished from cold and starvation in the forests. M. I. Orfánof, a Russian officer who served many years in Eastern Siberia, says that he once found 200 "Ivan Dontremembers" in a single prison—the prison of Kaidálova, between Chíta and Nérchinsk.[1]

Some of the *brodyágs* with whom I talked were men of intelligence and education. One of them, who was greatly interested in our photographic apparatus, and who seemed to know all about "dry plates," "drop shutters," and "Dallmeyer lenses," asked me how convicts were treated in the United States, and whether they could, by extra work, earn a little money, so as not to leave prison penniless. I replied that in most American penitentiaries they could.

"It is not so," he said, "with us. Naked we go to the mines, and naked we come out of them; and we are flogged, while there, at the whim of every *nariádchik*."[2]

"Oh, no!" said Captain Gudím good-naturedly, "they don't flog at the mines now."

"Yes, they do, your Nobility," replied the *brodyág* firmly but respectfully. "If you are sick or weak, and can't finish your stent, you are given twenty blows with the cat."

I should have been glad to get further information from the *brodyág* with regard to his life at the mines, but just at this moment Captain Gudím asked me if I would not like to see the loading of the sick and infirm, and the conversation was interrupted.

[1] "V' Dali" (Afar), by M. I. Orfánof, p. 226. St. Petersburg, 1883.

[2] A petty officer who directs the work of the convicts in the *razréiz* or cutting, and who sets their tasks.

SICK AND INFIRM EXILES IN TELÉGAS.

The *telégas* intended for prisoners physically unable to walk were small one-horse carts, without springs of any kind, and with only one seat, in front, for the driver and the guard. They looked to me like the halves of longitudinally bisected hogsheads mounted upon four low wheels, with their concave sides uppermost. More wretchedly uncomfortable vehicles to ride in were never devised. A small quantity of green grass had been put into each one to break the jolting a little, and upon this grass, in every cart, were to sit four sick or disabled convicts.

" All prisoners who have certificates from the doctor, step out ! " shouted Captain Gudím, and twenty-five or thirty " incapables " — some old and infirm, some pale and emaciated from sickness — separated themselves from the main body of convicts in the road. An under-officer collected and examined their certificates, and as fast as their cases were approved they climbed into the *telégas*. One man, although apparently sick, was evidently a malingerer, since, as he took his place in a partly filled *teléga*, he was greeted with a storm of groans and hoots from the whole convict party.[1]

The number of prisoners who, when they leave Tomsk, are unable to walk is sometimes very large. In the year 1884, 658 *telégas* were loaded there with exiles of this class, and if every *teléga* held four persons the aggregate number of " incapables " must have exceeded 2500.[2] Such a state of things, of course, is the natural result of the overcrowding of the Tomsk forwarding prison.

When the sick and infirm had all taken the places assigned them in the invalid carts, Captain Gudím took off his cap, crossed himself and bowed in the direction

[1] Some convicts are extremely skilful in counterfeiting the symptoms of disease, and will now and then succeed in deceiving even an experienced prison surgeon. If necessary for the accomplishment of their purpose, they do not hesitate to create artificial swellings by applying irritating decoctions to a slight self-inflicted wound, and they even poison themselves with tobacco and other noxious herbs.

[2] Report of the Inspector of Exile Transportation for 1884, p. 31 of the MS.

A CONVICT PARTY PASSING A SHRINE NEAR TOMSK.

of the prison church, and then, turning to the convicts, cried, "Well, boys! Go ahead! A safe journey to you!"

"Party — to the right! Party — march!" shouted one of the under-officers, and with a clinking of chains which sounded like the jingling of innumerable bunches of keys the gray throng, hemmed in by a cordon of soldiers, began its long journey of 1800 miles to the mines of the Trans-Baikál. The marching convicts, who took the lead, were closely followed by the *telégas* with the sick and the infirm; next came three or four carts loaded with gray linen bags; and, finally, in a *tárántas* behind the rear guard of soldiers rode Captain Gudím, the *nachálnik* of the convoy. The column moved at the rate of about two miles an hour; and long before noon it was enveloped in a suffocating cloud of dust raised by the shuffling, fetter-incumbered feet of the prisoners. In warm, dry weather, when there is no wind, dust is a source of great misery to marching parties — particularly to the sick, the women, and the children. There is no possible way of escaping it, and when a prisoner is suffering from one of the diseases of the respiratory organs that are so common in *étape* life it is simply torture to sit in a cramped position for six or eight hours in an open *teléga*, breathing the dust raised by the feet of 350 men marching in close column just ahead. I have traced the progress of an invisible exile party more than a mile away by the cloud of dust that hung over it in the air.

Five or six miles from Tomsk the party passed a *chasóv-naya*, or roadside shrine, consisting of an open pavilion, in which hung a ghastly wooden effigy of the crucified Christ. Here, as upon our departure from Tomsk, I noticed that two-thirds of the convicts removed their caps, crossed themselves devoutly, and muttered brief supplications. A Russian peasant may be a highway robber or a murderer, but he continues, nevertheless, to cross himself and say his prayers.

The first halt of the party for rest was made about ten miles from Tomsk, at the entrance to a small village. Here,

HALT OF A CONVICT PARTY FOR LUNCH.

on a patch of greensward by the roadside, had assembled ten or twelve girls and old women with baskets of provisions, bottles of milk, and jugs of *kvas*, or small beer, for sale to the prisoners. At first sight of these preparations for their refreshment, the experienced *brodyágs*, who marched at the head of the column, raised a joyous shout of *Privál! Privál!* — the exiles' name for the noonday halt. The welcome cry was passed along the line until it reached the last wagon of "incapables," and the whole party perceptibly quickened its pace. A walk of ten miles does not much tire a healthy and unincumbered man; but to convicts who have been in prison without exercise for months, and who are hampered by five-pound leg-fetters united by chains that clash constantly between the legs, it is a trying experience. In less than a minute after the command to halt was given, almost every man in the party was either sitting on the ground or lying upon it at full length. After a short rest, the prisoners began buying food from the provision venders, in the shape of black rye-bread, fish-pies, hard-boiled eggs, milk, and *kvas*, and in half an hour they were all sitting on the ground, singly or in groups, eating their lunch. With the permission of Captain Gudím, Mr. Frost took a photograph of them, which is here reproduced, and about two o'clock the party resumed its journey.

The afternoon march was without noteworthy incident. The *brodyágs* talked constantly as they walked, raising their voices so as to make themselves heard above the jingling of the chains, while the novices generally listened or asked questions. There is the same difference between a *brodyág* who has been to the mines half a dozen times and a novice who is going for the first time, that there is between an experienced cowboy and a "tenderfoot." The *brodyág* knows the road as the tongue knows the mouth; he has an experimental acquaintance with the temper and character of every convoy officer from Tomsk to Kará; and his perilous adventures in the *taigá*—the primeval Siberian

"BRODYÁGS" OR RUNAWAY CONVICTS.

forest — have given to him a self-confidence and a decision of character that make him the natural leader in every convict party. It is the boast of the true *brodyág* that the *ostróg* [the prison] is his father and the *taigá* [the wilderness] his mother; and he often spends his whole life in going from one parent to the other. He rarely escapes from Siberia altogether, although he may reach half a dozen times the valley of the Ob. Sooner or later he is almost always recaptured, or is forced by cold and starvation to give himself up. As an *étape* officer once said to a *brodyág* rearrested in Western Siberia, "The Tsar's cow-pasture is large, but you can't get out of it; we find you at last if you are not dead."

The conversation of the *brodyágs* in the party that we accompanied related chiefly to their own exploits and adventures at the mines and in the *taigá*, and it did not seem to be restrained in the least by the presence of the soldiers of the convoy.

The distance from Tomsk to the first *polu-étape* is twenty-nine *versts* (nearly twenty miles), and it was almost dark before the tired prisoners caught sight of the serrated palisade within which they were to spend their first night on the road.

A Siberian *polu-étape*, or half-way station, is a stockaded inclosure about 100 feet long by 50 or 75 feet wide, containing two or three low, one-story log buildings. One of these buildings is occupied by the convoy officer, another by the soldiers, and the third and largest by the convicts. The prisoners' *kazárm*, which is generally painted a dirty yellow,[1] is long and low, and contains three or four *kámeras*, each of which is provided with a brick oven and a double row of plank *nári*, or sleeping-platforms. According to the last official report of the inspector of exile transportation, which is confirmed by my own observation, " all of the *étapes* and *polu-étapes* on the road between Tomsk and Áchinsk — with

---

[1] Yellow is the *étape* color throughout Siberia.

a very few exceptions — are not only too small, but are old
and decayed, and demand capital repairs." Their principal
defect is that which is characteristic of Siberian prisons
generally; namely, lack of adequate room. They were

A POLU-ÉTAPE ON THE TOMSK-ÁCHINSK ROAD.

built from thirty to fifty years ago, when exile parties
did not number more than 150 men, and they now have to
accommodate from 350 to 450. The result, as stated by
the inspector of exile transportation, is that "in pleasant
weather half the prisoners sleep on the ground in the court-
yard, while in bad weather they fill all the *kámeras*, lie on
the floors in the corridors, and even pack the garrets."
The cells are not even as habitable as they might be
made with a little care and attention. They are almost
always dirty; their windows are so made that they cannot be opened; and notwithstanding the fact that the overcrowding, at certain seasons of the year, is almost beyond

belief,[1] no provision whatever has been made in them for ventilation.

When our convicts, after their toilsome march of twenty-nine *versts* from Tomsk, reached at last the red-roofed *polu-étape* of Semilúzhnaya, they were marshaled in rows in front of the palisade and again carefully counted by the under-officers in order to make sure that none had escaped, and then the wooden gate of the courtyard was thrown wide open. With a wild, mad rush and a furious clashing of chains, more than three hundred men made a sudden break for the narrow gateway, struggled, fought, and crowded through it, and then burst into the *kámeras*, in order to secure, by preoccupation, places on the sleeping-platforms. Every man knew that if he did not succeed in preëmpting a section of the *nári* he would have to lie on the dirty floor, in one of the cold corridors, or out-of-doors; and many prisoners who did not care particularly where they slept sought to secure good places in order to sell them afterward for a few *kopéks* to less fortunate but more fastidious comrades.

At last the tumult subsided, and the convicts began their preparations for supper. Hot water was furnished by the soldiers of the convoy at an average price of about a cent a teakettleful; " brick " tea was made by the prisoners who were wealthy enough to afford such a luxury;[2] soup was obtained by a few from the soldiers' kitchen; and the tired exiles, sitting on the sleeping-platforms or on the floor, ate

[1] The well-known Russian author Maxímof cites a case in which 512 human beings were packed into one of these *étapes* in Western Siberia (" Siberia and Penal Servitude," by S. Maxímof, Vol. I, p. 81. St. Petersburg, 1871); and Mr. M. I. Orfánof, a Russian officer who served ten years in Siberia, reports that an East-Siberian *étape* (at Vérkhni Údinsk), which was intended for 140 prisoners, never contained, when he visited it, less than 500, and sometimes held more than 800. (" Afar," by M. I. Orfánof, p. 220. St. Petersburg, 1883.)

[2] Brick tea is made of a cheap grade of tea-leaves, mixed with stems and a little adhesive gum, and pressed into hard dry cakes about eight inches in length, five inches in width, and an inch and a half in thickness. It resembles in appearance and consistency the blackest kind of " plug " tobacco.

the black bread, the fish-pies, or the cold boiled meat that
they had purchased from the provision venders.   The evening meal is sometimes an exceedingly scanty one, on account

A "KÁMERA" OR CELL IN A POLU-ÉTAPE.

of the failure of the peasant women to bring to the *étape*
for sale an adequate supply of food.   They are not obliged
to furnish subsistence to convicts on the road, and the exile
administration attempts no regulation of the commissariat

beyond furnishing the prisoners with money for rations, and allowing the peasants or the soldiers of the convoy to act as purveyors. In times of scarcity it is impossible to buy, with the money given to each exile for his subsistence, enough food to satisfy hunger. In one district of Eastern Siberia, where there had been a partial failure of the crops, the exiles could scarcely buy, with five cents a day, a pound and a half of black rye bread. The *étape* officers complained bitterly to me of the indifference of the Government to the sufferings of the prisoners, and declared that it was unjust and cruel to give men only a pound and a half of black bread, and at the same time force them to march twenty miles a day in leg-fetters, and in bitterly cold weather.[1]

After supper the roll of the party was called in the courtyard; a sentry was stationed at each corner of the quadrangular stockade, and another at the gate; a cheap tallow-candle was lighted in each *kámera; paráshas*, or large uncovered wooden tubs for excrement, were placed in the cells and corridors; and the prisoners were locked up for the night. More than half the party lay on the dirty floors without blankets or pillows, and the atmosphere of the rooms in the course of the night became foul and polluted to an extent that can be imagined only by one who has been present at the opening of the doors in the morning. How human beings, under such conditions, live to reach the mines of Kará, I do not know. It was my intention to ask a friendly *étape* officer to allow me to spend one night with the convicts in an *étape kámera;* but after

[1] This was in the Vérkhni Údinsk district of the Trans-Baikál. According to the statements made to me by the *étape* officers, black bread of the poorest quality cost from six to seven *kopéks* a pound, and the prisoners received only eleven *kopéks* a day. This state of affairs existed throughout the entire fall of 1885, growing worse and worse as winter came on. No attention whatever was paid, so far as I know, to the complaints and suggestions of the *étape* officers, notwithstanding the fact that a circular had been issued by the Prison and Exile Department providing for such an exigency, and requesting the Siberian governors to increase, in times of scarcity, the daily allowance of prisoners on the road. (Circular Letter of the Prison and Exile Department, No. 10,887, December 15, 1880.)

breathing the air of one of those cells when the doors were reopened in the morning, I decided not to make the experiment.

The second day's march of the convict party that left Tomsk on the 24th of August differed little from the first. A hasty and rather scanty breakfast in the *kámeras* was followed by the assembling of the convicts, the morning roll-call, and the departure; the day's journey was again broken by the *privál*, or halt for lunch; and early in the afternoon the party reached the first regular *étape*, where it was to change convoys and stop one day for rest.

The *étape* differs from the *polu-étape* only in size and in the arrangement of its buildings.

The courtyard is more spacious, and the *kámeras* are a

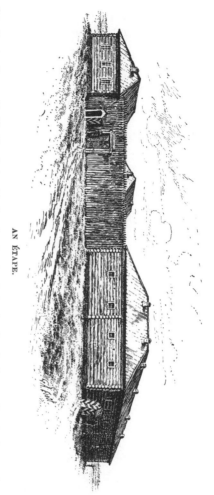

AN ÉTAPE.

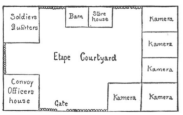

PLAN OF ABOVE.

little larger than in the *polu-étape;* but the buildings are old and in bad repair, and there is not room enough in them for half the number of prisoners now forwarded in every party. General Anúchin, the governor-general of Eastern Siberia, who saw the *étapes* along the great Siberian road at their best, describes them, in a report to the Tsar, as follows:

During my journey to Irkútsk I inspected a great number of penal institutions, including city prisons, forwarding prisons, and *étapes ;* and I regret to have to say that most of them are in a lamentable condition. The *étapes* are particularly bad. With a very few exceptions they are tumble-down buildings, in bad sanitary condition, cold in winter, saturated with miasm, and offering very little security against escapes.[1]

I have not myself said anything worse of *étapes* than this. If these buildings, after they had been put in the best possible condition for the governor-general's inspection, made upon him such an impression as this, the reader can imagine what impression they made upon me, when I saw them in their every-day aspect. I am quite content, however, to let Governor-general Anúchin's description stand as my own, with a few qualifications and exceptions. All of the *étapes* on the Tomsk-Irkútsk road are not of this character. I examined one at the village of Itátskaya, near Marínsk, which was clean, well cared for, and in perfect order, and I have little doubt that if I had had time to visit every exile station-house on the road, I should have found many to which the governor-general's description would not fairly apply. In the main, however, it is truthful and accurate.

The "lamentable condition" of the Siberian *étapes* seems to me to be mainly attributable to corrupt and incapable administration, and to the inherent defects of a bureaucratic system of government. For these very *étapes*, bad as they are, an immense amount of money has been appropriated; but the greater part of it has been divided between fraudulent contractors and corrupt Government officials. An inspector of exile transportation, who had excellent opportunities to know the facts, told me that it was hardly an

[1] First and second reports of Governor-general Anúchin to the Tsar. Appendix H.

exaggeration to say that if all the money that had been appropriated for the construction and maintenance of these "tumble-down buildings" could now be gathered together, it would be enough to pay for the erection of a line of solid silver *étapes* along the whole route from Tomsk to the city of Irkútsk. Governor-general Anúchin himself says, in the same report to the Tsar from which I have already quoted:

Large sums of money have been spent in repairs upon these buildings, and 250,000 *rúbles* have recently been appropriated for the erection of new *étapes* in the territory of the Trans-Baikál. I doubt, however, whether it will be possible to accomplish anything of serious importance without a change in the existing conditions. There is even danger that the new *étapes* in the territory of the Trans-Baikál will share the fate of the *étapes* in the provinces of Yeniséisk and Irkútsk.

General Anúchin's foreboding has been fully justified. Both the inspector of exile transportation for Eastern Siberia and the assistant chief of the prison department in St. Petersburg admitted to me that the new *étapes* in the Trans-Baikál were "very unsatisfactory."

Our convict party spent Tuesday night in the first regular *étape* at Khaldéyeva, under almost precisely the same conditions that prevailed the previous night in the *polu-étape* of Semilúzhnaya. Half the prisoners slept on the floor, under the *nári*, and in the corridors, breathing all night an atmosphere poisoned by carbonic acid and exhalations from uncovered *paráshas*. Wednesday was a day of rest; and the exiles lounged about all day in the prison courtyard, or studied the "record of current events," on the walls of the *étapes*. The sleeping-platforms and the walls of every Siberian *étape* bear countless inscriptions, left there by the exiles of one party for the information or instruction of their comrades in the next. Among such inscriptions are messages and greetings to friends; hints and suggestions for *brodyágs* who meditate escape; names of exiles who have died, broken jail, or been recaptured; and items of news, of all sorts, from the mines and the forwarding prisons. For the convicts, therefore, the *étape* walls are equivalent to so many pages of a daily newspaper, containing an exile directory, open letters, obituary notices, a puzzle department of *brodyág* ciphers, and a personal intelligence column of the highest interest to all " travelers on Government account." One of the first things that an experienced convict does, after his arrival at an *étape*, is to search the walls for news; and his fortunes not infrequently turn upon the direction or the warning contained in a message that he finds there from a comrade who has preceded him. Mr. Gálkine Wrásskoy, chief of the prison administration, has come at last to appreciate the significance and importance of these mural inscriptions, and has recently ordered *étape* officers to see that they are carefully erased. I doubt, however, whether the order will secure the desired results. The prison authorities are constantly outwitted by convicts, and the latter will soon learn to write their messages in places where an *étape* officer would never think of looking for them, but where an experienced convict will discover them at once.

Soon after leaving Tomsk, usually at the first regular *étape*, every exile party organizes itself into an *artél*, or "union," elects a chief or head man known as the *stárosta*, and lays the foundation of an *artél* fund by levying an assessment upon each of its members, and by selling at auction to the highest bidder the privilege of keeping an exile sutler's store or *maidán*, where the prisoners can openly buy tea, sugar, or white bread, and where they can secretly obtain tobacco, playing-cards, and intoxicating liquor. The organization of the party into an *artél* has for its primary object concerted and combined action against the common enemy — the Government. A single convict, regarded as an individual, has neither rights nor means of self-defense. He is completely at the mercy, not only of the higher authorities in the forwarding prisons and the provincial towns, but of every petty officer in the convoy command that escorts him from *étape* to *étape;* and the only way in which he can acquire even a limited power of self-protection is by associating himself with his fellow-convicts in an *artél,* or union. This *artél,* as an organized body, exercises all of its functions in secret, and strives to attain its ends, first, by enforcing solidarity and joint action on the part of all its members, and, secondly, by deceiving, outwitting, or bribing the officers and soldiers with whom it has to deal. It concerts plans of escape; it contrives means of obtaining forbidden articles, such as playing-cards and tobacco; it hires *telégas,* or sleighs, from the peasants along the road, and sells, or grants, to its members the privilege of riding in them for short distances when exhausted; it bribes executioners to flog lightly; it pays soldiers for smuggling intoxicating liquor into the forwarding prisons and *étapes;* and, finally, it sanctions and enforces all contracts and agreements entered into by its convict members. It is, in short, the body politic of the criminal world; and it fills, in the life of the exile, the same place that the *mir,* or commune, fills in the life of the free peasant. Within the limits of its prison environment the power of the *artél* over its members is absolute. It has its own unwritten laws, its own standards of honor and duty, and its own penal code. Its laws recognize only two crimes,—disobedience and disloyalty,—and its penal code provides for only one punishment—death. The exile may lie, he may rob, he may murder if he will, provided his action does not affect injuriously the interests of the *artél* to which he belongs; but if he disobeys that organization, or betrays its secrets to the prison authorities,—even under the compulsion of the lash,—he may count himself as dead already. Siberia is not large enough to furnish a safe hiding-place for the exile who has been unfaithful to his *artél.* More than once, in the large convict prisons, I saw criminals who had been condemned to death as traitors by this merciless

Siberian Vehmgerichte, who, therefore, dared not associate with their fellow-prisoners, and who were living, by permission of the prison authorities, in the strictest solitary confinement. Over the head of every one of these men hung an invisible sword of Damocles, and sooner or later, in one place or another, it was sure to fall. The records of Russian prisons are full of cases in which the sentence of death pronounced by an *artél* has been executed years afterwards, and in a place far removed from the scene of the offense. In one recent case the traitor was choked to death one night, at sea, while on his way in a convict steamer to the island of Saghalín, and in another the informer was found one morning with his throat cut in a Caucasian *étape*.

The prison officials throughout Siberia have long been aware of the existence of this secret criminal organization, but they have never been able to suppress it, and they now give to it a certain sort of recognition—putting up with its inevitable evils and making the most of its merits. A convoy officer, for example, wishes to be able to report to his superior at the end of the year that not a single exile has escaped while in his charge. He summons the *stárosta*, or chief of the *artél*, and says to him, "Call the boys together and tell them, from me, that if the *artél* will agree not to allow any escapes from the party on my beat, I will look the other way when they take off their leg-fetters."[1] The *stárosta* replies, "Slúshiu, S'" [I hear, sir], and goes back into the *kámera* to lay this proposition before the *artél*. The *artél* accepts it, and every chained convict begins pounding at the ankle-bands of his leg-fetters. The convoy officer, of course, has himself committed a penal offense in entering into this sort of an agreement, but he knows that the *artél* will never betray him, and he is relieved at once from all anxiety with regard to escapes. If, after the

[1] The ankle-bands of Russian leg-fetters fit so loosely that when they have been pounded with a stone into the form of an ellipse they can generally be slipped off over the heel. Of course this cannot be done, however, without the connivance of the convoy officers and the soldiers of the guard.

negotiation of such a treaty, an exile should attempt to get away from the party within the limits of that officer's jurisdiction, he would have to answer for it to the *artél*, and sooner or later he would pay dearly—perhaps with his life—for thus breaking faith and dishonoring the organization of which he was a member. The late Colonel Zagárin, inspector of exile transportation for Eastern Siberia, told me that he himself had often made a substantial contribution to the fund of an exile *artél* merely in order to secure from the latter a promise that no attempts to escape should be made within the limits of his jurisdiction. Such promises, he said, were always faithfully observed by the *artél* in its corporate capacity, and were rarely disregarded even by individuals. If, however, an inexperienced "first-timer," tempted by a favorable opportunity, should try to escape, in defiance of the *artél's* prohibition, the veterans of the party, namely, the *brodyágs*, would always undertake either to recapture the fugitive, or to bring in some other runaway convict as a substitute, and thus save the honor of the *artél*. He could not remember a single case, he said, in which the *artél* had broken faith. It must not be supposed, however, that the prison commune, in such dealings with the authorities, is actuated by any high or honorable motives. In keeping its promise, in enforcing solidarity, and in punishing disloyalty and disobedience with death, it is merely protecting its own existence and securing what a majority of its members believe to be the greatest good of the greatest number. It has no sentimental regard for truthfulness or faithfulness in the abstract. It simply knows that, at certain times and in certain circumstances, honesty is the best policy, and then it enforces honesty under penalty of death. If, however, circumstances so change as to render dishonesty the best policy, then the *artél* sanctions and compels the practice of deception, fraud, untruthfulness, and treachery, under the same tremendous penalty.

One of the most important functions of the exile *artél* is the enforcement of agreements entered into by its members, and particularly agreements to exchange names and identities. Every exile party is made up of two great classes, namely: A — criminals sentenced to hard labor with imprisonment; and B — criminals sentenced merely to forced colonization without imprisonment. Every convict in class " A " strives to escape the hard labor and the imprisonment by exchanging his name and identity for the name and identity of some convict in class " B." It would seem, at first thought, as if the difficulties in the way of such a transaction would be virtually insuperable. It is not only strictly forbidden by law, but it is a transaction in which one of the parties, apparently, gets all the benefit. Why should convoy officers allow such exchanges of names, and why should the colonist be willing to go to the mines in the place of the hard-labor convict, even if permitted to do so? The difficulties are only apparent, and the questions are easily answered. The convicts in every marching party that leaves Tomsk for Eastern Siberia number about 400, and they change convoy every third day. It is utterly impossible for a convoy officer to so familiarize himself, in three days, with the faces of 400 convicts, that he can tell one from another. If Iván Pávlof answers to the name of Mikháiel Ivánof at the roll-call of the party, he virtually becomes Mikháiel Ivánof. The convoy officer does not know either of them by sight, and even if he called the roll himself, and looked attentively at every man, he would not notice the substitution. So far as the authorities are concerned, therefore, names and identities can be exchanged without the least difficulty or danger. The willingness of the colonist to exchange names with the hard-labor convict and go into penal servitude in the latter's stead may be explained almost as easily.

In every exile party there are a few reckless, improvident, hard-drinking peasants who have been condemned to forced colonization. When one of these poor wretches has spent all his money, and perhaps has gambled away all of his clothing and mortgaged his food-allowance for weeks in advance, he gets into such a condition that for five or ten *rúbles* and a bottle of *vódka* he will sell his very soul. The hard-labor convict, who is generally a bold, enterprising, experienced recidivist, and a man, moreover, who has won and saved some money on the road, then approaches the hungry, thirsty, half-naked, and wholly destitute colonist, and says to him, " If you will exchange names with me and go in my place to the mines, I 'll give you my warm *shúba* [overcoat], five *rúbles* in money, and a bottle of *vódka*. You won't have to stay at the mines long. After I have had time to reach your place of colonization and run away, you can tell the *nachálnik* [chief] at the mines who you really are, and say that you have been sent there by mistake. He will make inquiries, and as soon as he finds out that you are not me, he will send you back to your place of colonization; and then we 'll both be all right."

The persuasive eloquence of the hard-labor convict, backed by five *rúbles*, a warm *shúba*, and a bottle of *vódka*, is generally too much for the resolution of the unfortunate colonist. He consents to the proposed exchange of names and identities, and the *artél* is at once convened to note, sanction, and mentally record the transaction. At the next and at every subsequent roll-call of the party, the hard-labor convict answers to the name of the colonist, and the colonist must answer to the name of the hard-labor convict. The more dangerous criminal, who, perhaps, should serve out a life sentence at the mines for murder, is turned loose in some East-Siberian village from which he immediately makes his escape, while the petty thief, drunkard, or wife-beater goes into penal servitude at the mines of Nérchinsk or Kará.

Although the exchanging of names has been practised by convicts in Siberia from time immemorial, and although it is manifestly unjust, prejudicial to the interests of the state, and detrimental in the highest degree to the welfare of the Siberian people, all suggestions made by experienced *étape* officers with regard to methods of stopping it have been disregarded. Ten years ago Colonel Zagárin, the inspector of ·exile transportation for Eastern Siberia, made a report upon the subject to Governor-general Anúchin in which he recommended that hard-labor convicts, as a class, be made distinguishable from forced colonists, as a class, by means of a different shaving of the head. Both classes now have their heads half shaven on the same side. Colonel Zagárin suggested that the heads of all hard-labor convicts be shaved on the right side and of all forced colonists on the left. The exchanging of names and identities between the two classes would then become impossible, for the reason that every *étape* officer and every soldier of the convoy could see at a glance to which class any particular criminal belonged. The forced colonist Iván Pávlof might answer, as before, to the name of the hard-labor convict Mikháiel Ivánof at roll-call, but it would be perfectly useless to do so, because the cut of his hair would at once betray him.

"What did the governor-general say to your suggestion?" I inquired, when Colonel Zagárin finished telling me about this report.

"Nothing," he replied. "It was never acted upon. Anú-chin referred, even in his report to the Gossudár, to the bad results of this practice of changing names, but he never tried to stop it in the way that I suggested."

"What preposterous stupidity!" I exclaimed. "The method is simplicity itself, it would cost nothing, and it would make the exchanging of names absolutely impossible. What conceivable reason could Anúchin have for not adopting it?"

"I don't know any reason," replied Colonel Zagárin, "except that he did n't happen to think of it himself. Our high officials don't take suggestions very kindly—especially from their subordinates."[1]

Since my return from Siberia an attempt has been made to secure certainty of identification in criminal parties by means of small photographs of the convicts attached to their *statéini spíski*, but I do not know how it has resulted.

Deportation by *étape* in Siberia is attended by miseries and humiliations of which a European or an American reader can form only a faint conception. I had many opportunities, during our journey from Tomsk to Irkútsk, to see convicts on the march in sunshine and in rain; to inspect the wretched *étapes* in which they were herded like cattle at night; to visit the lazarets where they sometimes lie sick for weeks without skilled medical attention or proper care; and to talk with intelligent officers of the prison department who had been familiar for years with every feature of the exile system. The result of my investigation was a deliberate conviction that the suffering involved in the present method of transporting criminals to Siberia is not paralleled by anything of the kind that now exists in the civilized world outside of the Russian Empire. Some of this suffering is due, of course, to negligence, indifference, or official corruption; but a very large part of it is the necessary result of a bad and cruel system, and it can be removed only by the complete abolition of the system itself, and by the substitution for it of imprisonment for life,

[1] This remark, "Our high officials don't take suggestions very kindly," was made to me, in substance, by at least a dozen experienced officers of the exile administration in Siberia, including the inspector of exile transportation, the warden of one of the largest of the convict prisons, and two successive governors of the Kará mines. I have, in my note-books, a score or more of suggestions made by these officers to their superiors with regard to methods of reforming the exile system, or of dealing with some of the evils that had been found, in practice, to arise. Most of these suggestions seemed to me to be wise and judicious, and all of them deserved serious and attentive consideration. Not one, so far as I know, was ever adopted, and in several cases the higher authorities distinctly intimated to their over-zealous subordinates that when they — the higher authorities — felt themselves to be in need of information or advice, they would make a requisition for it in due form.

or for a term of years, in European Russia. Only a moment's reflection is needed to satisfy any one that, even under the most favorable circumstances, six or eight thousand men, women, and children cannot march two thou-

A PARTY OF EXILES CROSSING THE YENISÉI.

sand miles across such a country as Eastern Siberia without suffering terrible hardships. The physical exposure alone is enough to break down the health and strength of all except the most hardy, and when to such inevitable exposure are added insufficient clothing, bad food, the polluted air of overcrowded *étapes*, and the almost complete absence of medical care and attention, one is surprised, not that so many die, but that so many get through alive.

The exile parties that leave Tomsk in July and August are overtaken by the frosts and the cold rains of autumn long before they reach Irkútsk. They have not yet been supplied with winter clothing, and most of them have no better protection from rain, sleet, or cold wind than that afforded by a coarse linen shirt, a pair of linen drawers, and a gray frieze overcoat. Imagine such a party marching in a cold, northeast storm along the road over which we passed between Áchinsk and Krasnoyársk. Every individual is wet to the skin by the drenching rain, and the nursing women, the small children, and the sick lie quivering on water-soaked straw in small, rude *telégas*, without even a pretense of shelter from the storm. The mud, in places, is almost knee-deep, and the wagons wallow through it at the rate of about two miles an hour. The bodies of the marching convicts, kept warm by the exertion of walking in heavy leg-fetters, steam a little in the raw, chilly air, but a large number of the men have lost or removed their shoes, and are wading through the freezing mud with bare feet. The Government, influenced, I presume, by considerations of economy, furnishes its exiles in summer and fall with low shoes or slippers called *katí*, instead of with boots. These *katí* are made by contract and by the thousand, of the cheapest materials, and by the Government itself are expected to last only six weeks.[1] As a matter of fact they frequently do not last one week.

A high officer of the exile administration told me that it was a common thing to see exiles leave Tomsk or Krasnoyársk with new *katí* and come into the second *étape* barefooted—their shoes having gone to pieces in less than two days. Even when the *katí* hold out for their nominal period of service, they are not fitted to the feet of the wearers ; they cannot be secured, because they have no

[1] Circular Letter of the Prison Department, No. 180.

laces; they are so low that they fill with mire and water and are constantly sticking fast or coming off in mud-holes; and on such a road as that between Áchinsk and Krasnoyársk scores of convicts either remove their shoes and hang them around their necks, or throw them away altogether, and walk for days at a time with bare feet, through mud whose temperature is little above the freezing-point.

As the party, wet, tired, and hungry, approaches one of the little log villages that lie along its route, the *stárosta*, or chief of the *artél*, asks the convoy officer to allow them to sing the "begging song" as they pass through the settlement. The desired permission is granted; certain prisoners are designated to receive the expected alms; the convicts all remove their gray caps; and entering the village with a slow, dragging step, as if they hardly had strength enough to crawl along, they begin their mournful appeal for pity.

I shall never forget the emotions roused in me by this song when I heard it for the first time. We were sitting, one cold, raw, autumnal day, in a dirty post-station on the great Siberian road, waiting for horses. Suddenly my attention was attracted by a peculiar, low-pitched, quavering sound which came to us from a distance, and which, although made apparently by human voices, did not resemble anything that I had ever before heard. It was not singing, nor chanting, nor wailing for the dead, but a strange blending of all three. It suggested vaguely the confused and commingled sobs, moans, and entreaties of human beings who were being subjected to torture, but whose sufferings were not acute enough to seek expression in shrieks or high-pitched cries. As the sound came nearer we went out into the street in front of the station-house and saw approaching a chained party of about a hundred bare-headed convicts, who, surrounded by a cordon of soldiers, were marching slowly through the settlement, singing the "exiles' begging song." No attempt was made by the singers to pitch their voices in harmony, or to pronounce the words in unison;

there were no pauses or rests at the ends of the lines; and I could not make out any distinctly marked rhythm. The singers seemed to be constantly breaking in upon one another with slightly modulated variations of the same slow, melancholy air, and the effect produced was that of a rude fugue, or of a funeral chant, so arranged as to be sung like a round or catch by a hundred male voices, each independent of the others in time and melody, but all following a certain scheme of vocalization, and taking up by turns the same dreary, wailing theme. The words were as follows:

> Have pity on us, O our fathers!
> Don't forget the unwilling travelers,
> Don't forget the long-imprisoned.
> Feed us, O our fathers — help us!
> Feed and help the poor and needy!
> Have compassion, O our fathers!
> Have compassion, O our mothers!
> For the sake of Christ, have mercy
> On the prisoners — the shut-up ones!
> Behind walls of stone and gratings,
> Behind oaken doors and padlocks,
> Behind bars and locks of iron,
> We are held in close confinement.
> We have parted from our fathers,
> From our mothers;
> We from all our kin have parted,
> We are prisoners;
> Pity us, O our fathers!

If you can imagine these words, half sung, half chanted, slowly, in broken time and on a low key, by a hundred voices, to an accompaniment made by the jingling and clashing of chains, you will have a faint idea of the *milosérdnaya*, or exiles' begging song. Rude, artless, and inharmonious as the appeal for pity was, I had never in my life heard anything so mournful and depressing. It seemed to be the half-articulate expression of all the grief, the misery, and the despair that had been felt by generations of human beings in the *étapes*, the forwarding prisons, and the mines.

As the party marched slowly along the muddy street between the lines of gray log houses, children and peasant women appeared at the doors with their hands full of bread, meat, eggs, or other articles of food, which they put into the caps or bags of the three or four shaven-headed convicts who acted as alms-collectors. The jingling of chains and the wailing voices of the exiles grew gradually fainter and fainter as the party passed up the street, and when the sounds finally died away in the distance, and we turned to reënter the post-station, I felt a strange sense of dejection, as if the day had suddenly grown colder, darker, and more dreary, and the cares and sorrows of life more burdensome and oppressive.

At the first *privál*, or halt, that a party makes after passing through a village, the food that has been collected is distributed and eaten, and the convicts, somewhat refreshed, resume their march. Late in the evening they arrive, wet and weary, at an *étape*, where, after supper and the *pereclíchka*, or roll-call, they are locked up in the close, unventilated *kámeras* for the night. Most of them are in a shiver— or, as they sometimes call it, a "gypsy sweat"—from cold and from long exposure to rain; but they have neither dry clothing to put on nor blankets with which to cover themselves, and must lie down upon the hard plank *nári*, or upon the floor, and seek warmth in close contact with one another. Some of them have, perhaps, a change of clothing in their gray linen bags, but both bags and clothing have been exposed for eight or ten hours to a pouring rain, and are completely soaked through. If the Government really cared anything about the comfort or health of exiles on the road, it would furnish convoy officers with tarpaulins or sheets of oilcloth to put over and protect the exiles' baggage in rainy weather. This would add a mere trifle to the cost of exile transportation, and it would make all the difference between life and death to hundreds of weak or half-sick human beings, who come into an *étape* soaked to the skin after a march of twenty miles in a cold rain, and who have no dry clothing

AN OLD CONVICT BEGGING FOOD.

to put on. The very money spent for the burial of the poor wretches who die from croup, pleurisy, or pneumonia, as a result of sleeping in wet clothes on the road, would buy a substantial tarpaulin for every exile baggage-wagon in Siberia—and yet the tarpaulins are not bought. If it be asked why not, I can only say, because the officials who care have not the power, and the officials who have the power do not care. I went through Siberia with the words " Why so ? " and " Why not ? " upon my lips, and this, in effect, was the answer that I everywhere received.

" I have recommended again and again," said a high officer of the exile administration to me, " that the convicts be taken to their destinations in summer and in wagons, instead of being obliged to walk throughout the whole year. I have shown conclusively, by exact figures and carefully prepared estimates, that the transportation of exiles from Áchinsk to Irkútsk in wagons, and in summer, would not only be infinitely more merciful and humane than the present method of forwarding them on foot the year round, but would actually cost fourteen *rúbles* less per man, on account of the saving in time, food, and winter clothing."

"Why, then, is it not done?" I inquired.

His only reply was a significant shrug of the shoulders.

"I have repeatedly protested," said another exile officer, "against the acceptance, from dishonest contractors, of articles of exile clothing that did not correspond with the specification or the samples; but I have accomplished nothing. Shoes so worthless that they fall to pieces in two days are accepted in place of the good shoes that ought to be furnished, and the exiles go barefooted. All that I can do is to lay before my superiors the facts of the case."

While in the city of Irkútsk, I called one day upon Mr. Petróf, the acting-governor of the province, and found in his office Colonel Zagárin, the inspector of exile transportation for Eastern Siberia. The latter had brought to the governor some *katí*, or exile shoes, that had just been accepted by the provincial administration, and was exhibiting them side by side with the original samples that had been furnished as models to the contractor. The accepted shoes did not resemble the models, they were perfectly worthless, and might have been made, I think, by the thousand, for ten or fifteen cents a pair. Colonel Zagárin was protesting against the acceptance of such shoes, and was asking for an investigation. The fraud was so manifest and so glaring, and the results of it would be so calamitous to thousands of poor wretches who would wear these *katí* for a day or two and then be forced to walk barefooted over icy ground or through freezing mud, that I thought something would certainly be done about it. Upon my return from the mines of the Trans-Baikál five months later, I asked Colonel Zagárin what had been the result of the protest that he had made to the governor in my presence. He replied, "It had no result."

"And were those shoes issued to marching exile parties?"

"They were."

I asked no more questions.

I could furnish innumerable illustrations of the way in which the life of convicts on the road is made almost intolerable by official indifference or fraud; but it is perhaps unnecessary to do so. The results of that life are shown by the records of the hospitals and lazarets, and by the extraordinarily high rate of mortality in exile parties. Hundreds of prisoners, of both sexes and all ages, fall sick on the road, and after being carried for a week, or perhaps two weeks, in jolting *telégas*, are finally left to recover or to die in one of the *étape* lazarets between Áchinsk and Irkútsk. It seems barbarous, and of course it is barbarous, to carry forward in a springless *teléga*, regardless of weather, an unfortunate man or woman who has been taken sick with pneumonia or typhus fever on the road; but, under existing circumstances, there is nothing else for a convoy officer to do. He and his soldiers must go on with the exile party, and he cannot leave the sick for five days in a deserted *étape* wholly without attendance. He is forced, therefore, to carry them along until they either die or reach one of the widely separated lazarets, where they can be left and cared for.

Many times on the great Siberian road, when I had been jolted until my pulse had become imperceptible at the wrist from weakness, sleeplessness, and incessant shocks to the spinal cord and the brain, and when it seemed to me that I could endure no more, I maintained my grip by thinking of the hundreds of exiled men and women who, sick unto death, had been carried over this same road in open *telégas*; who had endured this same jolting while their heads ached and throbbed with the quick pulses of fever; who had lain for many hours at a time on water-soaked straw in a pitiless storm while suffering from pneumonia, and who had nothing to sustain them except the faint hope of reaching at last some fever-infected lazaret. If men can bear all this, I thought, we ought not to complain of our trivial hardships, nor break down under a little unusual fatigue.

The sick who live to reach an *étape* lazaret may hope to die under shelter and in peace; but, if the reports of the exile administration are to be trusted, they can hardly expect to be restored to health. Mr. Gálkine Wrásskoy, the chief of the prison administration, in an official report to the Minister of the Interior, describes the condition of the lazarets between Áchinsk and Irkútsk as follows:

Up to the year 1885 the lazarets necessary for the accommodation of exiles taken sick on the great exile road had not been built, nor had any provision been made for regular surgeons, or even for *feldshers*.[1] According to paragraph 5 of section 363 of the " Laws relating to Exiles," it is the duty of civil and military surgeons, in places where *étape* officers are quartered, to examine the sick and give them necessary aid. Civil surgeons, however, do not live in *étape* villages, and army surgeons are found only at the *étapes* of Sheragúlskaya, Birusínskaya, and Tirétskaya. In these places there are army lazarets with six beds each, for the accommodation of sick soldiers belonging to the convoy commands. All prisoners taken sick on the road between Áchinsk and Irkútsk, up to the

[1] A *feldsher* is a sort of hospital steward, who, in the absence of a regular surgeon, performs the latter's duties.

year 1885, have been treated at these three *étapes* [1] — not, however, in the army lazarets, but in the common cells of the *étape* buildings. There they have been kept, not only without separation according to age, sex, or nature of disease, but without any of the conveniences and appliances that a lazaret should have. In the cells set apart for sick exiles there were neither nurses, nor hospital linen, nor beds, nor bedding, nor even dishes for food. [2]

A sick exile who reaches one of the *étapes* named in this report, and who is put into a common prison cell where there are "neither nurses, nor hospital linen, nor beds, nor bedding, nor even dishes for food," cannot reasonably entertain a very sanguine expectation of recovery. Most of them do recover, but, nevertheless, the death-rate in exile parties during their march from Tomsk to Irkútsk, if carried through an entire year, would amount to from twelve to fifteen per cent. [3]

It is not surprising that exiles sometimes endeavor to escape from a life so full of miseries as this by making a break for liberty between *étapes*. The more experienced *brodyágs*, or recidivists, generally try to get away by exchanging names and identities with some forced colonist who is soon to reach his destination; but now and then two or three daring or desperate convicts attempt to escape "with a hurrah"—that is, by a bold dash through the line of soldiers. They are instantly fired upon, and one or more of them is usually brought to the ground. The soldiers have a saying that "A bullet will find a runaway," and a slug

[1] The distances between these *étapes* are as follows: Áchinsk to Birusínskaya, 352 miles; Birusínskaya to Sheragúlskaya, 200 miles; Sheragúlskaya to Tirétskaya, 90 miles; Tirétskaya to Irkútsk, 139 miles. A marching party of exiles makes, on an average, about 80 miles a week. The results of the state of affairs described by Mr. Gálkine Wrásskoy may be seen in the official reports of the sickness and mortality in the lazarets of these three *étapes*. (Appendix G.)

[2] Report of Mr. Gálkine Wrásskoy, chief of the prison administration, for the year 1885.

[3] In 1883 seventy exiles died between Tomsk and Áchinsk, in the course of a journey that occupies about twenty-one days. This rate of mortality, if it had been maintained for a year, would have resulted in the death of 1217 exiles out of the whole number of 7865 making the journey. (Vide Report of the Inspector of Exile Transportation in Western Siberia for 1884, pp. 32, 33.)

À BREAK FOR LIBERTY.

from a Berdan rifle is always the first messenger sent after
a fugitive who tries to escape "with a hurrah." Now and
then, when the party happens to be passing through a
dense forest, the flying convicts get under cover so quickly
that the soldiers can only fire into the bushes at random,
and in such cases the runaways make good their escape.
As soon as they reach a hiding-place they free themselves
from their leg-fetters by pounding the circular bands into
long ellipses with a stone and slipping them over their heels,
and then join some detachment of the great army of *brodyágs* which is constantly marching westward through the
woods in the direction of the Uráls.

The life of exiles on the road, which I have tried to
roughly sketch, continues, with little to break its monotony,
for many months. In sunshine and in storm, through dust
and through mud, the convicts march slowly but steadily
eastward, crossing the great Siberian rivers on pendulum
ferry-boats; toiling up the sides of forest-clad mountains in
drenching rains; wading through mire in swampy valleys;
sleeping every night in the heavy mephitic atmosphere of
overcrowded *étapes*, and drawing nearer, day by day, to the
dreaded mines of the Trans-Baikál.